THE NEXT AGE OF
UNCERTAINTY

THE NEXT AGE OF
UNCERTAINTY

How the World Can Adapt
to a Riskier Future

Stephen Poloz

ALLEN
LANE

ALLEN LANE

an imprint of Penguin Canada,
a division of Penguin Random House Canada Limited

Canada • USA • UK • Ireland • Australia •
New Zealand • India • South Africa • China

First published 2022

www.penguinrandomhouse.ca

LIBRARY AND ARCHIVES CANADA CATALOGUING IN PUBLICATION

Title: The next age of uncertainty : how the world
can adapt to a riskier future / Stephen Poloz.
Names: Poloz, Stephen S., author.
Identifiers: Canadiana (print) 20210237406 | Canadiana (ebook) 20210237597 |
ISBN 9780735243903 (hardcover) | ISBN 9780735243910 (EPUB)
Subjects: LCSH: Business cycles. | LCSH: Financial crises. | LCSH: Economic
history. | LCSH: Investments. | LCSH: Uncertainty.
Classification: LCC HB3711 .P65 2022 | DDC 338.5/42—dc23

Book design by Lisa Jager
Cover design by Lisa Jager
Printed in Canada

10 9 8 7 6 5 4 3 2 1

ALLEN
LANE

Penguin
Random
House

For my beloved Valerie

CONTENTS

INTRODUCTION

Uncertainty is everywhere, but especially when it comes to the economy. Concerned that the weather might disrupt weekend plans? There's an app for that. But there's no app for the uncertainty that really counts. Is my job secure? Will I earn more next year? Can I afford to purchase a home? Will I ever be able to afford one? Is now the right time to buy? Is the money I have set aside for a down payment growing? Is the stock market about to collapse? What will the interest rate be when I renew my mortgage? Should I renew for a short or long term? How long will I live—will I have enough savings for my retirement? And why is the price of gasoline so high this week, by the way? These questions pertain to important personal life decisions that have long-term consequences. We *all* live in the economy.

These everyday questions are difficult enough for individuals, but they are even harder for companies, which have more factors in play. Indeed, the quality of their decisions will determine not only their future but also whether you *do* still have a job tomorrow. To maintain a viable business that offers secure employment and ongoing profitability, companies must make forecasts about future economic trends such as sales, prices, interest rates, and exchange rates. They translate those estimates into a business plan that covers hiring, orders for raw materials, equipment purchases, expansion plans, and so on. They also must develop a corresponding financial plan, supported by a bank and perhaps public equity or bond markets.

In short, employers and employees face the same economic uncertainties together. Economic growth versus recession, the rate of inflation, the level of interest rates, the exchange rate, the stock market, job creation or cutbacks, salary levels, the state of the housing market, prospects for government spending and taxes, and so on—it matters to us all. From the street level, some macroeconomic concepts may seem abstract, but they are ingredients in all of our major economic decisions: whether to work and where, where to live and how, what to buy and when, when to borrow and how much, when to hire and when to fire, and when to take a chance and expand the business. Economics is the air we all breathe and the water we all swim in.

You don't need an economist to tell you that economic instability has risen in recent years. That means it is becoming a lot harder to make plans for the future. The question often posed is whether things will ever return to normal. The book-long answer to that question is that "normal" is not what most of us think it is. The short answer is we should expect even more volatility in the years ahead, not less.

A future with greater economic volatility means that things could turn out either worse or better than we expect and that the range of possible outcomes will expand. We all instinctively loathe uncertainty, even when we understand that it is two-sided, meaning that it can bring not just bad luck but sometimes good. Uncertainty is stressful. We make fresh economic decisions every day based on our expectations about the future. And the wrong decision is only going to get easier to make.

When economic uncertainty increases, so do the risks associated with making the wrong decision. The forces acting on the economy will produce more frequent and larger fluctuations in employment, inflation, house prices, interest rates, and stock markets in the future. For example, when buying a house, we will need to consider that the risk of losing our job, and therefore possibly losing the house, will be greater than it has been in the past.

In short, the more uncertain our future becomes, the more risk we take on when we make everyday decisions. How do people make decisions in the face of uncertainty? We base our decisions on our own average past experience, expecting the future to follow course. In other words, if things seem unusual right now, most of us expect that things will return to normal. But how confident can we be of that? The more uncertain we are, the more stressful that decision becomes. We may seek advice from family, friends, or experts to relieve the stress of the unknown.

Experts are a special breed. They don't form expectations like the rest of us do; they make forecasts based on a much wider information base, including an understanding of economics, reams of data, and computer-driven models to predict outcomes. They spend all day trying to understand these things, while the rest of us do our regular jobs and try to understand the world on evenings and weekends. We read newspapers, books, search the web, or watch business news shows to access a wide array of experts to help us understand how the world works. There are many experts on the economy, and even more opinions than there are experts. There is too much information available to us on the economy, much of it loud, excessively confident, and contradictory besides. Experts aren't always right. And there are things experts just *can't* know.

During my time as governor of the Bank of Canada, I made a habit of being honest about uncertainty in our economic outlook. This is especially important after the economy is hit by a significant disturbance, as economic models can easily lead us astray. A good example was the Global Financial Crisis of 2008 and the Great Recession that followed. Canadian exports fell dramatically and the situation was made even more difficult by a rising Canadian dollar, which eventually broke above parity in 2011, forcing many Canadian export companies out of business. As the dollar moved steadily lower in the next few years, economists expected Canadian exports to recover. This forecast was wrong because so many of the export companies no longer existed. Economists' models were simply not equipped to account for company destruction on such a scale. This experience illustrated perfectly that economic forecasts should always be interpreted as the midpoint of a range of possible outcomes—sometimes a *wide* range of possible outcomes. A forecast is only an expert's guess, usually supported by models based on historical data. Economists are a lot like scientists in that we take in a lot of information and come up with an hypothesis for how the economy works. But while a scientist can test an hypothesis in the lab, economists and central bankers can only develop models based on past behaviour. As a consequence, those models work best when the future resembles the past.

This book was written in the wake of the COVID-19 pandemic, a case study in extreme economic uncertainty. From my vantage point, the situation looked and felt like chaos. For several weeks in spring 2020, my life consisted of an erratic and relentless sequence of virtual meetings, at all hours of the day, all taken from my rarely used home office using an internet connection of questionable reliability. Financial market programs and monetary policy tools were deployed on the fly, with most of us guided by instincts rather than actual data.

Whenever something extreme happens to the economy like that, economists are immediately called upon to opine on what it may mean for the future. Personally, I had very little confidence in our ability to predict how the pandemic would affect the global economy, and yet, as usual, confident forecasts about the future were not in short supply. The vast majority were predicting a major economic convulsion, one that would last for a long time. I was skeptical. Perhaps it was my sunny disposition rising to the surface, but I had the sense that economies would show some resilience. The situation reminded me of September 11, 2001, and the confident pronouncements in the wake of that event, some that very day.

"People will never travel again," said some economists. "The global economy will see a deep and prolonged recession," said many. I was chief economist at Export Development Canada (EDC) at the time, and I still remember wrestling with forecast uncertainty then. As it turned out, we realized that uncertainty itself was the most useful insight. We called our forecast update "The New Age of Uncertainty," to acknowledge that the future may never be as certain as it had seemed in the past. I carried a copy of John Kenneth Galbraith's 1977 book *The Age of Uncertainty* with me as a prop for the next few weeks as I delivered some twenty public speeches setting out our thinking on the future. We did not call for a global recession but said that increased uncertainty would throw sand in the wheels of international business. Business risk would be higher in a world in which the risk of terrorism was ever-present, and companies would adapt. For the record, the world economy did not experience a recession after 9/11; it picked up speed.

Galbraith's book was written during 1973 to 1977, a time of great uncertainty for the economics profession as the concept of "normal" was being upended. The arrival of the baby boom generation in the global workforce was disrupting labour markets. The price of oil skyrocketed in the wake of the Arab oil embargo, creating convulsions in oil-importing countries. The international monetary system in place since the end of World War II—under which most national currencies were fixed against the U.S. dollar, which was locked to a fixed price of gold—broke down, and exchange-rate volatility erupted. These were gigantic shocks to the world economy and represented a fundamental shift in what previously had been regarded as "normal." What emerged was a combination of rising inflation and rising unemployment, an outcome the economic models of that era had never predicted. Clearly, something had gone wrong.

Over the next decade, those models were given a complete rethink. A new generation of models was emerging while I was in graduate school in the late 1970s. This was Galbraith's point: economics had always progressed from one big new idea to another, to another, and each time the new idea's proponents delivered it with absolute but unjustified conviction.

This critique of economists did not originate with Galbraith. He quoted none other than John Maynard Keynes himself, from the very last paragraph of his 1936 book *The General Theory of Employment, Interest and Money*:

> . . . the ideas of economists and political philosophers, both
> when they are right and when they are wrong, are more power-
> ful than is commonly understood. Indeed, the world is ruled
> by little else. Practical men, who believe themselves to be
> quite exempt from any intellectual influences, are usually
> the slaves of some defunct economist.

When the world changes, economic theory must change with it. Economists who fail to adapt will be wrong, and so will everyone who follows them.

While history may not always repeat itself, it often rhymes, as famously pointed out by Mark Twain. As financial markets calmed in the late spring of 2020, I found myself thinking again about economic forecasts made at important turning points in the past and how wrong they had turned out to be. Not just in the decimal points but even in *direction*. The only reasonable interpretation of such forecast errors is that these major events had altered our economic foundations. Our theories had lost their power to predict the future.

Economists all carry in their minds a foundation for the economy, a conceptual set of elements and relationships between them that will be constant through time. The economy is always being disturbed by one event or another, so it is rarely observed in an unchanged setting, but this foundation is the place to which the economy will gravitate after a disturbance. Economists refer to this as a long-term equilibrium or steady state. Economic models are based on this foundational structure and attempt to explain the fluctuations around that steady state that the economy experiences. And the model is used to forecast how the economy will return to that steady state from today's starting point. Given the magnitude of the COVID-19 shock, I wondered what constants in the economy we could rely upon to act as an anchor for the future, a resting position to which we would return, once the pandemic was behind us.

I soon realized that there may be very few such constants in our economy today. I had been thinking about the destabilizing effects of long-term forces acting on the economy since 2019. That year, I had the honour of outlining my early thoughts on the subject in the marquee lecture at the Spruce Meadows Changing Fortunes Round Table, an annual high-level international gathering of business leaders and policymakers, begun by the late Ron Southern over twenty years ago and continued by the Southern family. As I prepared for that lecture, I came to understand that several of our key economic foundations are not constants—they are actually in motion—and their force would shape our future. This book grew out of that Spruce Meadows lecture.

Projecting our future while taking account of these long-term forces is far more difficult than it sounds. When several forces are acting on the economy at the same time, they can produce inexplicable instability, even crises, because of the complexity of their interactions. Some of these same forces were in motion in the 1970s when Galbraith was writing *The Age of Uncertainty*. This is how I came to think of our future as the "next" age of uncertainty, making the title of this book an obvious choice, if a sentimental one. The title is also meant to convey the idea that this next age of uncertainty surely will not be the last.

This book is aimed at those who wish to understand better what they see outside their windows, the risks they take on in everyday life, in order to make better decisions. It argues that a rising tide of risk is about to land on our doorsteps and it offers specific advice for navigating the future.

Whether you're a CEO or an economist or a parent thinking about your kids' education, it is easy to lose sight of the big economic forces already in motion, which will affect us long into the future, when we find ourselves in a daily struggle for survival. But it is those big economic forces that ultimately shape the outcomes of those struggles. This book aims to help us all think more clearly about, and prepare for, the next age of uncertainty.

Ottawa, Canada
June 2021

TECTONIC FORCES

Reflections: Bali, 2018

My work has meant a lot of travelling over the years. Travel around the U.S., Canada, and Europe became routine over time, but the trips to China, India, Australia, South Africa, and the Middle East never did, quite simply because of the distance involved. It gives you a true sense of the size of the world when it takes more than a day to get somewhere at close to a thousand kilometres per hour.

A trip to Bali, Indonesia, in October 2018 was especially long. The purpose was to attend the annual meetings of the International Monetary Fund (IMF) and World Bank, which generally are moved from Washington, D.C., to a member country every second year. A mass of humanity descends on the host country—central bankers, finance ministers, teams of officials, commercial bankers, media, and so on—straining the security and accommodation infrastructure. Bali being a dream tourist destination, this trip made it onto my lifetime list of real perquisites. Of course, almost the entire time was to be spent in meetings, but the hotel was on the beach so at least the prospect was tantalizing. It was late spring in Bali—and hot. The men were told in advance to wear a batik shirt, instead of a suit and tie. This sounded quite adventurous to me.

When we landed at the airport, we were given VIP treatment, taken to a private room for refreshment while officials took care of the immigration process. Then we were whisked down to the beach and checked into the hotel. While being shown to my room, I was briefed on earthquake and tsunami protocols. Although deep in a jet-lag fog, I paid attention to this spiel, because only a couple of weeks earlier there had been a catastrophic seismic event in Central Sulawesi, in the north part of Indonesia, accompanied by a gigantic tsunami. Tragically, more than four thousand people were killed and many thousands more displaced. This was top-of-mind for all of us, and it is a mark of Indonesian resiliency that the meetings in Bali went ahead as planned. The person who showed me to my room pointed out where to go—upstairs, as it turned out, to be above a major wave—in case the alarms sounded. The room was lovely, with lots of large windows divided into small panes. I went straight to bed, as is my custom on such trips, and was instantly deep asleep.

There is nothing quite like the chilling sound of rattling glass in the dead of night. I was on my feet in a split second, only to discover that the floor was moving. The entire room was rocking back and forth. I stood in the bathroom doorway until the shaking ended. I had little information to go on. The earthquake was much stronger than one I had experienced in the mid-1980s in Ottawa, where the rocking was sufficient to spill water out of our kitchen sink onto the floor. But it was weaker than a Tokyo earthquake a friend had described to me, when half the water in an outdoor swimming pool had sloshed out. My mind was preoccupied with the possibility of a tsunami, which would come ashore later. The earthquake might have felt modest where I was if the epicentre was far away, in which case it could still create a major wave that would land on our doorstep. But there was no alarm sounding in the hotel, no one else in the corridors. I did what anyone else would do—I checked Google. The earthquake had been a 6.4. No tsunami predicted. So I went back to bed but did not fall back asleep for quite a while. I suppose the locals grow accustomed to living with such risk every day, but it gave us visitors plenty to discuss at breakfast the next morning.

Beginning with a Metaphor

The world as we know it has taken some 200 million years to form, and it remains in constant motion today, as Indonesians know all too well. Even young children can look at a standard map of our world and notice that the shores of western Europe and Africa line up very nicely with the eastern shores of North and South America. They were once a single land mass, referred to by scientists as Pangaea, which began breaking up during the Jurassic period, about 150 to 200 million years ago.

Scientists believe that convection currents originating deep inside the semi-molten mantle of our planet cause the tectonic plates that make up the Earth's crust to float around. This is an extremely slow process, measuring perhaps as little as ten centimetres per year. But the sheer power behind this tiny change is incalculable. Over 200 million years, this cumulative motion was enough to create the Atlantic Ocean, as the Eurasian plate and African plate moved away from the North American plate and the South American plate. The world will continue to change over the next fifty million years as these tectonic forces widen the Atlantic Ocean further, and Australia will drift further north toward the equator.

A particularly interesting situation occurs when two tectonic plates are grinding past each other. Much of the time, the plates drift in this way without major incident. Perhaps the most famous of these boundaries is the San Andreas fault that runs through California, heading inland from the Pacific Ocean at San Francisco and angling south toward Palm Springs. Along that fault line, the Pacific plate is gradually moving northward, while the North American plate is drifting southward, resulting in almost continuous modest earthquakes in the region. This regular tectonic motion, or drift, accompanied by occasional tremors, is a form of equilibrium.

However, when the two plates stick together, the motion stops and stresses build up as the plates try to move. At some point, the pent-up force becomes great enough that the plates break free of one another, moving rapidly for a few moments, as if to make up for lost time. The result is a major earthquake, like the one that brought death and destruction to Sulawesi. Humankind can do little about such forces of nature, except try to understand them, perhaps predict them, and, most important of all, be prepared for them.

Five Economic Forces in Motion

Like tectonic forces, economic forces can deliver Earth-shaking power when they are released. While tectonic forces operate over millions of years, natural economic forces operate over decades, a significant period of time in a human lifetime. Like tectonic forces, natural economic forces are essentially imperceptible and rarely move in a straight line. Predicting the consequences of economic forces is never a straightforward, mechanical exercise, even if some economists make it sound that way.

Many casual observers think an economy operates like a car with lots of moving parts and fancy electronics. But the operation of a car is not complex in a behavioural sense. If you step on the accelerator, it moves forward. While there is a lot going on under the hood, everything is purely mechanical and therefore easy to predict. For every input you give the system, there is a corresponding output.

With a moving economic force, the underlying complexity always gives rise to uncertainty about its consequences. This means that economic predictions should always be expressed as probabilities, like weather reports. Economic forecasting is like driving a car in such disrepair that we can only say that it will probably move forward, but there is also a chance it will suddenly veer to the left or to the right.

The various linkages in an economy are far more complex than those in a machine like a car, because they are the product of the behaviour of individuals, viewed collectively. Economic forces sometimes amplify one another, pushing the economy in the same direction and creating a surprisingly large impact. Often, two forces partially counteract one another, each pushing the economy in opposing directions, and what is observed is the net effect of more than one force. Economists may not understand what brought those forces into balance. What is clear, though, is that a persistent imbalance can lead to a build-up of pressure, like when tectonic plates grinding past one another become stuck. Natural forces this powerful cannot be contained forever. At some point, the pressures exceed the friction holding them back and balance is violently restored. In geology, we call these episodes earthquakes; in economics, we refer to them as crises. Crises are the ultimate form of economic instability, outlier events; on the spectrum between economic stability and crisis lies a continuum of rising instability and growing uncertainty about the future.

It is one thing to contemplate the potentially violent interactions between two moving tectonic plates. It is quite another to consider the tectonic forces acting on the global economy, for there are more of them and their interactions are far more complex and unpredictable. This is not just an interesting theory to contemplate, for it may affect your employment security, your savings, or the value of your house.

This book examines five long-term forces that are in motion in the world today: population aging, technological progress, rising inequality, growing debt, and climate change. These forces are truly global in nature and in scope. All were already in motion long before the arrival of COVID-19 and will retain their potency long after the pandemic is behind us. In this sense, they are very much like the tectonic forces operating beneath the Earth's crust.

Consider population aging, my first tectonic force. While the fact that the world's population is aging is very well known, it is also perhaps the most underestimated force in the business world today. Because the population ages gradually, this force is unlikely to have a material effect over the horizon of the typical business plan. However, seventy-five years ago there was a major bulge in world population in the aftermath of World War II, lasting about twenty years; the peak year for births was around 1960. These people began to enter the global workforce in the 1970s. The bulge in workers peaked in the early 1980s, and many of them are exiting the workforce in the 2010–30 window. For many of us, our perceptions have been heavily influenced by the fifty-year bulge in the labour force driven by the baby boom generation, which is now reversing as the baby boomers slide through the retirement stage.

Economic growth consists of two elements: labour force growth and productivity growth. Therefore, economic growth is constrained by labour force growth. We are now entering an era of much slower labour force growth and therefore a slower growth trend in the economy. In the broad sweep of history, this is a return to more normal conditions, after a fifty-year disruption caused by the baby boom, which delivered quite rapid economic growth. This perspective is important because expectations for the future are generally anchored by our collective historical experience. Rapid population aging means that the experience of the past fifty years will not be a good guide for the future. That is, economic growth will not recover to its recent historical average. It will instead converge with the average of a much longer historical baseline—which will seem pretty lacklustre compared to the anomaly of the baby boom years.

Population aging also has implications for interest rates. When the economy is in a stable position, with no stresses or disturbances working through it, there emerges a natural relationship between the trend economic growth rate and the average level of interest rates. After adjusting for inflation, the two are roughly equal. For example, with inflation steady at 2% and an interest rate of 3%, the real (or after-inflation) interest rate would be 1%, and trend economic growth would also be about 1%. Of course, these relationships do not hold precisely at every point in time; reality is never as simple as an economics textbook. But they are true on average over longer periods, in much the same way that the average July temperature in Ottawa is around 21°C (70°F) and any given day can be quite different from the average. (I explain the implications for interest rates in more detail in chapter 2.)

As the baby boomers aged from their thirties to their fifties, their participation in the workforce boosted economic growth and pushed real interest rates higher, too. Observed interest rates rose even more in the late 1970s and early 1980s because inflation was rising at the same time. Both effects on interest rates peaked in the early 1980s.

Interest rates have been trending down since then. At first, this was mainly because of falling inflation, but in the last decade it is also due to aging baby boomers exiting the workforce.

The second tectonic force I examine in this book is technological progress, which is older than economics. Of the five forces, it is the only positive one. Documented from the beginning of human history, technological progress is always operating beneath the surface of and adding to economic growth. From time to time, however, humankind develops a technology that is applied throughout the economy with far-reaching effects on productivity. This is referred to as a general-purpose technology because of its wide applicability. Such episodes are sufficiently important to economic history that they are referred to as industrial revolutions, as in the deployment of the steam engine during the 1800s, electrification in the early 1900s, and the computer chip in the mid-1970s.

Each of these technological leaps delivered untold benefits to society, in terms of quality of life, productivity, and income. Economic growth was boosted above trend for several years, thereby permanently raising the level of national income. However, each technological leap also imposed significant hardships on individuals. Companies had to adapt to each new technology or be forced out of business, which is disruptive for company and employee alike. Many jobs were permanently eliminated and those affected remained unemployed for a long time before moving into something new. The First Industrial Revolution during the mid-1800s was followed by the Victorian depression of 1873–96. The Second Industrial Revolution of the early 1900s was followed by the Great Depression of the 1930s. The Third Industrial Revolution of the 1980s was managed better by policymakers, but considerable disruption and pain nevertheless followed. Rather than depressions, in the early 1990s and again in the early 2000s we saw so-called jobless recoveries—periods in which economic growth recovers but few new jobs are created.

Understanding the deep drivers of past industrial revolutions is important to understanding the future, because we are in the early stages of the Fourth Industrial Revolution. At its roots are the digitalization of the economy, the spread of artificial intelligence, and advances in biotechnology. So far, we have only seen the early consequences of this technological leap. We encounter artificial intelligence when we telephone our bank, or when we search the web for a product and later see targeted ads for that product the next time we go online. We saw new methods in biotechnology in action when it took only months to develop COVID-19 vaccines. The Fourth Industrial Revolution will have much in common with the first three. Accordingly, there is much to be learned from history, not just for policymakers but for firms and individuals, that will prepare us for the future.

My third tectonic force is rising income inequality. Income inequality has ebbed and flowed as an issue for society across the decades, as documented by Thomas Piketty in his 2013 book *Capital in the Twenty-First Century*, but it became front-page news during the COVID-19 pandemic. Historically, the main driver of rising inequality has been technological progress, but globalization has played an important supporting role. It is natural to expect that technological progress will improve the lot of everyone in society. It does eventually, but the first income gains from new technology tend to be scooped up by the inventive few. At the same time, people who are dislocated by new technology or by globalization may be jobless for a long time before finding new employment. Furthermore, the scars of that dislocation can remain for a lifetime, making it difficult for those affected to ever earn as much income as they did in the past. In short, technological change can make the future look very uncertain to individuals.

Those wealthy inventors of new technology and their shareholders will, in time, spend their new income gains throughout the economy, creating jobs in every sector to the benefit of society as a whole. However, few recognize this second-round positive economic effect as originating from the original technological disruption, particularly those who were displaced by the new technology in the first place.

These economic forces unfold not in a lab or a computer model but in a real world shaped by personal choices, giving rise to emotions ranging from fear to envy to anger. Consequently, rising income inequality and technology-led worker dislocation emerge as natural political issues. Not surprisingly, opportunistic politicians have long been tapping into this vein of popular discontent, offering hopes of a more equitable and less uncertain future. I will explain later that well-intentioned politics can easily prove to be counterproductive and lead to even more economic instability and future uncertainty, rather than less. Rising income inequality played a significant role in magnifying and prolonging the pain of the Victorian depression and the Great Depression and became front and centre during the COVID-19 pandemic.

My fourth tectonic force is rising debt, an issue that has attracted a lot of attention in recent years. The baby boomers boosted total household debt while in their peak borrowing years. However, total household debt continued to rise even as the eldest boomers began to retire, as their millennial children are even bigger borrowers. This is partly due to falling interest rates, which make it easier for both households and companies to manage a higher debt load, but innovation by banks has also been an important facilitator. Consider how much easier it is for households to borrow today, compared to in the 1970s or 1980s. Back then, a young couple would apply for a mortgage and wait for several days, on pins and needles, to hear the bank's decision. Metaphorically, we have gone from a fussy restaurant where one can only order from a set menu and then wait a long time for the food to arrive, to a casual restaurant with an all-you-can eat buffet of credit.

Furthermore, rising private sector indebtedness has been a natural side effect of the monetary policies of central banks. Among other things, central banks are charged with reducing the size of fluctuations in the economy in order to keep inflation steady. Whenever the economy weakens, interest rates decline to cushion the blow, encouraging households and companies alike to borrow to make large purchases and boost economic growth. This mechanism also helps weak companies survive the economic downturn, instead of failing, which minimizes job losses. Accordingly, each business cycle has seen indebtedness of both households and firms ratchet up to a new plateau, rather than being flushed out of the system through a tough recession and debt restructuring.

And then there is government debt. Using fiscal policy—increasing government spending or cutting taxes—to boost the economy when it weakens means running a deficit and increasing government borrowing. There has been a rising trend in government debt for at least a generation. Extraordinary government spending during the pandemic has increased global public debt back to levels not seen since the aftermath of World War II—truly, a force in overdrive.

My fifth tectonic force, climate change, has not played a central role in economic history so far, but it is attracting by far the most attention today. Climate change is widely—albeit not universally—acknowledged as a source of economic and financial volatility through specific weather events, such as floods, more frequent severe tropical storms, droughts, wildfires, and polar vortexes. These events cause dislocation of individuals, fatalities, destruction of homes and other infrastructure, and otherwise interrupt the normal flow of life and business. They put strains on government finances and can spill over into financial markets through their impacts on insurance companies and other financial institutions.

Increased attention to climate change is leading many governments to pivot toward policies that will encourage a transition to a net-zero carbon emissions economy by 2050. Examples include emissions regulations and carbon taxation. These carbon-reduction aspirations will face political challenges, of course. But whether a green pivot succeeds, is achieved partially, or fails, this forced energy transition will constitute a new source of volatility for the future. There are many possible paths to net zero, each with different implications for the economy, political outcomes, and compromises that may be unique to each country—all of which makes climate change a major source of uncertainty for individuals and companies.

Many of these paths will entail job losses in the fossil fuel sector and lower incomes in fossil fuel–producing countries. Under certain scenarios, major energy deposits may end up being stranded in the ground, with obvious implications for the market value of those companies and host countries. This volatility will be transmitted directly to the banks that lend to those companies, as investors look carefully for such connections and sell the stocks of both companies and connected banks that do not meet their new environmental standards.

In short, actively reducing carbon emissions, whether voluntarily, through regulation, or through the deployment of carbon taxes, will have extensive implications for economies and jobs. It will raise costs for firms directly by forcing them to invest in carbon-reduction technology, and indirectly as investors shun their securities, making borrowing more expensive. Many firms will adjust by deploying technology that reduces their carbon footprint and their workforce at the same time. The business environment will never be the same—that much is certain.

Interactions between Forces Create Instability

Importantly, all five of these forces are in motion and reaching critical stress levels at the same time. They are colliding with one another, building upon one another, and creating stresses just like the Earth's tectonic plates. The rising risk of economic and financial earthquakes will increase uncertainty about the future considerably.

Individual forces acting on the economy can produce orderly, understandable, and even predictable effects. For example, economists have thought about the impact of population aging for many years and have built models that capture some of its predicted effects on the economy. Most macroeconomic models assume that all consumers are the same and therefore only capture "average" consumer behaviour. This is obviously a serious limitation, but models are only intended to be rough approximations to the truth; simplifying assumptions are essential to building something that can be understood and used by economists. A richer model would allow for different behaviour between working households and retired households, for example, and then attach relative weights to the two groups before combining them to predict total consumer spending. Such a model would show how the aging population leads to slower economic growth than would a model based only on one typical household.

Economists' models are based on statistical averages. For example, when interest rises, household borrowing slows down, which is common sense. But by how much, and how quickly? The answer depends on other circumstances and varies across different households. In a macroeconomic model, a single number—economists call it an "elasticity"—summarizes all these possible outcomes. It is calculated based on average historical experience, say over the past ten or twenty years. The actual response of total borrowing in the economy to a given rise in interest rates may not match that specific elasticity, but on average it will, and the estimated elasticity is considered the most likely outcome. It is good practice for economists to acknowledge that predictions from their models are not certain and to provide some indication of the associated uncertainty. This can be done by making the prediction in the form of odds, as in a weather report, or as a range of possible outcomes. In the latter case, the greater the uncertainty between cause and effect, the wider the range of possible economic outcomes.

Acknowledging uncertainty in this way is appropriate but not widely practised. Imagine a media report where one economist is quoted as saying that interest rates could be between 1% and 4% next year, while another says confidently that interest rates will be 2.5% next year. The first is being honest and provides an understanding of the associated uncertainty, and that uncertainty remains with the audience. The second economist internalizes the uncertainty and gives the audience something simple to digest. They may feel no uncertainty at all. It is not surprising that it is the confident, simplifying economist who is quoted most often in the news media. People instinctively dislike uncertainty and are comforted by confident experts. And if interest rates turn out to be 3% next year, meaning that the first economist had a better forecast than the second, few will remember. This is unfortunate as the first economist could actually help people understand the risks they are taking when making financial decisions, and such knowledge could lead them to different decisions. The second economist, while more reassuring, leads people to take on more risk themselves, whether or not they realize it. In the future, better risk management practices by households will require pressing confident economists to elaborate on their forecasts and explain the upside and downside risks involved.

Analyzing multiple forces compounds the uncertainty problem profoundly. Each linkage between cause and effect has some uncertainty associated with it. Taking account of multiple sources of uncertainty at once means that the range of possibilities around an economic forecast becomes even wider. Further, that range of possibilities expands even more as the forecaster looks further into the future.

And that is just on paper. The real world is even more complex, because the multiple forces acting on the economy also affect one another. Economists call these dynamic interactions "endogeneity." Tracing all these endogenous interactions in an economic model is extremely difficult. The more complex and realistic a model becomes, the more difficult it is to measure the statistical uncertainty around the model's predictions. Indeed, it is my contention that when multiple long-term forces are acting together on the economy through time, and interacting with one another as well, the economy itself can behave erratically and appear unstable, perhaps even going into crisis. In this situation, the predictions of a model may have no value at all.

This idea has its roots in the mathematics of chaos theory. Its name says it all. Mathematicians have demonstrated that when well-understood dynamic processes interact with each other, they often produce predictions that are so volatile they are essentially chaotic. A simple example from everyday life is when a jet cruising through clear air encounters unexplained turbulence. The curvature of the wing—essential to creating the lift that allows the plane to fly—interacts with the resistance in the air to create minor elements of randomness, impossible to predict in advance, in the performance of the plane.

A parallel in medicine would be when someone contracts a well-understood illness and unexpectedly dies because of its interaction with another underlying condition that was believed to be under control, such as in the case of a very fit person suffering from PTSD suddenly dying of heart failure. Such outcomes appear incomprehensible until we allow for the possibility that the many interactions between health forces are far too complex for us to understand or attempt to model.

In terms of economic outcomes, even if we understand each individual force affecting the outlook, their interaction may produce outcomes that appear to be incomprehensible and therefore chaotic in a mathematical sense.

This reasoning offers an alternative explanation for "black swan" events, a term popularized by Nassim Nicholas Taleb in his 2007 book. Examples cited by Taleb include the rise of the internet or the terrorist attacks on 9/11, which were completely unexpected and game-changing. When an economist declares that an economic or financial event (such as the 2008 Global Financial Crisis) is a black swan, they are essentially absolving themselves of any responsibility for not foreseeing it. As Taleb points out, not all swans are as black as they seem, not even the one that landed in 2008. Once an event has happened, however, it switches from being unthinkable to potentially repeatable, and it becomes natural to offer rationalizations of it. After-the-fact rationalizations of unforeseen events are boundless in their ingenuity.

The new interpretation I offer in this book is that sometimes economies throw up what appear to be completely random events, such as crises, due to ordinary forces interacting beneath the surface in unusual ways. After crises happen, we understand them better, but that does not make them forecastable.

To illustrate this point, consider the tectonic plates along the San Andreas fault, which we know are in motion all the time. Earthquakes are inevitable. A prediction that a major earthquake is inevitable "someday" is not very helpful. However, if the prediction comes with ranges as to magnitude and timeline, it becomes valuable as a guide for risk management. Such a forecast would constitute a warning to prepare now to deal with the risk, whenever it does happen. If we get lucky, and experience two small earthquakes spread over a week instead of a single devastating one, the steps we have taken to manage the risk will not have been wasted.

Similarly, in economics, understanding the underlying forces that made an unforeseen event possible also guides us in risk management, because the event itself demonstrates what might happen. This is why airlines recommend that you keep your seatbelt fastened at all times when seated, even when turbulence is not expected; they are reducing the odds that you will be hurt should random clear-air turbulence happen, and experience shows that it might.

I will demonstrate that understanding these five tectonic forces provides a more complete explanation for many economic and financial crises, such as the Victorian depression of the late 1800s, the Great Depression of the 1930s, the Asian financial crisis of 1997, and the Global Financial Crisis of 2008. While these events have been studied extensively, the roles played by tectonic forces have received scant attention. Rather, emphasis has been given to more proximate triggers for these events, such as excessive speculation supported by financial leverage and stock market crashes. Many of us carry the impression that the Great Depression was caused by the 1929 stock market crash. I will show that a more compelling narrative is that the technological progress of the 1920s led to job disruption, rising inequality, and falling prices. Falling prices interacted with high levels of debt to put the economy into a deep and prolonged downturn.

With these learnings from past crises in hand, I will argue that the tectonic forces will generate increased uncertainty in the future, and that employees and employers will be seeking ways to manage that uncertainty to survive and prosper.

COVID-19: A Test of Resilience

When COVID-19 slammed the world, everything else was forgotten. The pandemic was a natural disaster of the first order, crushing tourism, entertainment, bars, restaurants, gyms, airlines, and in-person retail businesses of all shapes and sizes. It has altered work arrangements, shopping preferences, and educational settings. Some of these behavioural changes will have a permanent effect on our social fabric, and the experience will leave scars that affect perceptions for generations. Just as the Great Depression affected the perceptions and behaviours of our elders for the rest of their lives, so too will living through COVID-19 affect ours and those of our children and grandchildren.

The first few weeks of the pandemic were pandemonium, as I describe in some detail in chapter 8. Financial markets were in considerable stress. Investors sold just about everything to raise cash, and firms tapped every source of liquidity available. Central banks deployed all available tools—cutting interest rates effectively to zero, lending in unlimited amounts to financial institutions, purchasing government debt directly, and so on—to ensure that financial markets continued to function. The global banking system weathered the pandemic well, a testament to the changes made in the wake of the Global Financial Crisis. Governments supported individuals extensively, all around the world, with direct payments and wage subsidies that helped to maintain the link between employer and employee.

Importantly, the five tectonic forces were already in motion when COVID-19 arrived. Economic and financial volatility had been rising for some time, but the pandemic raised the volatility bar. It would be natural to expect a quieter post-pandemic world, but the tectonic forces will remain in motion, and some of them have been accelerated by COVID-19. Government debt has increased dramatically. The deployment of new technology is picking up speed. Factories are creating more space between workers using automation, more services are being delivered remotely with the help of artificial intelligence, and shopping from home is becoming the norm rather than the exception. Measures of income inequality have spiked in the wake of COVID-19, as the virus has mainly impacted workers in lower pay grades, in the service sector, and has had its greatest effects on women. Even the adjustments to climate change are being accelerated, as governments appear even more committed to rebuilding economies with a greener tilt, and investors are demanding greener behaviour on the part of companies.

Navigating the post-pandemic economy would be difficult enough in normal circumstances. But the five tectonic forces will come together to create even more economic volatility in the future, posing extreme uncertainty for individuals and for companies, long after the pandemic is behind us. Employers and employees alike will look to governments to protect them from rising economic and financial risk.

Higher Risk Must Land Somewhere

Like the waves in a stormy ocean, increased volatility must land somewhere. It will show up in several key channels, such as economic growth, unemployment, inflation, and interest rates. The economic ground beneath our feet is shifting. In the decades ahead, features of our lives we may think of as immutable are going to change, in some cases rapidly. What we consider to be traditional ways of working and learning, of borrowing and spending, of planning and innovating—this is all on the cusp of change. The role of corporations in our lives is likely to expand. The role of government social safety nets will be reconsidered, and probably reconsidered again.

Economics is not something that happens only in boardrooms and at think tanks. It comprises nearly all of our decisions. It is everyday life. Change the economic bedrock and you change everything.

2

POPULATION AGING

Reflections: Oshawa, 1959

In my earliest memory, I am in the living room of my parents' first home, on Grierson Street in north Oshawa. It is a modest neighbourhood, decidedly blue collar, but as I was taught from a young age, at least our home was in the north end. Modest as ours was, there were many other neighbourhoods visibly less well off.

My father was a tool and die maker for an auto parts company. His job entailed using a specialized machine, something akin to a router, to cut extra-hard steel into a die, which is essentially a reverse mould. The die was then fixed to a machine that would stamp thousands of identical auto parts out of sheet metal. It was a precision business using measurements of thousandths of an inch because, as my father would tell me, the stamped pieces needed to fit together perfectly to assemble the car. My mother was a homemaker and did office work at various times during my childhood—that is to say, during financially stressful times.

I am about four years old in this memory, making it 1959. I know it was after the cancellation by the Canadian government of the Avro

Arrow supersonic jet program, which took place in February 1959. My father had been working for an aerospace parts supplier and lost his job as a result.

It is nighttime, and there are a lot of people visiting—various aunts, uncles, and my maternal grandparents—seated around the room on a variety of casual and kitchen chairs as well as the forest-green sofa under the front window. There is a Christmas tree on one side of the room, with a few presents arranged under it. The room is filled with tobacco smoke; almost everyone is smoking. I can see my father drawing hard on his cigarette, the tip glowing brightly in the semidarkness. I can see my mother on the other side of the room, laughing heartily, cigarette in hand. "What's up, Stephco?" bellows my grandfather, using the nickname he gave me at birth, possibly because he already owned the name "Stevie" himself.

My parents grew up during the Great Depression of the 1930s, and they met and married in the late 1940s. Although my father was too young to have participated in the war, I am a part of the baby boom cohort. This chapter on demographics will demonstrate how important that cohort has been to our economic history. The bulge in births between 1945 and 1964 boosted the supply of workers in the 1960 to '80 window and we're seeing a massive exodus beginning in 2010 and lasting until 2030.

That demographic cohort also carried into the future important economic behaviours learned at the kitchen table. I heard many stories about struggling through the Depression, often beginning with the phrase, "You think you have it tough, do you? Well, let me tell you about when I was young . . ." My mother told me that an empty Corn Flakes box was cut up to make insoles to make her shoes last longer. My father had the grades in high school to attend university, but there was no money to pay for his tuition. He worked at his father's shoe repair shop—situated in the front of the family home on Simcoe Street South—while apprenticing as a tool and die maker in the late 1940s. Borrowing was always seen as an unfortunate family event. If you must borrow, say to purchase a house or a car, you would pay off the debt as quickly as possible, and invite your friends over for drinks and dinner the night you "burn the mortgage" or make your last car payment. These attitudes get passed down through generations and cause echoes in the future—in a way similar to the health consequences for children of smoking during pregnancy and raising them in a house full of second-hand smoke.

Economists often joke that demographics is easy to understand and predict, because we can be reasonably confident that one year from now, we will all be one year older. LOL, as they say.

Besides reflecting on the limited sense of humour of many economists, and their preference for inside jokes non-economists rarely appreciate, this truism does not do justice to the effects that demographic trends have on consumer spending, saving, interest rates, and economic growth. Economic models generally ignore demographics, because over the horizon that many are preoccupied with (say, a few quarters or up to two years), demographics can be taken as a constant. For investments that will last for ten years or more (perhaps as long as fifty years in the resource extraction business), understanding demographics could be critical to evaluating their present value.

But regardless of the horizon that is relevant to a company or to an individual, the outlook for economic growth and interest rates always matters. Demographics are a key ingredient of the trend line to which economic growth is expected to return by most forecasters. Even for companies with a short-term focus, demographic forces can make an important difference to the business outlook.

Economic Trends Courtesy of Mother Nature

Economic growth comes from two sources: growth in the number of workers, or growth in output per worker, which is called productivity growth. In an economy with a constant population—where there are just enough births each year to offset the number of deaths, and no immigration or emigration—economic growth would depend on rising productivity alone. Productivity is driven by production technology, which is a general term that encompasses such things as using machinery to speed up processes that previously were done by hand; replacing old machinery with faster machinery; organizing the factory floor to eliminate bottlenecks; upgrading workers' skills through training; or deploying an entirely new technology.

The number of available workers is limited by population growth. While it is possible that a change could cause more people to enter the workforce—subsidized daycare for preschool children, for example—in the absence of such structural changes, the available labour force basically tracks population growth. Population growth is relatively simple to predict by working with typical birth, death, and immigration rates.

Productivity growth is far more complicated as it depends on technological progress and its deployment, which is never smooth. Given this complexity, economists generally extrapolate from the recent trend in productivity growth, which amounts to an assumption rather than a forecast. A typical trend line for productivity growth is around 1% per year for advanced economies, and higher for emerging economies, which are catching up by importing technology from advanced economies.

Accordingly, an economy with 1% population growth and 1% productivity growth would exhibit about 2% trend economic growth. This trend in economic growth is often referred to as "potential growth": in normal times, it represents a ceiling on sustainable economic expansion. If the economy grows above that trend, inflationary pressures often emerge; if it grows below that trend, inflation is more likely to decline.

The economy would experience business cycles around that trend line as it is always being buffeted by disturbances. Suppose, for example, that oil prices rose suddenly because of a terrorist attack on a major oil production facility in the Middle East. Oil-importing countries would see their economies slow to a subtrend growth rate, while oil-exporting countries would pick up speed. After this disturbance settled, however, economies would make their way back to those original growth trend lines driven by population and productivity growth.

The economy returns to its potential economic growth rate after a disturbance naturally, although sometimes government or central bank policies can get it back more quickly. Because it is a state where the economy is in balance, economists refer to it as an "equilibrium" or "steady state." With the economy always being hit by one disturbance or another, we almost never observe it in a steady state. However, the idea remains relevant, for it describes the destination toward which the economy tends to return after a disturbance, in the same way that a bobblehead doll's head always returns to stillness. It is therefore a useful description of the economy "on average" over long periods of time, say five to ten years.

The main anchor to this description of the economy's steady state is global population growth, which has been slowing for most of my adult life. The global population has been steadily aging as the dominant cohort—the baby boomers—move through the world's age profile. In addition to this effect, lifespans have been lengthening due to better diet, lower smoking rates, and improved health care. As a consequence, the share of people sixty-five years or older in the total world population has been creeping up. The United Nations forecasts that this ratio will soon rise much more quickly, from less than 10% today to nearly 15% by 2050.

While population aging is a global phenomenon, it is at different stages in different parts of the world. Today, Japan and much of western Europe are the most advanced, with more than 25% of the population over age sixty-five. Canada, the U.S., central Europe, Russia, Australia, and New Zealand are a few years behind this trend, and China is only slightly behind that group. The youngest populations are in Latin America and especially Africa and the Middle East. Even so, all of us will be affected by the global aging trend.

Global population growth peaked in the mid-1960s at about 2% per year and has been steadily declining since. Global population growth is now at about 1% per year and is projected to slow to about 0.5% per year by 2050, and it may approach zero around 2100. That would put the global population somewhere between ten to twelve billion people, up from only three billion in the 1950s. The baby boom generation—those born between 1945 and 1964—are now between the ages of fifty-five and seventy-five. Even if better health and longer lifespans mean people remain in the workforce longer than in the past, the next ten to twenty years will still see a significant slowdown in global labour force growth.

Few people are surprised to hear these numbers, as they generally have a feel for the boomer phenomenon, but some of the implications for the economy are hidden in plain sight. Since economic growth is fuelled mainly by population growth, it follows that the trend in potential global economic growth, which has been slowing for the past decade, will continue to decelerate gradually for the next fifty years. At some point, population growth will cease altogether, and the world's only source of new growth will be from technological advances.

The concept of a "return to growth" is deeply embedded in our collective memories. Those of us who grew up in a world of 2% population growth fuelling economic growth are already wrestling with the idea of a deceleration of 1%. A further deceleration of 0.5% is in store for our children, and more deceleration for our grandchildren. It is difficult for people who have only lived for the past fifty years to contemplate this slowing trend line. They are accustomed to the economy growing solidly and think of it as a trend from which we have only fallen short in the last few years. Accordingly, many also consider recent weak growth as something that is temporary or can be fixed, which is only partly true.

In short, the economy will continue to return to normal, but that normal is being redefined by our aging population.

Giving Mother Nature a Helping Hand

Global demographics are one thing, but the situation in individual countries can vary considerably. In Canada, for example, homegrown workforce growth will hit zero sometime in the 2020s as the baby boomers retire. This raises the possibility that Canada will follow the same track that Japan did over twenty years ago. In the 1980s, the Japanese economy was a powerhouse; during the 1990s, a combination of population aging and low immigration levels caused economic growth to slow to a crawl. In the 2010s, Japan introduced policies to encourage more labour force participation by women, and as the workforce began to expand, economic growth picked up.

Canada has avoided this slowdown in the past through a welcoming immigration policy designed to foster about 1% population growth annually, thereby putting a floor under economic growth. Even so, if immigration levels are to remain unchanged, Canada's aging population would still be causing growth to slow over the next few years. Canada has recently raised its immigration targets and, provided that Canada remains a preferred destination, it may be able to avoid much of the global deceleration in economic growth. In other words, allowing more immigration is not just doing the world a favour, it is the world doing a favour for Canada.

A reoptimized distribution of people around the globe could also boost global economic growth. Talented, hardworking people can contribute more to global output in a society with more machinery and equipment, a better social safety net and other support systems, and more social and physical infrastructure, than they can trying to scratch out a living in an underdeveloped setting.

The point is, slowing population growth should not be thought of as some sort of doomsday scenario. The consequences of declining population growth can be offset, or at least delayed, by creating more labour force participation, by women or by older individuals. In developing countries, effective labour force participation can be increased significantly by structural reforms. However, such policies cannot alter the demographic forces that shape long-term economic growth.

Of course, simply having more people doesn't automatically mean more wealth. There are poor countries with no shortage of citizens, and there always have been. What allows an economy to harness the potential of its workforce is skills development and investment in capital, such as machinery and infrastructure. Together, these ingredients generate productivity growth, which is the amount of output each worker can produce and the other source of economic growth as mentioned above. In most economies, productivity growth is a steady source of new growth, like a rising tide. But occasionally there is a major technological wave that boosts productivity growth everywhere for a time; this phenomenon is examined in detail in the next chapter.

The most staggering example of economic growth in our lifetimes was driven not by technology but by a shift in government policy. China's economic miracle during the last thirty years was driven primarily by land ownership reform. The economy was transformed from a collection of single-family farms, each producing just enough to support its family, into one of commercial large-scale farming. Large firms can afford the purchase of farm machinery and investment in crop specialization, thereby boosting productivity and economic growth. Meanwhile, the displaced families moved from the countryside into the cities, where they fuelled a major expansion in China's workforce. That workforce expansion enabled a massive increase in manufacturing and services, just as China was joining the global trade system. The rest, as they say, is history—and we're living through it.

Still, it is impossible for any economy to sustain the rampant growth achieved during China's early economic breakthroughs. No country can grow by 10% forever. Economic growth in China has been in a declining trend now for many years. The reform process has matured, as it had to. But regardless of the rate of economic growth, the *level* of income will always be far higher than it was before the governmental policies that nudged the country into global markets. Eventually, as living standards approach those of other major countries, China's growth will look more like that of today's major economies.

This process of economic growth convergence by developing economies has happened many times before. It happened in Japan over the

1960–90 period, for example. Japan was able to benefit from technological advances in other countries and, by building from scratch, to
orchestrate true leaps in economic performance. As Japan made substantial inroads into such traditional North American bastions as motor
vehicle and television manufacturing, a fear emerged in Western societies that someday Japan might "take over." Movies like *Rising Sun* from
1993, starring Sean Connery, exemplified this fear.

We know that this fear was misplaced, but the underlying reasons
that Japan never "took over" are not well understood. The first reason
was demographic, as discussed above. The second reason is that an
economy's steady state growth rate also depends on its stage of development. Technological progress is spread around the world much like
fresh air. Ideas can be patented and even geopolitically hoarded but
remain easy to reverse-engineer and copy. Technological leaders are
like the leading goose in a V-shaped flock of Canada geese, breaking
the headwinds for the others that follow.

Over time, economies that are lagging can catch up in terms of per
capita income, either by importing the new technology or by copying
the ideas they see being developed by the leaders. Becoming the lead
goose, of course, requires technological and R&D leadership, which
is much harder to achieve. Korea is now well on its way to replicating
Japan's successful convergence during 1960 to '90 and, not coinciden-
tally, in many of the same product spaces, such as automobiles and
electronics.

The reader may find it ironic that the lead Canada goose in the
world is actually America, but I believe the metaphor is still apt (and
Canadians do not have a monopoly on Canada geese, as I regularly
see them on the golf course when I am in California).

This is all to say that trend economic growth is driven mainly by
population growth, whether homegrown or through immigration.

Productivity growth is usually a secondary source of economic growth, but it will become the primary driver as populations age. Given the gradual slowdown in population growth that is underway due to the aging baby boomers, in the absence of a new and long-lasting surge in productivity growth, worldwide economic growth is likely to remain on a gradually declining trend for the foreseeable future.

The Natural Rate of Interest

Population trends also affect interest rates. When the economy is on a stable path, with no stresses or disturbances working through it, there is a natural relationship between the trend economic growth rate and the average level of interest rates. After adjusting for inflation, the two are roughly equal. The immediate implication is that if global economic growth is expected to drift down in coming years, so will interest rates.

The explanation for this relationship is not complicated. The interest rates we observe consist of two components: the rate of inflation and the base (or "real") interest rate that excludes inflation. With inflation steady at 2% and an interest rate of 3%, the real, or after-inflation, interest rate would be 1%. The real rate of interest can fluctuate when the economy is disturbed but tends to return to what economists refer to as the "natural rate," again like a bobblehead doll. This interest rate anchors the system by maintaining a balance between saving and borrowing in the economy.

Suppose that households are the savers and companies are the borrowers. When rates are high, households save more, making more funds available for borrowing by companies, but if rates are high, companies will borrow less. This combination of high saving and low borrowing pushes rates down to make it less tempting to save and more tempting to borrow. Naturally, as more people borrow and there are fewer savings on hand to lend, rates go back up. All things being equal, saving and borrowing balance out.

Companies borrow to invest in their businesses, which contributes directly to faster economic growth. Therefore, when interest rates fall below the natural rate, borrowing and investment pick up, boosting economic growth. However, lower interest rates foster lower savings, which means less funds available to borrow, and so interest rates move back up, borrowing and investment gear back, saving and borrowing move back into balance, and economic growth subsides back to normal. This balanced situation is one where economic growth and the natural rate of interest are in alignment. Again, given that the economy is always fluctuating for one reason or another, this alignment is something that emerges on average over long periods, not at each moment in time.

The natural rate of interest is not observable directly, but economists have methods for estimating its value. The interest rates we observe in the market include "markups"—when taking out a mortgage, for example, you might pay the real rate of interest, plus 2% to account for inflation, plus another 1% if you want to borrow for five years instead of one year, because the lender wants protection in case rates go up. A company wishing to issue a five-year corporate bond would pay these same markups, plus an additional markup to account for the risk that they might default on the loan. The size of the risk premium would depend on their credit rating (BB, BBB, A, and so on).

As the baby boomers aged through their thirties to their fifties from the 1970s to the '90s, their participation in the workforce boosted economic growth. Because they were also in their peak borrowing years, the natural rate of interest and therefore real rates were being pushed up, too. Observed interest rates rose even more in the late 1970s and early 1980s because inflation was rising at the same time. The two sources of upward pressure on interest rates peaked in the early 1980s. Interest rates have been trending down since then.

At first this downward trend was mainly because of falling inflation, but in the last decade it has been the aging of baby boomers that has kept rates down. Older people tend to save more as they approach retirement: population aging brings with it more savings, which means more capital is available to firms to borrow for investment. At the same time, however, firms see the slowing overall economic growth rate as a reason to invest less, since it pushes down the likely return on their investments. The steady state interest rate—variously called the natural rate, the neutral rate, or sometimes "r-star"—will decline along with trend economic growth.

Much of the decline in interest rates we have seen in the past twenty to thirty years is really Mother Nature at work. Indeed, over the past 150 years, low real interest rates have been the norm, not the exception. Long-term nominal interest rates (uncorrected for inflation) were less than 5% for nearly forty years during the latter half of the nineteenth century, then again after World War I until the mid-1960s. At that point, the entry of baby boomers into the labour force boosted economic growth and real rates of interest, and this bulge in real rates was reinforced in terms of nominal rates by the outbreak of the Great Inflation in the 1970s.

What this means is that people in my age cohort tend to believe that higher interest rates are normal, but that historical experience is mostly because of demographics and inflation. Our children are learning quickly that low interest rates are much more the norm. We are returning to an era reminiscent of the 1950s and early 1960s. We are returning to "normal."

Another factor that has been weighing on interest rates in the last twenty years has been financial intermediation—innovation and competitive forces in banking. Interest is what one pays to buy something today rather than saving the money first and buying it later; essentially, interest is the cost of impatience. When the ability to borrow was subject to artificial constraints during the 1960s and 1970s, consumers were prepared to pay a higher rate of interest to satisfy their current wants rather than saving and waiting. However, the borrowing process at banks and other financial intermediaries has since evolved from that conservative, paternalistic, highly constrained system to one where households essentially manage their own borrowing in a self-serve credit system. This has been facilitated by increased competition in financial intermediation and technological advances that allow financial institutions to manage credit risk far more efficiently than in the past. People's degree of spending impatience no longer seems to be constrained by the real rate of interest, as it had been in the past.

Let's translate all these concepts into the observable world. If the economy were growing in inflation-adjusted terms at, say, 1% and inflation was 2%, then in nominal (or observable) terms the economy would be growing at 3%. The average company would see 3% revenue growth, and governments would see 3% tax revenue growth. If the steady state real rate of interest were 1%, the interest rates we pay— what we call the nominal rate of interest—would be based on 3% (1% real economic growth plus 2% inflation). Longer-term interest rates would be higher, and higher-risk borrowers would pay a risk-specific premium on top of those rates. This is how we end up with such a complexity of observed interest rates in the real world.

Even so, they are all tied together by the common factor of the natural rate of interest. Behind those rates are natural linkages between the natural rate and economic growth, population growth, productivity, and inflation. In the short term, they fluctuate independently for multiple reasons, so this long-term relationship between them may not be obvious to the casual observer. But they are anchored together, like a group of children on a school trip, tethered by a series of six-foot ropes. The most important of these "children" is the rate of population growth, as it has begun to hold the entire group back and will do so for the foreseeable future.

Trend global economic growth will not recover to its historical average. In fact, it will grind lower in the next ten to twenty years. The natural rate of interest, the anchor for our system of interest rates, will also remain low for the foreseeable future. Global workforce growth will trend down, and workers may be in short supply, particularly in economies with restrictive immigration policies. Aging countries may need to compete with one another to attract immigrants to fill workforce shortages. Meanwhile, the growing elderly population will put major demands on health care systems, both acute and assisted living, and government finances will be strained.

While individual countries may be able to postpone the inevitable through increased immigration, the world as a whole cannot do so. The best way to ensure continued increases in living standards and boost trend economic growth globally is to promote technological progress.

3

TECHNOLOGICAL PROGRESS

Reflections: Discovering Science Fiction

Technological progress is always happening, usually in increments small enough to seem underwhelming, at least to fans of science fiction. I developed my taste for science fiction in 1966, at the tender age of eleven, when *Star Trek* first aired on television. We had moved from Oshawa to the nearby rural community of Mitchell's Corners, in time for the arrival of my little brother in 1961. *Star Trek* was a real mind-opener for me—travelling at warp speed, beaming people here and there, handheld devices for communications and medical exams, and reading reports on what today we call a tablet. Many of these concepts still seem quite outlandish fifty years later, but some proved to be highly prescient.

The next few years were typical rural living for my family. Then came the fall and winter of 1966–67, which proved to be very difficult for the Poloz household. My parents did not talk about it much in front of us, but I knew we were struggling. There was a year-long strike at my father's company, led by the production workers whose jobs were under threat from automation. Their job was to stand in front of a giant press, insert a piece of sheet steel, and step on the press trigger. The press holding the die would crash down, turning the flat steel into a car part; the worker would remove the newly formed piece, stack it in a rolling cart, and repeat. All day long. These jobs were obvious candidates for automation, not least for safety reasons. Many a day my father would return home with a story about one of the workers losing a finger or worse. The strike ended up sinking the company.

My father did a lot of odd jobs during that period, including picking apples for the farmer up the road. Eventually, he was able to find work as a tool and die maker at another auto parts supplier, and start again. But the cumulative financial strain proved too great, and in the summer of 1967 my parents sold their dream house and moved back to Oshawa to live with my maternal grandparents.

Theirs was a small, wartime house on Quebec Street, in the south end of town, government-built in the 1940s to accommodate returning veterans and their families. My grandfather was a veteran of World War II, and part of the family lore was that he served in an artillery unit in Europe alongside James Doohan. Twenty years later, Doohan went on to serve as chief engineer Montgomery "Scotty" Scott on the Starship *Enterprise*, in the original *Star Trek* series, which always made my connection to *Star Trek* seem more legitimate.

My grandparents' house had two bedrooms upstairs with sloped ceilings and two bedrooms on the main floor. There was one bathroom, and a coal-burning stove in the living room was the sole source of heat. Attached to the back was a shed piled high with coal that could be accessed easily by the back door. As a young fellow, I had always found it difficult to imagine my grandparents raising five children in that home in the 1940s and 1950s.

I was soon to discover how it could be done. My grandparents moved into the second storey of their home, where my father installed a tiny bathroom for them. One bedroom became a kitchen and a small sitting room, and the other bedroom was used by my grand-mother. My grandfather would make up the sofa with sheets and a blanket every night. The Poloz family lived on the ground floor, and my handyman father added a new room onto the back. The coal-burning stove was replaced by a gas furnace in the crawlspace, as the house had no basement. As a parent and as a grandparent today, I still marvel at this magnanimous gesture on the part of my grandparents.

Knowing no one in Oshawa, and impatiently waiting for eighth grade to begin, I sought out the McLaughlin Public Library, so named after its benefactor, Colonel R.S. McLaughlin, who founded General Motors. I discovered a shelf in the library dedicated to science fiction, with titles by Asimov, Bradbury, Clarke, Heinlein, Herbert, and a host of others. I read the whole shelf that summer. A year later, I watched the first lunar landing in awe—science fiction had become reality.

I think my exposure to science fiction has always made me an optimist when it comes to technological advances and their promise for society as a whole. And yet the year-long disruption of my father's work—the root cause of which was advancing automation—was a major setback for us as well as for my grandparents. Although we had a roof over our heads, it was a crowded one. We had lost the dream home, and there were no savings to finance a university education for me or for my brother. The scars are real ones.

Economics and Human History

The process of economic specialization began after millennia during which humans wandered all day, hunting and gathering their next meal. The discovery that by staying in one place, people could plant their own food and raise their own animals was a tectonic innovation.

That is, agriculture was our first technology. While at first this was a family-oriented subsistence operation, in time people discovered the economic benefits of specializing their work and trading what they produced with others. Some people grew plants, others raised animals, others hunted, and each produced more than if they had tried to do a variety of things all at once. They traded with one another to obtain a steady variety of food.

Eventually the system became good enough that there was a surplus left over after all the work was done—extra production, or savings. That gave our species the ability to create culture, government, a military, and the other things that define modern humans. This historical evolution has been described beautifully by Jared Diamond in his book *Guns, Germs, and Steel*. We're no different today: everybody specializes. And we all use the money we earn to trade for the things we need.

Taking trade international was the next step in this development process. The trade in goods and services was no longer only with neighbours; it was across borders, across oceans, and it required technology, such as shipbuilding and the use of animal power to move goods across distances. (Note that international trade is not between countries, but between people located in different countries.) Specialization in economic activity is what delivers high productivity, societal surplus, and trade (whether domestic or transborder trade) makes us all better off than if we did everything ourselves. Globalization as we refer to it today differs from two hundred years ago only in intensity and in the fragmentation of products and services into geographically distributed supply chains.

Technological progress has been a persistent feature of this history. Steady advances in human capability have been punctuated occasionally by significant leaps in productivity, driven by the widespread adoption of new general-purpose technologies. These leaps in economic performance are big enough to be labelled industrial revolutions.

Three Industrial Revolutions, Three Periods of Pain

The First Industrial Revolution, generally dated from the late 1700s until the late 1800s, was driven by the invention and widespread application of the steam engine, which replaced human or animal energy with something much more powerful. That revolution freed many people from hard labour, which is another way of saying they lost their jobs. Inventors and early adopters of this new technology profited handsomely, giving rise to a stock market boom. Established companies experienced a major shakeout, especially in Europe—those that adopted the technology could offer their wares at a huge discount relative to those that did not. A lot of this competition came from companies in the new economy in North America. It was barely getting started at the time of the First Industrial Revolution, so adopting new technologies was easier in North America than in Europe, where established companies needed to abandon their old technology and invest in the new, a highly disruptive and long process.

Economic theory makes these kinds of adjustment processes sound easy. The new technology can produce the same goods—cloth, say—far more cheaply than the old technology. Cloth prices fall, making it more affordable. New jobs are created in making the technology for clothmakers and in maintaining the machinery. At the same time, lower prices for cloth mean that everyone has more purchasing power than before, leading to more spending on all other goods. This extra spending creates new jobs across the entire economy. The result is that people who lost their jobs when the technology was introduced can eventually find new jobs in other sectors. Historically, every such innovation has eventually created more jobs than it destroyed.

That is the theory. In reality, the adjustment process to a new technology takes a long time. Workers displaced by technology must cut spending and the economy slows. Falling prices due to technological improvements are generally seen as a good thing, for they increase affordability. However, when the displacement of workers is widespread, spending can weaken dramatically, and falling prices and wages can become generalized throughout the economy—in other words, deflation sets in. Deflation works to magnify the burden of outstanding debts, for both individuals and firms. A firm with a large debt will struggle to meet its obligations when the prices it can charge for its products are declining. The same is true for people with mortgages: wages often fall during a deflation, while mortgage payments remain unchanged. Furthermore, when companies go into bankruptcy, or households stop making mortgage payments because people have lost their jobs, it puts their banks at risk of failure.

In other words, the interaction between deflation and debt slows spending even further, essentially trapping the economy in a weakened state for an extended period—a depression. In the economy, it can take a long time for the new growth in other sectors, and the brand-new jobs related to the new technology, to spread spending around and enable everyone to find their new place in the economy.

Between 1873 and 1896, the world went through what we now call the Victorian depression. I will argue in a Chapter 7 that the foundations for the Victorian depression were laid by the First Industrial Revolution. The accompanying stock market boom and collapse were important elements of the episode but were secondary rather than primary causes.

The Second Industrial Revolution had its origins in the spread of electrification, beginning in the early 1900s. The general-purpose nature of electricity catalyzed the development of many other technological advances. It is easy for people of our generation to take all of this for granted, and it helps to see reactions to new technology depicted meticulously and sometimes hilariously in various episodes of *Downton Abbey*. The debates between Downton's cook, Mrs. Patmore, and her apprentice, Daisy, over the relative merits of electric refrigerators over traditional iceboxes are a good example.

The economic adjustments to the new technology were interrupted by World War I, as normal production activity and labour relations took a back seat. Even more lethal than the horrors of that conflict was the global outbreak of the Spanish flu. Economists warned that another depression might follow. But what emerged in the postwar, post-pandemic period was the Roaring Twenties, a period in which survival relief combined with rapid industrial innovation led to a surge in optimism and a stock market frenzy.

There was real substance behind the optimism. A whole new world of motor cars, movies, and consumer goods was opening up to the advanced economies of the world, particularly the United States. Stock markets soared, and investors borrowed to bet even more on the new prosperity; stocks rose parabolically. All such stock market bubbles eventually collapse for lack of fresh oxygen, and it takes only a whiff of doubt to catalyze a reversal. After the stock bubble burst in London and then New York in the autumn of 1929, the global economy fell into the Great Depression for the next ten years. The economy contracted for several years, and widespread deflation of prices set in. The end result of decades of progress seemed to be the breadlines of the newly unemployed.

If such a situation arose today, central banks and governments would use their tools to stabilize the economy and prevent a deflation from becoming generalized. Although the U.S. had a central bank by then—and the Bank of Canada was created in 1935—the macroeconomic situation was poorly understood. In 1936, John Maynard Keynes offered the first economists' guide to policymaking to counter economic depressions. He argued for massive increases in government spending to halt the economic contraction and falling prices, financed through government borrowing. This advice was heeded to some degree in the second half of the 1930s. Unfortunately, when government spending came in substance, it was not with the objective of repairing the damage wrought by the Great Depression. Instead it was for the materiel needed to engage in World War II. Keynes's ideas became mainstream in the postwar period and were widely practised for the next thirty years.

The Third Industrial Revolution was driven by the computer chip—electronics and IT combined to allow the automation of production and the coordination of assembly and delivery logistics from a distance. New technology enabled companies to enhance the logistics of supply chains, which permitted even more specialization and allowed the production chain to go global. Beginning in the mid-1970s and through the 1980s, workers were displaced directly by these new technologies, as products and services were created that no one had dreamed of before. These ranged from personal computers, which largely eliminated typing pools, to mobile phones, which largely eliminated phone booths, to the internet itself.

Computers led to major advances in industrial automation, and the computer chip found its way into everything from cars to thermostats to refrigerators. Behind the scenes, IT services—maintaining hardware, developing code, and providing centralized services—spread everywhere. Again, there was a global stock market bubble, based partly on the valid implications of this new technological wave and partly on a thick layer of leverage and pure speculation.

Unlike the first two industrial revolutions, the third was not associated with a global depression. Something else was in store. Workers in many advanced economies were introduced to the phenomenon of the "jobless recovery" in the early 1990s and again in the early 2000s: there was recovery for some but not for all. Much of the growth in manufacturing happened in developing countries in Asia and Latin America. Japan presents something of a special case, as it exhibited some depression-like symptoms for much of the 1990s, after its 1989 stock market and real estate crashes.

Still, that is far better than a global depression. I would attribute this better macroeconomic outcome after the Third Industrial Revolution to smarter policymaking, compared to the previous industrial revolutions. By the 1990s, many central banks were pursuing inflation targets. The advice of John Maynard Keynes in the 1930s had contributed to the relative economic stability of the post–World War II period, but doubts about his theory began to emerge in the late 1960s, when global inflation became a problem. Milton Friedman advocated for a simpler monetary policy framework: central banks could simply control money supply growth to keep inflation low.

A true convulsion in macroeconomic theory came in the 1970s, during the time when John Kenneth Galbraith was writing *The Age of Uncertainty*. What emerged was a strong focus on controlling inflation as the foundation for macroeconomic policymaking. Within this framework, the tendency for prices to fall during industrial revolutions, as observed in the past, would automatically be countered by persistently easy monetary policy. This allowed the economy to grow into the new capacity being created, without experiencing deflation, as in past industrial revolutions. It is now well understood that there would be seismic side effects of this policy, felt in 2008—rising leverage, a housing market crash, and the failure of a number of financial institutions around the world. The Global Financial Crisis then gave way to the Great Recession.

Nevertheless, one could take hope from the fact that the 1930s Great Depression was less prolonged and severe than the Victorian, and the global adjustments to the Third Industrial Revolution were milder still. This progression suggests that monetary and fiscal policies are becoming increasingly effective. At the same time, the pace of change within each industrial revolution has been increasing, which points to even greater risks as the next industrial revolution unfolds.

The Fourth Industrial Revolution

It is important that we fully understand the past three industrial revolutions, as we find ourselves living early in the Fourth Industrial Revolution, a widely used term coined by Klaus Schwab of the World Economic Forum. The Fourth Industrial Revolution is about the digitalization of the global economy, which is bringing huge advances in machine learning, artificial intelligence, and biotechnology—all of which are likely to have far-reaching effects. The same fears that confronted individuals during the first three industrial revolutions are once again widely apparent with conventional jobs that include a wide range of repetitive tasks—such as fabrication, driving, operating agricultural machinery, financial advising, call centres and other forms of customer service, such as retail sales—at risk.

Economic history was aptly described in 1942 by Joseph Schumpeter in *Capitalism, Socialism, and Democracy* as a process of creative destruction. Technological innovation creates economic growth. But it also destroys relationships, ways of life, and capital investment based on old technology. Focusing only on the job losses associated with technological progress misses more than half the picture. Hundreds of years of actual experience supports that contention.

Consider the mechanization of agriculture as one example. When Canada was formed in 1867, about 50% of the population was engaged in agriculture. Today it is less than 2%, and agricultural output per person has increased massively. The 48% of the population that was displaced from the agricultural sector found gainful employment somewhere else in the economy. More that 5% of the economy consists of IT workers, and employment in that sector is growing at a rate of 7% to 8% per year. None of those jobs existed before the Third Industrial Revolution. Note also that just prior to the COVID-19 pandemic, Canada's unemployment rate was at a forty-year low, despite the displacement of jobs caused by the Third Industrial Revolution during the preceding forty years.

This historical experience is encouraging, but it still leaves open the possibility that the other features of the first three industrial revolutions—two depressions, various financial crises, jobless recoveries, the Great Recession—will figure prominently in the fourth. We can expect that there will be falling prices for goods and services, possibly generalized deflation, and the dislocation of workers, all of which could again create depression-like symptoms while the economy adjusts. No doubt, these stresses will cross over into the political domain.

Nevertheless, our experience with the previous three industrial revolutions suggests that policymakers are learning as they go along and are even better equipped to deal with the Fourth Industrial Revolution than they were for the third.

Steady technological progress means that every advanced economy moves along two tracks. There is the upper track, with above-average growth, where new technology is being deployed and new employment channels are opening. Then there is the bottom track, where jobs are being destroyed. The destruction of some jobs is the very essence of technological progress.

The challenge for economies and their policymakers is to ensure that these two economic tracks reconverge, and quickly, unlike in past industrial revolutions, which lasted for years and even decades. In time, the same technology that creates wealth for some and hardship for others can enable more and more people to move from the bottom track onto the upper track. It has done so throughout modern history. That is why we are better off today than we were at the beginning of the First Industrial Revolution, as rising incomes and expanding purchasing power create jobs throughout the economy.

The adjustment to new technology, however, can be catastrophic for some individuals. People can be left behind. The Fourth Industrial Revolution may have even more destructive potential than the first three, because it has the capability not only of augmenting human work but of replacing it entirely, in wide swaths of the economy. Every technological advance in history has driven an income wedge between those on the top track and those on the bottom track—which leads us to the tectonic force of rising income inequality.

4

GROWING INEQUALITY

Reflections: The View from Below

Income inequality became an issue in economics the day that human-kind transitioned from subsistence farming to an organized economy. I can certainly say from personal experience that income inequality is most visible from below. Growing up in Oshawa and hanging out with other blue-collar kids underscored for me that society was not simply divided into haves and have-nots. There are many more degrees of having and not-having than can be described by the difference between white-collar and blue-collar families. My father was a skilled tradesperson in the auto sector but had never managed to get a job at General Motors, the largest local employer. Working for a small auto parts supplier meant a substantially lower income than his counterparts at GM. There were blue collars everywhere, but in Oshawa some were a richer shade of blue.

Indeed, around my house GM usually stood for "Generous Motors." There was a visible difference between us and GM kids: they had more than one pair of jeans, they had dental plans, and they had cottages. The GM pay scale was driven by a unionized workforce, which over time managed to extract an extraordinary level of income from the company. Few of my high school classmates were motivated to go to university: in the seven years it took for me to earn a PhD in economics, a GM assembly worker was earning a high wage, accumulating fifteen points in an inflation-indexed defined-benefit pension plan, getting married, buying a house, and starting a family. The starting salary in 1981 for the PhD in economics at the Bank of Canada was less than that for the GM assembly worker.

One interpretation of this narrative on relative incomes is that GM's pay policies back in the 1960s and 1970s represented an early form of what is today called "stakeholder capitalism." Labour unions first emerged as weapons against income inequality and egregious workplace practices, and the auto sector in North America must represent a major victory viewed through that lens.

However, it is also true to say that the high wages at GM were the result of a powerful labour union pushing a company with little incentive to push back. Complacency, or what economists would call "moral hazard," can easily arise in a large firm, simply because its scale might make it believe it is too big to fail. Such a company might simply accede to the demands of labour unions and avoid the financial consequences of a strike, comfortable in the knowledge that the government would help out if it was to run into trouble. In the end, there is no need to blame either unions or management. What matters is the outcome.

Evidence that GM went too far to keep labour happy was demonstrated in 2008, when the collapse in motor vehicle sales in the wake of the Global Financial Crisis brought some major auto companies to the brink of disaster. GM was considered too big to fail at a time when economic confidence was already fragile. In Canada, a bailout was organized by the federal and Ontario governments. The design and implementation of the agreement was undertaken by a task force of bureaucrats, including yours truly as head of the lending group at Export Development Canada. It was a profoundly disappointing chapter for Oshawa, and I took little pride in being part of the resolution.

Today, industrial Oshawa is a shadow of its former self, even though there remains some vehicle assembly and a number of parts suppliers. Recent developments point to a modest renaissance in coming years. Economies adjust, and life goes on.

Inequality Attracts Politics

Economics and politics often collide in the real world. Economics matters to people and people vote. What we call "economics" today was called "political economy" and seen as part and parcel of political science. The split between economics and political science began as economists moved away from an oral tradition to use mathematical tools that developed the logic of their research. In recent years, however, political considerations have come to dominate discussions of the economic outlook, and economists would ignore political considerations at their peril. One of my favourite sayings is that it only takes a little bit of politics to spoil a great economic forecast.

It is natural to ask why politics is intruding into economic analysis so forcefully nowadays. The global order we have enjoyed through most of our lives was the product of two world wars and has served us well for some seventy-five years, so far. Under this global order, international trade was always considered essential to productivity, economic growth, and rising living standards. Governments focused on providing infrastructure, education, and health care and used policies to smooth economic fluctuations and to redistribute income to protect the disadvantaged. Central banks were primarily responsible for providing low and predictable inflation to foster good economic decision-making and helping to smooth economic fluctuations. It was not a perfect economic order, but it has worked and has even improved over time.

The Global Financial Crisis and the subsequent Great Recession raised serious questions about this paradigm. All the ingredients of another great depression were present in 2008. Even though avoiding a depression constituted a major policy victory, the fact that the pre-conditions to the crisis were even allowed to build up was inexcusable to many. Furthermore, the means used to avert a depression left a broad perception that Wall Street was bailed out and taxpayers paid for it, while still having to suffer from the lingering effects of the Great Recession. The eventual recovery from the Global Financial Crisis was very gradual and characterized as jobless, as the economy laboured to adjust to the ongoing effects of the Third Industrial Revolution. Many of the usual characteristics associated with a depression lingered: the widespread dislocation of workers, a two-track economy with slow overall economic growth, and rising income inequality. In short, rising popular discontent, with political consequences.

Data from the United Nations show that global income inequality has declined during the past generation when measured country by country. In other words, the gap in incomes between countries has narrowed over time. However, within-country income inequality has risen for over 70% of the world's population. Although the reasons for this vary from one country to another, the common characteristics include technological progress, rising corporate concentration, eroding labour bargaining power, and globalization. While each of these factors may be influenced by others, the primary driver is generally acknowledged to be technological progress.

The famous American economist Arnold Harberger offered an important insight into income inequality in 1998. He mused that technology-led economic growth is often presumed to act like yeast: spreading everywhere as it grows, so that everyone eventually gets some. However, technology-led economic growth behaves more like mushrooms, which pop up here and there and are plucked by those well positioned to do so. As a result, a majority of individuals are left out of this growth.

Technology and Globalization Fuel the Income Divide

Considerable research by economists supports the view that technological progress has been the main driver of economic restructuring, or job displacement, in our times. By economic restructuring, I mean the need for firms to adapt to technology, which means laying off existing workers and creating new jobs requiring different skills. Technological change is ever-present, a continuous incremental process fuelling productivity growth in a modern economy and leading to a constant churn in jobs. However, periodic transformational waves of technological progress, as experienced during the three industrial revolutions, give rise to wrenching adjustments, in which the gains initially go mainly to capitalists while displaced workers have their lives upended. It is not hard to see why people are generally resistant to technological change.

Despite extensive evidence that technological change has been mostly responsible for job losses historically, it is far more popular to blame globalization instead. On the ground level, the effects of globalization look identical to those of automation: firms must adapt to forces of international competition, or their businesses will fail. To reduce production costs, they produce some of their components in a lower-wage country, laying off workers in the domestic economy. To the worker, the difference between being laid off because of foreign competition or because of the deployment of new technology is almost semantic. The fact that the big wave of globalization in the 1990s was accompanied by, and facilitated by, the Third Industrial Revolution makes it even harder to separate the two.

It is worth pointing out that this is exactly how international trade is *supposed* to work. As they say, it's not a bug, it's a feature. Consider a situation with no international trade between two countries. Everything is made domestically, no matter how inefficiently; every country would need its own automobile industry, for example, and the domestic diet would be restricted to the sorts of food that could be grown on domestic soil.

Countries are not all the same—they have different natural resources, different workforces, and so on. Accordingly, when we allow for the possibility of trade between them, each can specialize in what they do best and trade with one another to satisfy what consumers in each country wish to buy. For example, one country might specialize in making cars, as they possess all the necessary raw materials, while the other specializes in making wine, given a perfect soil and climate, and then they trade with one another.

What happens on the ground when trade opens up is that an inefficient, high-cost domestic company is at risk of being put out of business by an offshore company. In the example of two countries that are both making cars and wine, when trade opens up auto workers in one country lose their jobs while wine workers in the other country lose their jobs. Those displaced domestic workers may be unemployed for some time while looking for a new job, and income inequality rises as one consequence. By the same token, the winning domestic company grows.

In theory, the workers who are displaced from the inefficient domestic company can get jobs in the growing, efficient domestic company, assuming their skills are transferable. This may not happen easily in practice, or overnight. Instead, there may be a long period where the inefficient domestic company tries to compete with the offshore producer, domestic wages in that sector are compressed in the process, and governments may even be moved to bail out their stressed domestic producers. Finding a new balance can be a long, painful, and messy process. As for income inequality, the final outcome depends on the relative wages of auto workers as opposed to wine workers.

Trade negotiators spend entire careers debating the complexities of this adjustment process, sector by sector. It is why trade negotiations between two countries take so long and why trade agreements rarely even happen. When agreements are reached, companies are given years to adjust to them. Imagine the complexity when all the countries around the World Trade Organization table try to find common ground on shared issues.

This interpretation misses the most important benefit of engaging in international trade: consumers in both nations pay lower prices for everything. Going back to our two-country example, before trade was allowed, everything consumers in both countries bought was expensive. Even the efficient companies in the domestic economy were only so large and could have reduced costs and therefore prices for consumers if they could have become bigger. The inefficient companies were producing expensive products. And many products were simply unavailable, even though they were produced in the other country, because there was no trade.

To complete our understanding of what trade liberalization means for people, we need to take account of these price effects. Once international trade begins, the efficient domestic company grows in scale and becomes even more efficient as a result. This translates into lower prices for consumers. The inefficient domestic company goes out of business, and their products are replaced by inexpensive imported goods from the successful offshore company, which is itself growing because of trade and becoming even more efficient as a result. Consumers in both countries see lower prices for everything, which effectively means they are suddenly richer. With reduced costs for the goods they buy, whether domestic or imported, they have money left over. They spend that money on other things—on more of everything—and this creates expansion and new jobs in every single sector of both economies.

Trade liberalization produces both winning and losing companies in both countries, with obvious and visible implications for their workers and for income inequality. Economists call this the "substitution effect," and its complexity makes trade negotiations laborious; it is also what raises opposition to trade liberalization, on behalf of those who will be hurt by the opening-up of international trade. As significant as this hardship is for the affected individuals, it is dwarfed by the widespread macroeconomic benefits of trade liberalization. The expanded availability of goods and increased purchasing power in both countries comprise what economists call the "income effect." It is lamentable that this effect rarely finds its way into trade negotiations or debates at the kitchen table. Even though it is the more important channel, the income effect is much harder to trace and to prove that it is due to international trade.

By way of illustration, let's return to our example of two countries, with one exporting autos and the other exporting wine. Once both cars and wine become less expensive in both countries, consumers have more purchasing power and spend that extra money on houses, renovations, restaurant meals, clothing, vacations—in short, on more of everything. Unfortunately, few accept the argument that these new jobs (created in housing construction and maintenance and in restaurants and so on) actually derive from increased trade in automobiles and wine, but they are. This job creation is driven by trade-induced increases in purchasing power. The focus of popular debates on trade lies instead on those who lost their jobs in auto manufacturing in one country and in winemaking in the other country.

And how does trade affect income inequality? This is a very complex question. The worker who is displaced from the auto sector might never re-enter the workforce, in which case income inequality has clearly risen. Or that displaced auto worker might end up as an electrician in the homebuilding industry, possibly with a higher income. Even so, few would acknowledge that the existence of that electrician's job was due to the overall income gains coming from the new international trade. The fact is, resisting trade and insisting that every country should make its own automobiles is similar to someone insisting that we should each grow our own vegetables, cut our own hair, and do our own dry cleaning. Doing these things for ourselves would leave little time for us to do our own jobs, in which we specialize, and would constrain our ability to create economic value.

The level of purchasing power that people enjoy today is generally not understood to depend on international trade arrangements. It is taken for granted that this level of prosperity would persist even if trade restrictions were put in place that erode the incomes being earned through international trade. As usual, all the attention is given to the substitution effect—trade restrictions are believed to help a stressed company here at home prosper again—while the accompanying loss of the past income effect, which will matter much more in the end, is ignored.

As a concrete example, putting tariffs on home appliances manufactured abroad in an attempt to force companies to move that production onshore may create or restore some domestic jobs. However, it will also increase the price of home appliances for every household in the country, thereby reducing everyone's purchasing power and leading to lost jobs in many other sectors of the economy.

These illustrations are simplified; the real world is highly complex. Globalization has allowed companies to increase specialization and reduce costs in the production of all manner of things, right down to the smallest components of the items we buy, which directly increases productivity and profitability. Products and parts are made wherever the specialists are and connected by international trade, an architecture we call global supply chains.

Globalization is often cast as an either/or proposition—either a firm produces a product onshore or produces it offshore. In fact, the situation is far more complex than this. A given product may be broken down into numerous components. Some of those are easy to manufacture—they are essentially commodities and as such may be possible to make far less expensively offshore in a low-wage economy. Since the product is so simple, it is easy to get the appropriate quality, and there is no need to pay a high wage domestically for the same thing.

Other components of the product may require highly skilled workers, using specialized capital equipment, and therefore are more naturally done domestically by higher-paid workers. The capital intensity of each component also comes into play. If a component is made by machinery with very few workers, its costs will be about the same regardless of where in the world the operation is located. Mandating that a labour-intensive process be brought back onshore where wages are higher simply forces the company to choose a higher capital intensity so that worker productivity can justify those increased labour costs. In other words, fewer jobs will be created by forcing such a move than most people expect.

The optimal allocation of supply chains is a complex problem to solve and requires matching the necessary productivity and skill levels with the right wage rates in the right countries. This specificity also makes any supply chain fragile. A low-wage country may not remain a low-wage country if it succeeds in trade and its living standards rise; that country will move up the value chain. Domestic companies will then seek lower-wage economies to incorporate in the labour-intensive portions of their supply chains. It can also lead them to discover that the cost advantage of locating part of their supply chain in a foreign country has eroded sufficiently that it makes sense to bring that element home, a process called reshoring.

How Global Supply Chains Really Work

Consider a smartphone, an incredibly complex combination of components—some of which are easier to manufacture than others. The most complex of all is the software. For simplicity, suppose that some of the components can be produced by workers with high-school education, some require university education, and a few require further specialization. It would be bizarre for a company to use its most highly paid workers to make each and every component. Instead, the company looks around the world for companies that best produce each component, choose the ones offering the best combination of price and quality for that work, and farm each component out. It is the fragmentation of the product that allows this granular matching of skill sets, wages, and components. With those supply arrangements in place, the company coordinates component supplies so that they arrive in the final assembly place at the right time. This is no small task—Apple's global supply chains cover more than forty countries, for example.

The worker with a high-school education in an advanced economy may not be able to compete to make these low-value components. This is because over time, social pressures, minimum wage laws, or other constraints have made their wages higher than those in other countries. These domestic workers see a successful smartphone company offshoring many jobs—jobs that could be done domestically, albeit at a higher cost—and they cry foul.

The offshoring may make the difference between a $500 smartphone and a $1,000 smartphone and therefore drastically impact how many smartphones the company can sell and how many jobs it can create. Indeed, if that company were to insist on using local labour to produce a $1,000 smartphone, a competing foreign company might build a global supply chain, produce a $500 smartphone, and put the domestic company out of business. Some consumers may be persuaded to buy local, especially if the domestic government puts tariffs in place to make the foreign smartphones cost $1,000. Even so, the domestic company will sell far fewer smartphones at $1,000 than it would at $500, limiting job creation. It would also mean that domestic consumers who purchased $1,000 smartphones would have $500 less available to spend in other parts of the economy. This is how policies that try to force companies to increase local content in their products generally backfire and cause job loss in every other sector of the economy.

In this globalization example, many of the high-paying jobs remain local: management, design, engineering, marketing, software creation, and perhaps the production of the most complex components requiring highly skilled workers or special capital equipment. This is a positive, for it means that the largest share of the income generated by that company falls into the local economy, even if a high number of lower-wage jobs are created offshore. Those high incomes are largely spent in the domestic economy, supporting jobs in all sectors.

Despite this, the most visible impact of that successful company may be that lower-skilled domestic workers lose their jobs to low-wage foreigners. These workers are forced to transition elsewhere in the economy—to somehow find their way from the low-growth track into the higher-growth track. If the forces acting on the economy are persistent ones—and globalization surely qualifies, as it has been active for some thirty years—then there is a steady flow of disrupted workers into the low-growth track of the economy, and constant churn in labour markets as they try to move to the higher-growth track. There will always be some people who end up in the low-growth track, working various low-wage jobs in order to survive, because they cannot make the transition. Accordingly, even if many people do make the transition into the top track of the economy, income inequality is very likely to rise during the adjustment process, which could take a long time. The most visible evidence will suggest that the highly successful local company has contributed to higher income inequality, because it is almost never given credit for its over-all impact on total domestic income, spending, and job creation.

Nevertheless, there can be little doubt that technological progress and globalization have contributed to rising income inequality over horizons that matter to individuals. The leading economy with the most multinational companies with aggressive offshoring is the United States. According to data published by the Organisation for Economic Co-operation and Development (OECD), the U.S. also has one of the highest levels of income inequality in the advanced

OECD countries. The measure used to determine this is the Gini coefficient; it captures the deviation from perfect equality along a scale from 0 to 1, where 0 indicates a perfectly equal income distribution, and 1 indicates a perfectly unequal distribution (theoretically, one individual gets all the income). The Nordic countries lead the world in terms of favourable income distributions, with Gini coefficients averaging around 0.26–0.28, whereas the U.S. is just below 0.40. Turkey, Chile, Mexico, and South Africa have much higher income inequality than the U.S., with Gini coefficients well above 0.40, and over 0.60 in the case of South Africa. The U.S. Gini coefficient is around 40% higher than the Nordic countries and around 30% higher than Germany, France, and Canada. The U.K. Gini is around 10% lower than the U.S., Japan around 15% lower. It is one thing to have a less progressive distribution of income than other countries at a single point in time, but it is quite another if income inequality also trends higher over time. The U.S. Gini coefficient has risen by around 8% in the past ten to fifteen years.

Government policies are quite capable of preventing rising income inequality in the face of technological progress and globalization. The principles involved are as old as the legend of Robin Hood. It is noteworthy that while the U.S. Gini coefficient has been rising, Canada's has declined by about 5% over the same time period. This single observation can go some way in explaining the different political climates in the two countries. Canada has one of the most progressive tax systems among the major economies. As reported by the OECD, the all-in income tax rate at the average wage, accounting for various tax transfers, for a single-income family with two children is only 2.4% in Canada. The comparable figure for the U.S. is 12.2%. Even highly egalitarian Sweden has a figure of 17.8%. Denmark is 25.2%. In Canada, the consumption tax rebate and family allowance programs effectively create a negative income tax at the low end of the tax system. This has changed significantly in the past decade, as the comparable figure in 2010 for Canada was 8.1%, whereas the U.S. was 11.2%. In other words, net income conditions at the low end of the spectrum have improved significantly in Canada and deteriorated marginally in the U.S.

Even so, regardless of geography, people learn about spectacular income gains at the top of the income spectrum and perceive their wages as remaining stagnant by comparison. Nowhere is this clearer than in the finance sector, which may be one of the reasons why the U.S. and the U.K. have the most skewed income distributions. Stagnant or falling wages are a likely outcome for the lower-skilled workers of companies newly exposed to foreign competition, according to basic international economic models.

Another way to look at this is to consider what has happened to income levels within companies. Back in the 1960s, it was common to see companies with an income hierarchy in which the CEO would earn ten to fifteen times the lowest-paid worker. This ratio trended steadily higher, particularly once stock options became a popular form of compensation for senior leaders. By the late 1980s, the ratio had reached the forty times range and nowadays it is more than two hundred times.

Politics Can Increase Volatility

Understandably, these relentless economic forces create discontent in large swaths of advanced economies, which is bound to capture the interest of politicians. Today, the amplification effect of social media guarantees that these issues become political. The typical economist response that market forces are ultimately good for everyone can sound like some sort of phony religion to those directly affected. Former prime minister of Canada Stephen Harper wrote in his 2018 book *Right Here Right Now* that these tensions are being manifested in political polarization between "globalists" and "localists." The colloquial terms are "anywheres" and "somewheres." It is the somewheres who are most disrupted by technology and trade and are tied to their communities, so they cannot adapt to such powerful changes the way anywheres can. In a similar vein, author Jeff Rubin called these people "expendables" in his 2020 book of the same title. The point is not to cast blame but to understand that rising inequality is very likely to be politically polarizing. Indeed, the concept of democratic compromise appears to be on the verge of extinction.

Countries with weak redistributive policies were first to show increasingly polarized politics and emergent populism, but there appears to be a shift in that direction globally. This would, of course, include the election of Donald Trump as president of the U.S. in 2016, along with growing numbers of populists and anti-immigration parties in European parliament and the Brexit movement, just to name a few. Given all the acting forces, shifts toward domestic focus and more rivalrous international posturing are at least explainable, whether there are unintended consequences or not. Certainly, the economic underpinnings of this shift imply that it will not go away just because Trump is no longer president. The growing importance of the tectonic forces is likely to polarize politics more deeply.

Ian Bremmer of Eurasia Group calls this future a "G-zero world," where there is diminished global leadership, nations focus more on their own narrow interests, and international relations are more rivalrous. One consequence would be that co-operative international fora, such as the G7 and G20, designed to make enlightened decisions about the future of the world, will lose their relevance. Meanwhile, domestic political consensus is becoming ever harder to achieve as social media amplify voices, create echo chambers, and polarize politics. Good policies may become exceedingly difficult to develop and execute, especially growth-enhancing structural reforms that can have negative consequences for some individuals in the short run.

A global shift toward nationalist policies runs the risk of reversing many of the past benefits of globalization. Trade restrictions will directly erode the specialization in production that has delivered big productivity gains. Economic growth will slow even further for a given rate of population growth in a trade-restricted world. The losses from deglobalization will not be uniform: economies most dependent on trade and supply chains will be hurt the most, while relatively closed economies (especially large ones) may be less affected.

For highly vulnerable economies, deglobalization will mean an immediate loss of productivity and a lower level of national income. Little inefficiencies in many parts of the economy eventually add up to slower trend economic growth overall. Deglobalization is like throwing sand into our economic machine. These same effects would be present in larger, less trade-dependent economies, too, but perhaps less visibly so because the pure domestic economy is so much bigger. Transition to a lower economic growth rate will entail firms dismantling global supply chains and rebuilding them, destroying existing capital stock, and building new capital stock, only to achieve less than before. We could go through an extended period of disruptive adjustment and slower economic growth, before settling into a new lower level of global income, with a slower growth trend. In other words, instead of creative destruction, we are likely to see uncreative destruction.

The biggest effects of deglobalization, however, will be on consumers. The consumer sees more product choice and lower prices through trade, which increases real purchasing power. This is the channel through which most of the gains from international trade are delivered. Deglobalization through trade restrictions or tariffs has exactly the opposite effect, resulting in significantly lower purchasing power for consumers. The most direct effect is that of tariffs, which are always paid by domestic consumers. Even this can be hard for consumers to see. For this reason, anti-trade politicians often seem persuasive, as they claim to save domestic jobs. But they always fail to mention that there will also be higher prices for everyone.

The ongoing rise in income inequality has deep roots in our economic system, driven mainly by technological advances and facilitated by globalization. The natural emergence of political polarization because of this trend makes a consensus about how to address it elusive. The COVID-19 pandemic has added more urgency to this tectonic force.

In the long sweep of history, income inequality has seen major swings, both up and down. Past peaks in income inequality were associated with economic depressions, which created the conditions for a reduction in income inequality, whether self-initiated by employers or forced by government policies or rising unionization. Such turning points are examples of the sort of economic and financial instability that can arise due to the action of our tectonic forces. The world may be close to such an inflection point now, as the political pressure to address income inequality intensifies. Even so, consensus on this issue will be difficult to achieve, and compromise policies run the risk of reducing total national income in an attempt to improve its distribution. Furthermore, it is important to understand that even if politicians act soon to reduce the level of income inequality, the unfolding of the Fourth Industrial Revolution will cause it to resume its worsening trend in the years ahead.

A constant companion of rising income inequality has been growing indebtedness, and it is to that fourth tectonic force that we now turn.

5

RISING DEBT

Reflections: Modest Beginnings

I managed well in school, getting good grades and awards for academic achievements. I was smart enough to work hard to make up for whatever talents I lacked, which were many. Certainly, I have little to report on the athletic side of the scorecard, beyond playing a bit of soccer and error-prone softball. My parents were especially meticulous in reminding me of my academic shortcomings and took special care not to overdo the praise when things went well. In other words, the pursuit of excellence and the preservation of humility were actively nurtured.

Hard work came naturally, driven by my desire to achieve a higher standard of living than our family had. Frankly, I was a nerd. I even looked the part. I was not permitted to switch from a military brush-cut hairstyle until 1969, several tough years, socially speaking, after all my friends began letting their hair grow. My view of society was shaped by my parents, and they put our family doctor and our dentist at the top of the economic pyramid. I surmised that if you were smart enough, worked hard enough, and went to school long enough, you could be a doctor or a dentist and earn a substantial income—sufficient even to live in the far north end of Oshawa.

I was the first member of either of my parent's families to go to university, riding a scholarship from Queen's University and the income from holding down three jobs during high school. I worked for my uncle's swimming pool company, on construction sites, and in sales in the record department (what today they call vinyl) at Eaton's department store in the Oshawa Centre, after school and on Saturdays. And I had my own disc jockey business on Saturday nights, spinning discs at wedding receptions, curling bonspiels, and other gatherings. I maintained this business from the age of fifteen through my under-graduate years at Queen's, driving from Kingston to Oshawa virtually every weekend to spin discs on Saturday nights.

When I went to Queen's University in 1974, I had every intention of becoming a medical doctor. The first step was to take at least two years of life sciences, which has a well-defined track—biology, chem-istry, physics, and math in the first year, with one slot left for any subject you want. I had no idea what to choose, for I had a one-track mind. I considered a second math course, but during my first week on campus, someone suggested I try economics, just for fun.

It was probably the best piece of advice I ever received. I fell in love with economics. It had the power to help us understand how the world works and to devise policies that would make everyone better off. Imagine making everyone better off all in one go, not just one person at a time as doctors do. I learned about the role played by the Bank of Canada and was instantly drawn in. I knew I wanted to work at the bank, and I wanted to run the place someday. Not many kids have such a specific vision at such a young age and go on to see it realized, nearly forty years later. Of course, the path I followed was not a straight line.

Always the cautious one, though, in my second year at Queen's, I still took the courses needed to apply to medical school but switched my major from life sciences to economics. After that year, I was totally sold on the idea of becoming an economist, and I never applied to medical school—to the profound and vocal disappointment of my parents.

I had also fallen in love with a young woman sitting in the next row one seat ahead of me in my grade ten geography class in 1971. Valerie and I were married in 1976 when I was halfway through my undergraduate degree at Queen's. Valerie was working in customer service at a bank and that—combined with my DJ gigs most Saturdays, summer jobs, and scholarships—kept us in the black through my remaining years at Queen's and in graduate school at the University of Western Ontario.

While in my fourth year at Queen's, Valerie and I were watching *Dallas* on television when the phone rang. It was my professor who was supervising my undergraduate thesis.

"Steve, I need to see you down at the Donald Gordon Centre immediately," he barked in his charming British accent.

"What's up?" I replied, with one eye still on the onscreen shenanigans of J.R. Ewing.

"There are some people from the Bank of Canada attending a conference down here. I told them about your research, which shows that most of the work at the bank is a load of rubbish, and they want to talk to you right away."

I was quite taken aback. My research was on irregularities in how much money people were holding in their bank accounts, an important measure central to the policies of the Bank of Canada at the time. But I definitely had not demonstrated that researchers at the bank were producing "rubbish." It sounded to me like my good professor might have embellished things a little. I was thinking this through, and I suppose I was not showing sufficient enthusiasm.

"Why are you hesitating? Put on a suit and get down here!"

I threw on a suit and tie and headed to the conference facility, where I met a couple of people from the bank. One of them I knew by reputation: he was one of the researchers whose work I supposedly had demonstrated was rubbish, an impression I immediately attempted to correct. They sat me down and grilled me for half an hour and told me they would be in touch. The following Monday, I was offered the summer job of a lifetime: a fabulous learning experience with a wonderful mentor. At the end of the summer, I was guaranteed a position at the bank when I finished graduate school. A lifelong attachment to the Bank of Canada was born.

At the time, the bank was very focused on getting high rates of inflation under control. Keeping inflation low remains the anchor for monetary policy for most central banks today. Targeting inflation means adjusting interest rates in response to significant fluctuations in the economy. One positive side effect is that these same interest rate adjustments also help to reduce volatility in economic growth and employment. There is an unintended side effect, however: they lead to rising debt levels.

Persistent Debt Accumulation

The accumulation of debt has become one of the hottest macroeconomic subjects of our times. Every type of debt keeps hitting a new record, producing much angst about the consequences "when the chickens come home to roost." Most observers attribute the rise in debt to low interest rates, which is another way of saying they blame central banks. As explained in chapter 2, this is a misperception.

Let's begin with household debt. The most cited measure of indebtedness is the ratio of debt to net disposable income. Though a convenient measure, it represents an average level of debt for the entire economy and is far from a complete picture. In Canada, for example, that ratio has risen continuously for the past twenty years, from 117% in 2000 to around 180%, meaning that the average household owes nearly twice their take-home pay. Since around half of households have no debt at all, this ratio is much higher for households with debt. Further, since the figure is an average, there are households with far higher debt ratios, especially in cities such as Vancouver or Toronto, where real estate prices are particularly elevated.

Canada has some company in this rise in debt, as reported by the OECD. Australia has seen a rise to over 200%, the U.K. to over 140%, and there have been big rises in such countries as France, Italy, and Sweden. There are important exceptions, however. The U.S. has about the same household debt ratio as it did twenty years ago, having seen a rise from 104% to 144% in the early 2000s and then a big reversal to about 105% in the wake of the Global Financial Crisis. This reversal is often pointed to as a warning to highly indebted countries, such as Canada and Australia. Germany's debt ratio was stable for the 2000s and then trended downward during the 2010–20 period. Obviously, the track of debt depends on the cyclical financial experience of each country, and the state of the local housing market plays an important role.

Notably, all these so-called highly indebted countries have household net worth well in excess of 400% of disposable income, many in excess of 500%. That is a clue that the use of this metric mixes apples and oranges. At the risk of oversimplification, we can say that countries with high housing prices have high household debt; since the households own the house as well as the mortgage, this tends to balance out in net worth data.

Even so, household indebtedness is persisting deep into people's life cycle. According to the latest data from Statistics Canada, only around 57% of Canadians over the age of sixty-five are debt-free, while ten years ago the figure was over 70%.

Motor vehicle finance has also made a significant contribution to rising indebtedness. In Canada, auto loans have become very long in duration, with seven years a quite common term length. Since payments are fixed, the immediate depreciation of the vehicle on the drive home from the dealer means that its value falls below the outstanding loan amount until well down the road. Many individuals attempt to trade their vehicle for a new one before the end of the loan period and are encouraged to roll the remaining balance into the next loan. In the last twenty years, the average loan-to-value ratio for all motor vehicles has risen from around 23% to 33%, and the share of all households with vehicle loans has risen from around 20% to over 30%.

Similar concerns have been raised with respect to corporate debt, commonly measured by the ratio of outstanding debt to annual profits, as reported by the OECD. In this measure, too, Canada stands out, with a ratio in excess of 8 in the past couple of years. The U.S. ratio is even higher. Japan and France have ratios around 6, the U.K. around 5, and most other OECD countries around 4. Overall, the rise in corporate indebtedness is less than that for household debt.

Policies Foster Rising Debt

Although casual observers might be skeptical, there is solid empirical evidence that macroeconomic stabilization policies have steadily become more effective over the last fifty years or so. Certainly, the targeting of inflation by central banks has an economy-stabilizing value that is beyond dispute. Variations in employment, unemployment, and national income have all been smaller as inflation has become lower and more predictable.

However, it is hard to see what would have happened in the absence of these effective monetary and fiscal policies. Economists use models to decompose actual outcomes to show what would have happened without policy—this is how they measure the effectiveness of a course of action. Achieving an inflation target means anticipating future pressures on inflation due to fluctuations in economic growth and unemployment and then adjusting interest rates to moderate those effects. This is akin to steering your boat a few degrees left to compensate for the waves that are pushing the boat to the right. In attempting to keep inflation stable, the central bank also helps to stabilize economic growth and employment. The economy can still experience large fluctuations in growth and employment, but those fluctuations turn out to be smaller than they *would* have been without the benefit of an inflation-targeting framework.

But not all side effects are so benign. In experiencing fewer deep recessions than in the past, economies have missed out on some of the "cleansing" effects associated with economic downturns. It is during downturns in the economy that fragile firms fail, and their debts are written off by banks, which usually lowers economy-wide indebtedness. Once the economic recovery gathers momentum, new firms with relatively low debt emerge to take their place. It is widely believed that this cleansing action of downturns also helps to boost the average productivity growth rate, as new companies are more likely to use the latest technology and have higher efficiency than old ones. Preventing those recessions, or at least reducing their severity, leads to the build-up of fragile, low-productivity "zombie" firms, thereby lowering trend productivity for the economy as a whole.

It also means that the economy becomes increasingly indebted through time. When the economy slows, the central bank lowers interest rates as an inducement for both households and firms to spend more, through increased borrowing at the lower rate of interest. As a result of these policy actions, the rise in unemployment is reduced and eventually reversed. Those who blame the central bank for the attendant increase in indebtedness almost never seem to appreciate what would have happened if stabilizing policies had not been put in place: that without the rise in indebtedness due to lower interest rates, unemployment would have been much higher and more persistent, and everyone would have been worse off as a result.

All of which is to say that debt is crucial to the functioning of the economy. It is only through borrowing that households, firms, and governments can operate over time. Consider the alternative. It is obviously not preferable for a couple to save for twenty-five years and then buy a house just when their children are ready to leave home, rather than using a mortgage to buy the house when they actually need it. Similarly, for a firm looking to expand to meet increased demand for its products, waiting to accumulate enough retained earnings would mean missing the opportunity to grow the company and add new workers to the payroll. For governments using borrowed funds, building infrastructure creates an asset that delivers returns to society, while facilitating private-sector growth and generating tax revenues for years to come. It makes little sense to force governments never to borrow for such a purpose. In short, there are structural reasons for debt to exist, not only cyclical ones, and separating the two can be extraordinarily difficult.

The interaction between fluctuations in the economy and monetary and fiscal policies leads to a third side effect of effective stabilization policies: the creation of the so-called financial cycle, as distinct from the more conventional business cycle. The financial cycle describes the build-up of risk in the financial system during the positive part of the business cycle and its correction during a downturn.

While one might expect financial risks to be low when the economy is growing but to be high during a downturn, there are dynamics under that surface. Risk builds up during an expansion when lenders are happy to lend, and that risk actually materializes in a downturn. All too often, the risks are only identified once it is too late.

A policy of strong intervention can hide risk in plain sight. Over time, the global financial cycle has lengthened and grown in amplitude, because the effectiveness of stabilization policies has prolonged economic expansions and led to ever higher borrowing. In short, investors, firms, and households become complacent and take on more risk the longer an expansion is maintained by good policies. That makes the day of reckoning potentially that much more severe when it does arrive.

Furthermore, the accumulation of debt makes the economy more sensitive to interest rate increases. Essentially, every percentage point increase in rates causes a much bigger increase in required debt service payments—the greater the stock of debt. After an economic downturn, interest rates do not always return to where they were beforehand, as central banks worry about the potential fallout in the financial system. Therefore, interest rates may never rise sufficiently to cleanse the system of low-quality debt and underperforming companies. As the story goes, the economy essentially becomes addicted to debt and more fragile over time.

The accumulation of debt clearly played an important role in the Global Financial Crisis of 2008. And yet fast-forward another decade to 2019, aggregate global debt—related to households, firms, and governments—had nearly doubled to about three times total national income for the world. That was before the arrival of COVID-19, which caused global government debt to rise to about 100% of global income, nearly 20% higher than the year before.

Government Debt Sustainability

Although the underlying reasons differ, the global post-pandemic debt situation is not unlike that seen at the end of World War II. Big surges in government debt have historically been associated with wars. In advanced economies, indebtedness rocketed from around 30% of total national income to over 80% during World War I. Indebtedness generally declined during the Roaring Twenties, reaching around 60% of national income, but then rose again during the Great Depression. World War II took debt in the advanced economies well above 120% of national income, but this debt overhang shrank very rapidly during the next generation, bottoming at around 30% in the mid-1970s.

The next forty years saw a persistent rise of government debt, driven by the use of fiscal policies such as tax cuts and extraordinary government spending financed through borrowing to stabilize economies during recessions, as discussed earlier.

In the U.S., presidential philosophies around government deficits also played a contributing role. Ronald Reagan (1981–89) saw U.S. government indebtedness rise from around 30% of national income to around 50%; George H.W. Bush (1989–93) moved the debt ratio above 60%; Bill Clinton (1993–2001) lowered the debt ratio to below 60%; and George W. Bush (2001–2009) boosted the debt ratio to over 80% for the first time. Barack Obama (2009–2017), who took over in the midst of the Global Financial Crisis, saw the debt ratio rise to about 100%. Donald Trump's presidency (2017–21) saw the arrival of COVID-19 and the biggest peacetime increase in government spending in history. President Joe Biden has continued with these policies, bringing the U.S. debt ratio well above 100%.

The advanced economies as a group have followed the U.S. indebtedness ratio upward, starting at around 30% in the mid-1970s, reaching 75% to 80% by the turn of the millennium, ratcheting to above 100% during the Great Recession, and then rising a further 20 percentage points during the COVID-19 pandemic. In Canada, the government debt picture has been brighter than the average. Including provincial debt, the debt ratio peaked in the mid-1990s at around 100%, fell to about 70% just prior to COVID-19, and then moved back above 100% during the pandemic.

Government debt levels as high as 200% of national income have been managed in the past—such as the U.K. in the early 1800s and again in the 1940s, and Japan and China today—but what risks do today's debt levels present for the future? There is more than one way to manage a debt burden, some more insidious than others. This analysis is particularly relevant when considering the other long-term forces acting on the economy, as discussed earlier.

I like to ask other baby boomers if they recall growing up in the 1950s or 1960s under the gigantic debt burden incurred by their parents during World War II. It is extremely rare to find anyone who can remember that subject coming up at the kitchen table. Although taxes on individuals increased in the wake of World War II, government debt ratios fell mainly because of strong economic growth. True, economic growth was much higher in the 1950s and 1960s than we are likely to see in the next decade or so. But the same demographic forces that will keep economic growth low in the future will also keep the natural rate of interest low, making it easier for governments to service their debt.

At a technical level, the macroeconomic conditions that make government debt sustainable are quite simple. If the interest rate that governments must pay on their outstanding debt is lower than the growth rate in the economy, then the ratio of debt to income will shrink over time. This is true even if the government never actually pays down the debt and instead only pays the interest: the growing economy will cause the debt ratio to fall over time. We can think of this either in real terms (the real interest rate needs to be below the real economic growth rate for the economy) or in nominal terms (nominal interest rates need to be below the headline growth in the economy, including inflation).

As discussed above, the aging global population will have a moderating effect on world economic growth and on the natural rate of interest in the years ahead, given the gradual convergence of the two. However, individual governments are in a position to lock in low rates of interest on their debt now, while at the same time undertaking policies that will enhance long-term economic growth in the future. As long as those rates are lower than economic growth, the debt will gradually decline relative to the size of the economy, thereby meeting the requirement of sustainability. There is a range of options for achieving this, as elaborated in Chapter 12. Reducing government debt ratios faster than this natural decline might be preferable, in order to restore fiscal firepower in preparation for a future crisis, but that is a political question.

The inexorable rise in indebtedness is the product of population aging, declining real interest rates, financial innovation, and macroeconomic policies. There can be no doubt that debt creation has been a great facilitator of economic progress, whether by households, firms, or governments. If we could imagine where we would be if debt was constrained like it was, say, during the 1950s, we would not like what we saw. Almost all measures of economic performance, both individual and in aggregate, would have fallen far short of society's actual progress.

None of that alters the fact that debt accumulation makes households, firms, and governments increasingly vulnerable to future disturbances to the economy. When debt loads are high, the consequences of any shock to the economy are magnified and can become catastrophic. For households, a temporary job loss can mean financial ruin if the debt load is sufficiently high. For a firm, a recession can interact with excessive debt and lead to bankruptcy, destroying all the firm's jobs permanently. When individuals or companies are wiped out, so are their debts, which means that their financial institutions also incur major losses. Governments do not have unlimited capacity to borrow, either. They must present a credible fiscal plan or face the harsh judgment of investors who will sell their debt, force interest rates higher, and cause a day of reckoning.

Being increasingly vulnerable to future economic disturbances through rising indebtedness is one thing. Having the tectonic force of rising debt crash into another tectonic force is quite another, with potentially far more profound consequences for the global economy. One such interaction is with technological progress, which historically has led to declining prices as the benefits of a new technology spread. Falling prices make existing debts appear even larger. Another important interaction is that between rising indebtedness and climate change, for the volatility of weather is placing growing financial burdens on already heavily indebted governments.

6

—

CLIMATE CHANGE

Reflections: Childhood Weather

When I was a young lad growing up in Oshawa, I didn't have a lot—except for jobs, that is. Mowing lawns, shovelling snow, and babysitting were big businesses for me. I can attest that there was a lot of snow every winter of the 1960s. In those days, it was the law that homeowners were responsible for shovelling the sidewalk in front of their home before eight a.m. Some days, the task was gargantuan, and I know it was not because I was just a little guy.

I am told that there was even more snow in Oshawa forty to fifty years earlier, when my grandfather was my age. If he were to be believed, the snow was regularly up to the top of the hydro poles, and he still had to walk to school and back—uphill both ways. No doubt, my grandfather was prone to exaggeration, but from personal observation I can say that there is less snow in Oshawa these days than when I was a kid.

Fact is, gradual warming of the Great Lakes and less ice cover in winter has meant more moderate winter weather, albeit punctuated with the occasional large snowstorm due to the vagaries of the lake effect.

These personal reflections underscore that resistance to the science of climate change would fly in the face of common experience over the past half-century. Of course, the existence of a global warming trend is not really in dispute; the issue that remains to some, as argued by Steven Koonin in his recent book *Unsettled*, is whether human behaviour is behind that warming trend or if it was happening anyway. However, the rise in global temperatures has not been gradual but meteoric and highly correlated with Earth's pace of industrialization; there is a growing consensus that immediate behavioural shifts are necessary to avert the worst of the predicted scenarios. Shareholders, employees, customers, and governments are all taking actions based on this belief. A transition to a lower-carbon economy is coming.

Carbon Emissions and Externalities

There is widespread and growing agreement that a continued rise in accumulated greenhouse gas (GHG) emissions will mean increasingly volatile weather, flooding, destruction of certain communities, and growing shortages of drinking water. The effects will continue for a long time even if we change our ways now, because modifying the atmosphere's trajectory will be much like turning a proverbial aircraft carrier. Harder and slower, in fact. Changing the direction global civilization has been travelling for the past 250 years will be a feat unlike anything humanity has ever pulled off.

Reducing emissions means finding ways to change the behaviour of billions of people. Hydrocarbons are a key source of energy, and the most important common factor of economic development is energy use. Rising living standards mean rising energy demand, and hydrocarbons remain the most important source of energy in the world by far. GHG emissions are a by-product of economic progress. How do we stop one without stopping the other?

The short answer is that there are alternative sources of energy that do not create GHG emissions. Solar, wind, geothermal, tidal, hydro-electric, and nuclear energy are all technologies we have on the shelf—all more expensive than hydrocarbon-based energy is today, but scale and new technology are causing the cost gaps to narrow over time. Even so, much of our existing technology has been grown on a comparatively cheap hydrocarbon base. Slowing and then stopping growth in GHG emissions looks to be exceedingly disruptive economically.

Why hydrocarbon-based energy is less expensive than other forms can be explained more easily by economics than physics: greenhouse gas emissions have historically been free. That is, there is a steep and accumulating environmental cost to the planet, but those who emit greenhouse gasses have almost never been required to pay it. Today, when you purchase a new television, you are charged a small recycling fee, which helps to pay the costs associated with disposing of it at the end of its life in such a way that the plastic, wire, and other materials can be reused rather than going to a landfill. Few such recycling fees apply to the emissions associated with burning a tank of gasoline in your car, or a ton of coal in a factory. In effect, we are all disposing of toxic waste directly into the atmosphere.

Economists refer to this gap as a "market failure" or "the tragedy of the commons." For the most part, people act in their own personal self-interest. Sometimes their activities result in side effects that negatively impact other people or society at large. If markets do not in some way force that individual to compensate others for those side effects by attaching a cost to the behaviour, that person is effectively getting something for free. Any time you can accumulate wealth without fully paying for it, chances are you're not going to stop. Not surprisingly, the side effects of market failure tend to grow unsustainably. Governments can sometimes impose rules to control the situation, thereby reducing the side effects.

A simple example would be a neighbour who opens a snack bar in their garage. They put up a big sign, welcoming people to drop by for a quick snack of poutine, say, and a cold drink. Soon the neighbourhood is overrun with parked vehicles and the odour of deep-frying potatoes. The property values of the surrounding homes fall, while the neighbour with the snack bar makes good money from his enterprise. There has accordingly been a transfer of wealth from the surrounding people to this one neighbour.

This actually happened to me. When we bought our first home in the Ottawa suburbs, the backyard bordered on an unpaved secondary road. Across the road, there were cows in the field, a lovely view each morning, even if they are now chastised as a source of GHG. The road behind our house had a small bend in it, a jog, and at that point the gravel shoulder of the road was especially wide. One Saturday morning I looked out the bedroom window and saw that a chip truck—equipped with a kitchen for cooking French-fried potatoes—had taken up residence there. Soon the air was filled with the aroma of frying potatoes, and cars were stopping to partake. Fans of poutine love that smell when they pass by it. But all weekend long?

Economists call the side effects in this parable "externalities": undesired outcomes that are not captured, or "internalized," in the market prices. If they were, the neighbour with the snack bar (or the owner of the chip truck) would compensate the neighbours for the loss of market value of their homes and need to charge far more for the poutine. Chances are, no one would come to the snack bar, because the fries would be too expensive. This is how a market-based mechanism can prevent economic activities whose effects will spill over onto innocent bystanders. Clearly, this would be a complex market system to develop. A government could possibly do so, taxing the poutine business sufficiently to transfer funds to the affected neighbours. A simpler alternative would be for the city to have a rule that no one in a residential neighbourhood is permitted to operate a business from their home—or on the road behind their house. This is a more typical non-market approach to the externality problem.

Now, consider how this reasoning works for GHG emissions and climate change. People drive their vehicles and burn gasoline, releasing various forms of carbon-based gases into the atmosphere. No one owns the atmosphere—it is a commonly held resource, in effect owned by society at large. Because of global air currents, the atmosphere arguably is owned by global citizens, not just local ones. Over time, carbon released into the atmosphere exceeds the ability of the planet to absorb it, whether by plants or by animals eating the plants. Released carbon builds up, the Earth's atmosphere traps more and more of the sun's heat, and the planet warms.

Conceptually, the externality of GHG emissions is no different from the odour of deep-frying potatoes and the traffic related to the bad neighbour's snack bar. GHGs accumulate in the atmosphere like fryer exhaust because no one must pay to release those emissions. And since the atmosphere belongs to some eight billion people scattered across the globe, how on Earth are they to get together to force GHG emitters to pay? This is a classic failure of markets to find a balanced outcome, or a tragedy of the commons—a situation that always arises when many people share a common resource without having to pay for it.

This depiction of the drivers of climate change is a vast oversimplification. Climate change is not solely an issue in the moment but has a profound time dimension. As explained by Mark Carney in his 2021 book *Value(s)*, the true tragedy is that the catastrophic effects of climate change will not be felt until far beyond the horizon of people alive today. This greatly reduces the incentive for the current generation to address the problem. Who wants to bear the costs of benefits they will never see? In Carney's words, "climate change is the tragedy of the horizon," not just the commons.

Emission Standards, Carbon Taxes, and Investor Activism

Like the neighbour cooking French fries, the obvious way to encourage people to take account of the negative GHG side effects of their behaviour is to charge them for the emissions they create. In the case of GHGs, this would be extremely simple to implement. Since everyone who burns fossil fuels must first purchase them, we need only add a tax to that price designed to capture the GHG side effects. People would then use less fossil fuel, and greener alternatives would be made relatively less expensive. Drivers would find the step up to an electric vehicle more sensible, public transit would seem inexpensive, and so on. Raising the cost of fossil fuels lowers demand, and with diminished use of fossil fuels, there would be less GHG emissions. It would only be necessary to raise prices to the point where the remaining carbon emissions from fossil fuels could be absorbed by the planet.

Of course, simple economic theory, even when supported by Mother Nature, often does not translate well into simple politics. The political cycle is never more than a couple of years—and social media makes it seem even shorter. The tragedy of the horizon means that, left alone, it is difficult to find a political solution to a problem that has its greatest effect on future generations.

Not surprisingly, carbon taxation has been very difficult to implement. In Canada, the federal government has taken extreme measures to make it palatable, refunding carbon tax revenues to the general public in advance of receiving the funds. This clever structure ensures that a typical family does not face a reduction in disposable income due to the carbon tax, while leaving intact the fact that fossil fuel becomes relatively more expensive, thereby encouraging switching and a reduction in carbon emissions.

Despite the plan's elegance, it has not prevented the emergence of life-and-death political drama over the issue. The plan has even incited skepticism that it will have any effect on consumer behaviour—why should people switch if you refund the tax before they even pay it? The answer is that consumers can save even more money by reducing their use of taxed gasoline. What the issue really boils down to is the sensitivity of fossil fuel demand to small increases in price. Meanwhile, a carbon tax can have a profound effect on large emitters of GHGs. Since the objective of such a policy is to promote GHG reductions, not to put the emitter out of business forever, reducing corporate taxes for big emitters so they have the capacity to invest in emissions-reducing technology might also be a useful avenue to explore.

Many would argue that imposing carbon taxes and then hoping that consumers will reduce emissions misses the point. If total emissions (as opposed to individual emissions) don't go down, the planet would be no further ahead. Even if a carbon tax causes each individual to generate fewer emissions, total emissions might continue to grow because of population growth or increased energy use in developing economies. Or maybe people will adjust but not fast enough. Some argue instead for regulations to limit GHG emissions directly. Big industrial emitters would be given new emissions targets and fined for not meeting them. Stricter emissions standards would also be put on motor vehicles, but perhaps not as extreme as dictating that all vehicles must have zero emissions (such as electric cars). Consider that today's hybrid vehicles use about half as much fossil fuel as standard internal combustion engines. If all new vehicles were hybrid, it would create an enormous reduction in emissions, while leaving much of our current energy infrastructure intact.

Emissions regulations are more complex to implement than a carbon tax, as each regulation must be customized to a particular part of the economy. But they will have the indirect effect of raising costs for those responsible for GHG emissions and therefore should lead to similar adjustments in behaviour as envisioned under carbon taxation. One advantage of a regulatory approach is that it leaves a firm's revenues intact, thereby maximizing its financial ability to deploy technological solutions to carbon emissions. In contrast, a carbon tax leads to an immediate loss in cash available to the firm, thereby reducing its ability to make emissions-reducing investments and possibly making it more fragile besides.

Since all such policies are political issues, we are likely to see a range of different outcomes around the world, even with a shared global goal. These gaps will emerge as an important business risk. There may be a need for border mechanisms that adjust the prices of traded goods to account for their carbon footprint, to level the carbon playing field between domestic and offshore producers. A carbon tax on domestic companies would put them at a competitive disadvantage if offshore producers did not face a carbon tax. A border adjustment mechanism would operate like an automatic tariff that would decline as the foreign producer reduced its carbon footprint. Provided the ultimate user of fossil fuels pays the costs associated with GHG emissions, there would be a steady realignment of economic activity around lower carbon usage over time.

Whether adjustment to a lower-carbon economy occurs through regulation or carbon taxation is of little difference from a theoretical point of view. Even so, all such policies are guaranteed to be politically contentious, and polarization of politics makes finding a consensus on such issues increasingly difficult. It may be particularly hard to find common ground across different countries, potentially causing the transition to a lower-carbon global economy to go more slowly than many would hope.

There is another channel of behavioural adjustment that could prove equally powerful in managing climate change, one that is happening without government intervention—the investor channel.

Investors have begun to speak out against carbon emissions and to vote with their portfolios. As investors shun securities of companies with large carbon footprints, and banks and other lenders follow suit to satisfy their shareholders, companies with large carbon footprints will find it increasingly difficult to finance themselves. Over time, they will need to pay more to borrow, which is effectively what economists call a "risk premium," to capture the risks they pose to the environment. This risk premium will be paid whether they are borrowing in bond markets, stock markets, or directly from a bank. With a higher cost of capital, large GHG emitters will find it necessary to invest in carbon-reduction technologies to reduce their carbon footprints. Otherwise, they will be forced to exit their business for lack of affordable finance.

Consider two companies in the same space, one with an extensive program of carbon footprint reduction and one without. The second firm will end up paying more to finance their operations than the first firm. The first will have a combination of higher operating costs (those associated with GHG-emission reductions) and lower financing costs. The profitability comparisons will depend on the structures of the firms, but the reputation effects alone could mean a significantly higher stock price for the first firm. These mechanics are already observable in markets.

Some have lamented this market mechanism as it means "closing" capital markets for traditional GHG-emitting firms. This is not true. The market is forcing firms to pay a higher capital cost if they continue to produce excessive negative side effects. There is a strong incentive to correct those side effects, and to do so in an efficient way that preserves profitability. Strategies include deploying carbon capture technology and, in theory, passing the extra costs on to the customer—which becomes, in effect, carbon taxation by the firm, rather than by the government.

This all sounds fine in theory, but some observers question the power of this mechanism to actually lead to lower carbon emissions, just as there are people who do not believe that carbon taxation will affect people's behaviour. A more relevant question is whether investors have enough information to make informed decisions about a company's carbon footprint. Company reporting tends to be lengthy and complex, and comparisons of carbon footprints between different companies may be very difficult to make. If investors conclude (or social media informs them) that a given company is a large GHG emitter and is likely to remain so, then that company's stock could fall to zero and the company could be stranded almost immediately. Managing this risk will require companies to offer full transparency on their carbon footprints, as well as their plans for and progress in reducing them, so that investors can adjust their portfolios in an orderly fashion. That way, a company with high GHG emissions would pay a tax in the form of a higher cost of financing and would have a stronger incentive to improve over time but would not be put out of business overnight. Enabling this transparency within a standardized international framework is the objective of such initiatives as the Task Force on Climate-Related Financial Disclosures (TCFD) developed under the auspices of the Financial Stability Board.

From a societal viewpoint, there is a very compelling incentive to make the transition to a greener energy economy an orderly process. The world is still highly dependent on fossil fuels and is likely to be for a long time. Around 80% of global energy needs are supplied by fossil fuels today, about the same share as thirty years ago. Global energy demand continues to grow, and it will take considerable investment in alternative energy sources solely to accommodate that growth while holding the use of fossil fuels unchanged, which would not reduce aggregate emissions. It is simply not possible to suddenly stop producing and using fossil fuels, as some idealists advocate, without traumatic consequences for living standards. The goal is to achieve net zero emissions—a situation in which humankind produces a level of emissions low enough that they can be absorbed by the planet. This can be achieved in a variety of ways, including reducing the use of fossil fuels, investing in green energy sources in compensation, capturing GHG emissions to keep them out of the atmosphere, and planting more trees to help Mother Nature absorb more.

The Paris Agreement of 2016 was designed to set a pace on this transition and is framed around keeping the rise in global temperature well below 2 degrees Celsius (above pre-industrial levels). According to climate change experts, this requires that the world reach net zero emissions by 2050. The Paris Agreement, signed by 195 countries, sought to create the international coordination necessary to prevent countries from evading the transition while others did all the heavy lifting. The world at large has a strong interest in reducing GHG emissions.

However, individual countries that take the lead could make themselves uncompetitive in the global marketplace against countries that do not. It is too easy for certain countries, especially small ones, to stick with the status quo on the grounds that their contribution to global emissions is too tiny to matter—a perfect illustration of the tragedy of the commons. The Paris Accord may prove to be an important supporting framework and a crucial source of peer pressure, but it will not be the driving mechanism. It is instead a political challenge for each individual country, which only adds to the uncertainty about the future for individuals and companies. The many possible paths to net zero—using combinations of emissions pricing, regulations, and subsidies—all depend on politics. The transition will therefore be an independent source of economic and financial uncertainty in the years ahead.

Given this uncertainty, the investor enforcement mechanism may prove to be the most significant, for the simple reason that it operates without the need for support from public policies or political consensus. More and more companies are offering sustainability reports with data on GHG emissions on an annual basis. They are also setting out objectives around carbon footprints, and some are even including these as part of the incentive structure for executive pay. In this respect, setting out a goal of net zero by 2050 is fine, but this must translate into measurable progress year by year. Indeed, the COVID-19 pandemic seems to have accelerated the deployment of such targets in the corporate world. The year 2020 saw an astonishing wave of corporate commitments to reach net zero emissions by 2050. Most of these commitments are around Scope 1 emissions, which are those under direct control of the company. Other commitments extend to Scope 2 emissions, which include the indirect emissions caused by the generation of the power used by the company. And there are companies committing to net zero emissions including Scope 3—those produced by consumer use of the company's products. 2050 is just shy of thirty years distant, yet it is enough time for people to believe that these goals may be met.

Since no government has required that firms do this, the progress we have seen is testament to the power of the investor. The promotion of the TCFD recommendations for corporate reporting, now supported by some 1,500 organizations worldwide, is playing a key role in this phenomenon.

Even so, the investor enforcement mechanism is not that well understood, certainly not by retail investors. Media reports have latched onto references to the risk that some corporate assets could become "stranded" in the transition to a lower-carbon economy. Such binary green or not green analysis of investing suggests that any company in the traditional fossil fuel business is about to disappear. This is unlikely, given the time it will take to develop alternative energy sources while still accommodating continued growth in global demand for energy.

Furthermore, achieving net zero can occur along with continued use of fossil fuels, whether for combustion or for the production of various materials in the petrochemical industry. With sufficient transparency, investors should be able to see which companies produce energy with the largest carbon footprint and penalize them the most. As the world reduces its reliance on oil, it will be the highest production-related carbon emitters that stop producing first. The GHG emissions related to the production and refining of oil into final fuels are a huge source of potential emissions reduction. Pressure from investors to reduce emissions sets the stage for an intense competition to be the most efficient providers of energy based on fossil fuels. This force alone could solve a high proportion of the world's GHG emission problem, and it is quite separate from the actual use of fossil fuels as a source of energy.

Another way for companies to adapt is to develop complementary businesses that are green, so that their overall business is a more

attractive shade. Over time, they can gradually grow the greener end
of their business as the non-green business tails off, in line with the
widespread transition to a net zero GHG emissions future. For example, BP has recently announced that it will develop renewable energy
projects to tilt its mix of activity in a green direction. Since this is a
space already occupied by specialized renewable energy companies,
BP shareholders will be asking whether BP can add more value to the
space than specialized renewable players.

A blending model might also prove helpful for Canada's oil sands
producers, which have a reputation as being big GHG emitters
despite having reduced those emissions considerably over the years.
Transforming the raw bitumen into a form that is useable requires
energy in some form, and low-cost and plentiful natural gas has
always seemed the easiest route. However, pairing oil sands production with a green source of refining energy (such as hydro, nuclear,
green hydrogen, or using carbon capture in conjunction with natural
gas) would vastly reduce the GHG emissions related to oil production. Companies are also making important strides in extraction efficiency, using smaller quantities of steam in conjunction with chemical
thinners, for example. The situation has changed dramatically compared to thirty years ago, and this makes claims that in the next thirty
years these companies can achieve net zero very credible.

Even if the use of fossil fuels as energy for transportation declines
steadily, other uses of oil and gas seem likely to continue to grow.
Today, about 80% of global oil production is refined into transportation fuels such as gasoline, diesel, and jet fuel. Those emissions-inten-
sive uses are likely to decline over time, at least as a share of total
energy use. However, the other 20% of oil production goes to a wide
range of other uses, including making plastics, synthetics, waxes,
asphalt, and other chemical products. Society will continue to pave

roads; build houses with asphalt shingles, vinyl windows, and siding; and make synthetic fabric for clothing and plastic components for motor vehicles, airplane wings, and spacecraft. Accordingly, producers of oil that lower emissions may be able to remain in a growth business for a long time, certainly well beyond 2050, along with the companies that deliver those products to manufacturers and end users. For the record, heavier oils, such as those produced in Canada, have the richest content for this end of the business.

Some may argue that this outlook for the oil business is altogether too sunny. Time will tell, but for a helpful bit of evidence, consider the global tobacco industry. Not only is it a significant source of carbon emissions but it is responsible for killing some eight million individuals every year. According to the World Health Organization (WHO), global consumption of approximately six trillion cigarettes each year produces some 2.6 million tons of carbon dioxide and over five million tons of methane. On top of this, the random disposal of trillions of non-biodegradable cellulose acetate cigarette filters is the biggest source of single-use plastic on the planet. A little perspective can go a long way in this space. In terms of GHG emissions, cigarette smoking is a small contributor compared to motor vehicles, which emit on the order of 2.5 billion tons of carbon dioxide in a year, or 1,000 times the emissions from smokers. The fact remains that investors have been shunning tobacco company stocks for many years, and yet the top three tobacco companies still have an aggregate market cap of over $300 billion. In contrast, companies in the oil business are actively facilitating society's transition to net zero. Surely, over time, financial markets will recognize this and value those companies accordingly.

Obviously, there are many possible futures in this space, each to be determined by politics that may vary from country to country. This all translates into heightened uncertainty for individuals and for companies. If widespread carbon taxation remains politically challenging, governments can at least focus on climate sustainability infrastructure, which includes setting international rules around corporate disclosure and helping to create carbon exchanges with global scope so that emissions reductions can happen everywhere, not just in advanced economies. In other words, if a company in China scraps its coal-fired power generation and switches to natural gas, there needs to be a way for that company to be rewarded for doing so, even if it continues to use large quantities of fossil fuels. A true global carbon exchange would facilitate exactly that, as companies looking to green themselves would purchase carbon credits while companies that had reduced their carbon emissions would sell them.

Climate change is already creating extreme, unpredictable weather events with economic and financial consequences for individuals, companies, financial institutions, and governments. The climate will become increasingly inhospitable over the next thirty years even if remedial actions to limit greenhouse gas emissions are taken immediately. This raises significant risks around food and water scarcity, mass migrations, and political instability in advanced economies. This is a tectonic force capable of changing everything.

It is inevitable that the forces emanating from climate change will be politicized. This is true for our other tectonic forces, but the politics associated with climate change may prove to be the most rancorous and divide previously stable constituencies. There are too many losers, winners, and doubters for it to be otherwise. Given that climate change itself is a collective problem arising from the failure of our system to capture the consequences of the behaviour of self-interested individuals, it absolutely demands a collective response—in other words, politics—to move forward. That addressing climate change is necessarily political makes it one of the most important sources of future economic uncertainty on the horizon.

Even if the direction of travel is clear, the forced energy transition to net zero by 2050—if it can be achieved—will add even more volatility to the mix. Given that there are many different possible paths to net zero, the policy response to climate change is likely to be a source of more uncertainty for the future, not less. Entire business models can be created or destroyed by the shift in relative prices implied by the move toward full pricing of GHG emissions.

Whether governments can bring a unified approach to the climate change problem is difficult to say, politics being politics. Even if they fail, investors are already voting with their portfolios, and this trend will continue, leading to profound shifts in capital allocation, business disruptions, and potentially stranded assets.

As a policy matter, emphasizing technological solutions to carbon capture and sequestration seems the best way to balance the world's green aspirations with its carbon backbone. Escalating carbon taxation is clearly one possible route. But governments can maximize flexibility by regulating emissions while creating incentives to build technology that removes carbon directly out of the air and buries it—the reverse of mining. Today, the methane emissions from municipal waste are being captured and fed into natural gas systems in some cities. Building on this idea, the conversion of municipal waste into hydrogen, or some other storable energy source, while capturing, storing, or reusing the embedded carbon holds considerable promise.

Such a circular technology would be truly liberating for society—imagine if single-use plastics were completely guilt-free, because the plastic was reliably converted to clean energy at the local landfill site. As a society, we owe it to ourselves and our children and grandchildren to find innovative ways to continue to exploit the benefits of the planet's natural resource wealth, while protecting the world from further climate change. Given the inevitability of more global warming, a two-pronged approach of reducing emissions immediately while developing new carbon-capture technologies for the future seems the best way to manage climate change risk.

The tectonic force of climate change clearly poses a daunting challenge on its own. But it is inevitable that it will collide with the other tectonic forces discussed in earlier chapters, leading to marked volatility and future uncertainty.

7

INTERACTING FORCES MEAN
A RISKIER WORLD

Reflections: Forks in the Road of Life

When you contemplate the number of possible paths a life can take, it is truly remarkable to find yourself where you are. How many decisions has it taken to progress from, say, high school to your current situation? If you had taken only one different turn on the road during the past twenty years, where would you be? The difference between that imagined scenario and where you are today could be gigantic—a different city, a different profession, a different spouse, kids versus no kids, and so on. A sequence of random events adds up over time to a tremendous amount of cumulative uncertainty. The people we are today are essentially the sum of all those decisions and the related experiences, which make us unique as individuals.

As Yogi Berra once said, "When you come to a fork in the road, take it." How is it that when I went to Queen's, I happened to meet someone who talked me into taking economics? Had I never met that person, I may have taken another math course instead of economics, entered medical school as planned, and ended up practising medicine somewhere near my hometown of Oshawa. The forks in the road and the cumulative uncertainty that lies between that starting point and today's outcome are beyond measure.

This simple thought experiment illustrates an important premise of this book: as in our lives, dynamic forces drift through time and never go in a straight line. Many random elements intrude along the way, and over time that uncertainty keeps adding up. Viewed from today, the uncertainty around where we will be five or ten years from now is huge, and where things ultimately end up is unique to each individual. This perfectly demonstrates the mathematics of chaos, or the butterfly effect, which is central to understanding the rising risks we will face in the near future.

Euphoria had been sweeping global stock markets for years, a wave of optimism driven by the latest technological advances. No end to the boom was in sight—investors were pouring money into new communications systems, transportation technologies, and the latest innovations in manufacturing. New ways of conducting payments were upending the old. A new era was underway.

Until Black Friday. Behind the wave of real economic progress hid the usual array of thinly veiled fraudsters luring undiscriminating investors beset by the fear of missing out. In a market that was out over its skis, discovering just one crack in the narrative was sufficient to turn sentiment on a dime. The market crashed that Friday morning: more than half of the stocks on the exchange evaporated, and over 100 financial institutions were thrown into insolvency. The market was closed by early afternoon, and the fallout was an economic depression that endured for some twenty years. Governments responded by putting in place tariffs to protect their economies.

That panic began on Friday, May 9, 1873, in Vienna, capital of the Austro-Hungarian Empire; it is widely seen as the catalyst of the Long Depression, or the Victorian depression. In subsequent weeks, credit dried up, suspicions grew, more investors exited, and more companies went bankrupt. Contagion was slower in those days, but over the next few months, the panic spread to other centres, including London, Berlin, and New York. The New York Stock Exchange closed for ten days that September.

While the 1873 panic clearly contributed to the Victorian depression, describing the episode as a classic boom-bust cycle—wherein investors simply lost their nerve—is far too simplistic. Economic historians do point to the boom that came before the bust, often citing excessive investment in railroads, but they also point to an important shift in payment systems. The German empire stopped minting silver coins in 1871 and shifted to a payment system based solely on gold in July 1873. A butterfly flapped its wings.

This seemingly innocuous decision in Germany led to ripple effects around the world, with significant consequences. Other countries, including the U.S., followed the German move to the gold standard, abandoning silver as a means of payment. The global money supply contracted, pushing interest rates up and causing heavily indebted farmers and railroads to default, taking their banks and other investors with them. This narrative makes it clear that the panic was not simply caused by a loss of investor confidence in Vienna and explains its international transmission.

I would also offer a deeper interpretation, based on tectonic forces. In the lead-up to the 1873 panic, the world was undergoing a tectonic shift of the first order. The First Industrial Revolution was humankind's first giant leap forward since people stumbled into agriculture. The colonization of North America brought an incredible wealth of new resources to the equation—arable land, timber, metals, minerals—and this combined with the deployment of the steam engine increased the supply capability of the world dramatically. In short, there was a surge in productivity the likes of which had never been witnessed before.

As discussed in chapter 3, that increase in global supply and shift to a new efficiency frontier resulted in declining prices for a wide range of goods, including food, cloth, and other manufactured items. Many people lost their jobs in the process, especially in the old economies of Europe, thereby compounding the demand-supply imbalance. The capitalists and railway barons were capturing the spoils of the First Industrial Revolution, while workers either lost their jobs or laboured long hours for low pay in the new factories. In other words, income inequality rose dramatically.

Meanwhile, declining prices were poison for companies with outstanding debt that were slow to adapt to the new technology, leading to eroding creditworthiness and growing suspicion in the minds of investors. The collision between three tectonic forces—technological progress, growing income inequality, and rising debt—laid the foundation for an eruption of economic and financial volatility.

All the situation needed was a catalyst to start the earthquake, and the Bismarck government obliged. Germany's shift from a bimetallic payment standard to the monometallic standard probably merits the label "tectonic" all by itself. The move proved to be highly contagious internationally and led to a shortage of gold and therefore of money. Just as the global economy experienced a massive increase in the supply of goods and needed more money supply to facilitate the growing volume of transactions, along came an outright cut in the global supply of money. Suddenly, there was too little money chasing too many goods, and deflation set in. The result was a perfect depression cocktail.

The Victorian depression illustrates perfectly how tectonic forces can interact and produce unexpected eruptions of economic and financial volatility. And not just volatility in the sense of fluctuating markets, but a true outlier, a black swan that delivered years of outright human misery completely out of proportion to the observed disturbances impacting the economy. The Victorian depression raised our collective level of uncertainty about the future permanently.

Understanding Uncertainty

Individuals and companies face uncertainty beyond measure every day. Uncertainty has always been a key part of practical economics, as it is the study of the behaviour of individuals and companies. Economists are always trying to capture broad shifts in aggregate behaviour—macroeconomics—based on what individuals do. You and I may react to a given situation differently, but when we add everyone's reactions together, we can define the average response across all individuals, and we acknowledge that the average is a statistical concept subject to uncertainty. In other words, when confronted with a certain situation, on average, people as a group will react this way, but each individual within the population reacts a little differently. Macroeconomics is not mechanical or precisely scientific; it is about a reasonable approximation of typical or average human behaviour.

A popular concept in economics is the standard or "normal" statistical distribution, commonly known as the bell curve. The normal distribution sketches the probability associated with each possible outcome. The most likely outcome is at the centre, at the top of the bell shape; this point is widely known as the average—the outcome you would expect. Perhaps in university you heard of professors using the bell curve to determine your grade. Because the difficulty of tests varies, and grading varies by professor, the university may want professors to make all the averages the same, say 70%. If the average in one class was 65%, the presumption is that the test was harder or the grading was more demanding, so each student has their grade moved up by 5% to make the class average the same as that of other classes. The rest of the bell curve represents all the other possible outcomes, each with lower and lower probabilities as we move farther away from the average. There is a very low probability of a student achieving 100%, a higher probability of 80%, and the highest probability is the average, 70%.

With this distribution of possible outcomes in mind, we can use mathematics to calculate the risk, or the probability, of a specific possibility occurring. If we believe we know what the statistical distribution of outcomes looks like, we can measure the risk associated with assuming that the future will be in line with the average demonstrated in the past. A very wide bell curve with a flat top would indicate that the probability of the average outcome is still highest, but not that high, as the probability of both higher and lower outcomes is significant. Assuming the average outcome will happen again tomorrow is risky.

In his book *The Black Swan*, Nassim Nicholas Taleb described the ever-popular bell curve as highly misleading, because it gives a false understanding of the concept of risk. When people think of averages described by bell curves, they tend not to consider the various highly unlikely outcomes that lie far away from the average, far out to the left or to the right of the average, in the tails of the curve. These improbable "tail risk" events are unfortunately littered throughout history, and people are almost never prepared for them, precisely because they are dismissed as extremely low risk. Calling the bell curve "that great intellectual fraud," Taleb writes, "Shockingly, the bell curve is used as a risk-measurement tool by those regulators and central bankers who wear dark suits and talk in a boring way about currencies." Mea culpa.

Much of our understanding of uncertainty in economics is built on the thinking of Frank Knight, an American economist who published a century ago. Knight used the term "risk" to describe situations where it is possible to calculate or measure the probability of specific outcomes. For example, an economist might use models to determine that there is a 30% probability of a recession a year from now. However, when calculating the odds is impossible for one reason or another, the uncertainty is so profound that it cannot be captured by economic models or approximated with average historical behaviour or bell curves. Uncertainty that cannot be measured is not considered "risk" but "Knightian uncertainty."

Correlations and Economic Models

Economic models rely on correlations in the data, regular associations between variables that can be used to make predictions. For example, consumer spending is positively correlated with consumer income; when income goes up, so does spending. The correlation is less than perfect, because on average some income is always saved, and the amount varies from person to person and with the underlying circumstances.

Even casual observers understand that correlation does not necessarily imply causation. There could always be something else going on that causes those two things to happen at the same time. This is where economic theory becomes important. By laying out predictions based on a tightly formulated theory, the economist is basically defining how causality should manifest itself in the economic statistics. If correlations in the statistics are consistent with the theory, then the economist has some confidence that the imagined relationships are reliable and uses them to forecast the future. Those relationships are collectively described as models.

In most cases, these relationships are not simple binary ones, such as "When this goes up, that usually goes down." Usually several things happen at once. The behaviour of one variable—say, the exchange rate—depends on the behaviour of several other variables, not only one of them. The analyst who relies on the historical correlation between the exchange rate and one other economic variable will discover a correlation that works only until it does not. When it does not, it will be because some other variable has taken over as the dominant driver of the exchange rate. Economists and the media often then explain how the usual correlation has "broken down" and been replaced with a "new theory." But in the end the new theory won't be much better. This new correlation, too, will work until it does not. This happens because the framework being applied is not complete.

The problem of deciding which correlations matter most and can be relied upon for forecasting is almost always multidimensional and much more difficult than it sounds. For example, the decision to purchase a house almost certainly depends on a person's income— the higher the income, the higher the propensity to buy a home rather than rent. At the same time, since the purchase of a house usually requires borrowing money, interest rates also matter to the decision. When interest rates are high, the mortgage payments are higher for the same home purchase than if interest rates were low. Lower interest rates tend to boost housing purchases; higher interest rates discourage them.

Now, suppose we observe a strengthening in house sales and a rise in interest rates at the same time. What are we to make of this reversal of the usual correlation? By setting aside the simple correlation in favour of a more elaborate model, we are reminded that housing sales are driven by incomes as well as by interest rates. If incomes are rising, house sales may rise, even if interest rates are rising as well. But sales will rise by less than they would have if interest rates had remained low. Understanding this intuitively requires that the observer imagine what house sales would have looked like if interest rates had not risen—sales would have been even stronger—and then understanding the effect of higher interest rates as a separate calculation. This thought process requires that observers imagine a counterfactual, which is difficult to do. People quite naturally think in terms of simple, two-variable correlations. Economists use statistical techniques to sort out the relative importance of such drivers in the data, essentially allowing for the possibility that two or more things may be going on at the same time.

And that is just a simple model for housing sales. The economist's model of the entire economy will include similar statistical relationships describing exports, imports, consumer spending, investment spending by firms, government spending, exchange rates, longer-term interest rates, and so on. Each of these elements interacts with many of the others, all simultaneously. As it becomes more complete, the model, like the economy, gradually loses the simplicity that allows the economist to understand how it should work.

When that happens, it is no longer possible to predict what correlations should be observed in the real world, or to understand the ones that are observed. The model can only be used to simulate history and to perform experiments that reveal its properties. Some parts of the model (housing, say) may explain history very well, while others (business investment, say) do so less well. Economists would say that the latter relationship is subject to more uncertainty than the former, because their tool is less able to replicate history. But all the components must work together to generate the variables we need to understand, such as overall economic growth or inflation.

A model's forecast for economic growth or inflation contains all of the uncertainty from the multiple relationships that describe each part of the economy. This complex confluence of uncertainty is referred to as "model uncertainty," and it is the most comprehensive measure of the risks that we take when we make economic decisions.

That is not the only source of uncertainty in economics. Ordinary measurement issues also play a role. Some important concepts in the economist's model are crystal clear in theory but muddy in practice. One example is the capacity of the economy to produce goods and services, which depends on both the capacity of firms to produce and the availability of labour. Another is the natural or equilibrium rate of interest, as discussed earlier.

To be honest, the economist must acknowledge that the uncertainty around the measurement of these elements will feed directly through the complexity of the model economy and magnify the bottom-line uncertainty around its forecasts for economic growth, inflation, interest rates, and so on. When seriously in doubt, the economist will produce multiple forecasts by making a series of assumptions about such variables and generate a "cloud" of possibilities for the future.

The Butterfly Effect, Black Swans, and Chaos Theory

If empirical economics appears challenging, predicting the weather seems even harder. There are just so many variables at work at any given time. As in economics, weather is inherently dynamic, evolving every moment of every day. Part of the problem is that even though the relationships in the weather are physical rather than behavioural or social (as they are in economics), the measurement of weather phenomena is even more imprecise than economic measurement.

Edward Lorenz was the first to observe in the early 1960s that the weather could appear to be chaotic—mathematically unpredictable—since it was so highly sensitive to starting conditions, and those were hard to measure precisely. Lorenz was engaged in the development of weather models and first talked about the "butterfly effect" in a study in 1972. According to his theory, it is possible that a butterfly flapping its wings in Brazil could set in motion a series of consequences that magnify through time and ultimately cause a tornado in Texas. In other words, small changes in starting conditions—or small errors in measurements of starting conditions—could have large consequences for the weather forecast.

Nowadays, forecasting the weather entails simulating many weather models with small variations in starting conditions to create multiple forecasts, which are then averaged out to give you the information on your weather app. This reduces the importance of the starting point measurement errors to the final weather forecast. Weather forecasters have become really good at their craft in recent years, with the hourly projection incredibly close to the actual outcomes.

Research by mathematicians has demonstrated that any system of moving forces with complex interactions, particularly one with some elements that are nonlinear, may generate chaotic outcomes. By "chaotic outcomes," they mean that one could not have predicted what might result from that particular combination of forces—the result is essentially random. If we replicated the same situation at some point in the future, a completely different outcome might result. This is mathematically true even when the forces are completely mechanical and known with certainty. This concept applies directly to the weather and to economies, both modelled with mathematical relationships, many of which are nonlinear. If a butterfly can change the weather, imagine what a convergence of tectonic forces can do to the economy.

Like the atmospheric forces that cause weather, the five tectonic forces are all relatively simple to describe. Populations age, technology progresses, income inequality worsens, debt loads rise, and our planet gets warmer. None of these is complex, really, but their consequences are. And when they all are evolving simultaneously, their interactions have the potential, in theory, to generate what appears to be chaotic or inexplicable outcomes for the global economy. In other words, the actual readings on economic growth, inflation, or interest rates in the future may be inexplicable given what we observe today and the models we create. This degree of uncertainty is, again in theory, incalculable and therefore needs to be regarded as "Knightian." For individuals, this means that the economic risks associated with ordinary decisions will be higher in the future.

Nassim Taleb's notion of a black swan is closely related to this concept of uncertainty. In Taleb's characterization, an event takes place that has never occurred before, and the whole world changes as a result. The internet is created, and the world is never the same. Two jetliners crash into the World Trade Center in New York City and the world is never the same. Or the U.S. housing market collapses, causing a global financial crisis, and the world is never the same. In the aftermath of such events, people can rationalize the crashing of the planes or the crashing of the housing market, which suggests to many observers that the events ought to have been foreseeable, by experts at the very least. The fact that the black swan has occurred means that in the future we should never be caught flat-footed again.

Taleb is absolutely right. There will always be major risks and opportunities hiding in the tails, events that will redefine our perception of risk from then on. But in a world of shifting and grinding tectonic forces, the issue is not just one of unpredictable tail risks. A more appealing explanation for unforeseen economic and financial events is that the complexity of our world and the forces acting on it are *guaranteed* to produce chaotic outcomes from time to time. Furthermore, as those forces become more powerful over time, we will experience more economic and financial volatility *on average*. Inexplicable events may appear to be black swans but will be the natural product of the growing complexity of our environment. If this book is about one thing, it is that the rising risk bearing down on us is right in the middle of the bell curve. It is something we can bet on—even if the events themselves are not forecastable, we know higher volatility is coming.

That is not a forecast in the usual economic sense. I am not plugging data into a model to see what it predicts. This is a deeper inference, a logical conclusion based on mathematics. Future interactions of growing tectonic forces will inject chaos into the global economy. Consequently, the statistical averages on which we base our understanding of the economy will become far less reliable, surrounded by more risk. Our economic decisions will by necessity be cloudier, and it will be much easier for us to be wrong and to suffer the consequences of poor decisions.

As Klaus Schwab and Thierry Malleret of the World Economic Forum put it so eloquently in their 2020 book *COVID-19: The Great Reset*, the one word that best captures the twenty-first century is "interdependence," a by-product of globalization and technological progress. Greater interdependence means more opportunities for specialization in economic activity and trade across borders, with complex global supply chains part of the inevitable outcome. But this degree of interdependence also makes economies more vulnerable to cascading shocks. Economies have become more synchronous as a consequence, regardless of the underlying disturbance.

To illustrate, consider how rapidly the COVID-19 pandemic spread around the world, with international travel far more common today compared to twenty or thirty years ago. In a recent study, Max Roser assembled data on global tourism from the UN World Tourism Organization showing that there were 278 million international arrivals in 1980 and 1,400 million arrivals in 2018, a 500% increase. This is a good proxy for the globalization of business, not just rising tourism. The increase occurred during a period when global population rose by roughly 70%. With people moving around a lot more than ever before, the globalization of any new virus is highly likely, whether from a bat in China, a mink in Denmark, or a mosquito in Toronto. Schwab and Malleret argue convincingly that the shockwaves from COVID-19 will reverberate long into the future, adding to economic and political instability. However, it is my contention that the world would have experienced a rising tide of risk in the future even if the pandemic had never occurred.

Politics and Geopolitics

The tectonic forces will not only interact with one another. The consequences of rising volatility for individuals and companies will inevitably draw politics into the mix, adding another layer of uncertainty to any economic issue. Well-intentioned government policies that take political considerations into account will suffer from compromise and may have unintended consequences for the business environment. Even if they do not, the uncertainty around what governments may do about a specific issue can be a significant impediment to business decision-making. In today's highly interdependent world, political tensions in one country can cascade into global geopolitics, bringing new dimensions of uncertainty to the kitchen table. We have seen exactly this mechanism in recent years in the domain of international trade. Rising income inequality has fuelled discontent in the U.S. and led to arbitrary trade restrictions with important consequences around the world.

Similarly, the collision of the tectonic force of climate change with continued population growth seems certain to turn water into a source of future geopolitical volatility. The World Health Organization estimates that by 2025 around half of the world's population will be living in water-stressed areas. On top of this, the transition to a lower-carbon economy may prove to be water intensive. Hydrogen is often touted as the greenest fuel, but its production often begins with fresh water. Electric cars use batteries made from lithium, the production of which uses enormous amounts of water. Nuclear power uses large amounts of water, as does geothermal energy. In short, global water stresses could cause major seismic events in the global economy, including human catastrophe, mass migrations of people, or even a war.

Interactions between tectonic forces offer a more coherent explanation for the major crises in history. The Victorian depression and the Great Depression were both the product of the interactions between a major technological wave, rising inequality, and debt. These same ingredients laid the foundation for the Asian financial crisis of 1997, which then infected Latin America and Russia. In the aftermath, the tectonic forces continued to rumble, creating the preconditions of the Global Financial Crisis.

The Fourth Industrial Revolution is underway and has probably been accelerated by the global pandemic. Combined with the forces of population aging, growing income inequality, rising debt, and climate change, we have all the necessary ingredients to predict more economic and financial earthquakes in the near future. Many of the tectonic forces will attract political debate, attempts at compromise, and unexpected shifts in policies, which will add another layer of risk to the outlook. A crisis like that of the late 1800s is very possible given these conditions. However, just as a series of smaller but serious earthquakes is not the same as a catastrophic one, predicting rising risk is not the same as predicting a crisis.

In practical terms, higher risk in the future will mean more frequent recessions and increases in unemployment but, by the same token, more frequent economic booms with occasional bouts of inflation. Periods with extremely low interest rates, alongside periods of unexpectedly high interest rates. Significantly more volatility in stock markets, both down and up, as well as in house prices. More volatility in prices for raw materials, including oil, which will be reflected at your local gas station. All of this means that any specific economic decision—to expand a business, or to renew a mortgage for a short or long term, for example—will bear increased risk of proving to be wrong.

It is not just that the five tectonic forces are in motion and growing. It is that they can reinforce one another to create magnified convulsions in the economy. Population aging means low or possibly even lower interest rates, which will cause the inexorable rise in indebtedness to pick up speed. Climate change leads investors to demand a risk premium for providing capital to firms that are less than pure green, and the future business environment suddenly becomes a political hot potato. Technological advances displace workers, increase income inequality, and invite governments to intervene in unexpected ways. This is how increased uncertainty about the future can make financial decisions far more difficult.

With the tectonic forces in motion and already causing increased volatility throughout the global economy, should we be surprised that a bat in Wuhan can flap its wings and bring the world to its knees?

8

MANAGING RISK IN REAL TIME

THE COVID-19 PANDEMIC

Reflections: The Homecoming

I returned to the Bank of Canada as governor after an eighteen-year absence full of interesting and rewarding forks in the road. Principal among these was the valuable time spent in corporate boardrooms while with EDC, gathering a ground-level understanding of how the economy worked that one can never achieve by poring over economic articles, models, and data. This experience proved to be of extreme value on several occasions during the next seven years, but none more important than in the early days of the pandemic of 2020.

The announcement of my appointment as governor was in early May, 2013, a lovely day for "the walk," which is a Bank of Canada tradition. The minister of finance (the late Jim Flaherty) and the outgoing governor (Mark Carney) walk the governor-designate down Wellington Street in Ottawa to the National Press Building, as reporters and photographers hustle along the sidewalk seeking the perfect shot of the trio. At one point, with traffic halted and photographers crouched here and there, I started to step forward and Minister Flaherty reached out and stopped me, rumbling, "Steve, this wouldn't be a good moment to get run over by a car," under his breath. In the press theatre, the three of us conducted an impromptu press conference.

Earlier that day, I had slipped away from my desk at EDC, only telling my executive assistant that I had an outside appointment. I was picked up at the curb and then secreted into the Bank of Canada building through the basement, where there is space to park a couple of cars and a loading dock for trucks to make deliveries. Governor Carney was waiting for me on the loading dock, and as he shook my hand, he exclaimed, "Steve, welcome home!" A special moment for a kid from Oshawa—truly a homecoming.

But my first day on the job a month later was easily the most memorable. For starters, Governor Carney had left me a nice hand-written note in my desk drawer, which I still have. Next, I persuaded the person in charge of such things to have the original 1930s desk of Graham Towers, the first governor of the Bank of Canada, brought out of storage and delivered to my office for my personal use. I'm big on tradition, and I could visualize the original Towers desk from my visits to the governor's office of John Crow and later Gordon Thiessen. I promised to treat it like the heritage piece it is. Next, it was time to meet Prime Minister Harper in his office, along with Minister Flaherty. When I returned to my office, the head of our currency department was waiting with a special sheet of paper and a special black pen, and they said, "Governor, I need your signature."

Since I first dreamed of running the Bank of Canada, nearly forty years earlier, I had pictured this very moment. There can be nothing more special for a monetary economist than having your signature appear on the money that Canadians carry in their pockets. The special sheet of paper had ten boxes on it for me to sign in, the idea being that I would sign ten times and then choose the signature I liked best to appear on Canada's banknotes.

With my pen poised, I thought I should alert them to my plan, which had been long in development. "I should mention," I said, "that I plan to sign with my full name, Stephen S. Poloz." Being a student of the matter, I had noticed that past governors had signed simply with their initials and their last name.

"Oh, Governor, you really shouldn't. Traditionally, the banknote signatures are with initials only."

I replied that I was fully aware of the tradition but nevertheless had made up my mind to do something different. My given name, Stephen, is also my mother's family name. But there was also a deeper story. My mother was a distant relative of George Stephen, who was president of the Bank of Montreal from 1876–81. He went on to manage the construction of the trans-Canadian railway that bound our country together and was the first president of Canadian Pacific Railway. The Bank of Montreal was the Government of Canada's bank before the Bank of Canada was created in 1935, which meant there was also a central banking connection between me and old "Uncle George." For these reasons I wanted both family names, Stephen and Poloz, on the money. And so that is how I signed my name.

In that same first meeting, I asked when we could expect to place an iconic Canadian woman onto one of our banknotes. The answer was, regrettably, that it would not be possible to achieve this during my seven-year term as governor. Needless to say, I was not happy with this answer and made it a personal mission to create a banknote with an iconic Canadian woman sometime during my term. Our first opportunity came when it was decided to issue a special bank note commemorating the 150th anniversary of Canadian Confederation in 2017, which included the image of Agnes Macphail, the first woman elected to the House of Commons. We then launched a process to update one regular banknote, rather than the entire series, and engaged Canadians in nominating candidates to appear on it. At the end of this process, the minister of finance, Bill Morneau, chose Viola Desmond, depicted in a striking new vertical design, with the Canadian Museum of Human Rights on the reverse side of the note. We were all immensely proud of that achievement, especially since in 2013 we had believed it to be impossible before sometime in the 2020s.

Another thing that seemed impossible back in 2013 was that the world economy could one day be almost completely shut down as the result of a global pandemic. If the Global Financial Crisis of 2008 seemed to alter some foundations of our economy and make the future difficult to predict, the COVID-19 crisis seemed to be many times worse. It put the learnings of a lifetime to the test.

The events of 2020 perfectly illustrate the idea of the interdependence of forces set out in chapter 7. COVID-19 cannot be regarded as a black swan in the sense of Taleb, for epidemiologists have long been expecting such a pandemic to happen someday. The risk of virus mutation and the transmission from animals to humans is a constant one, not unlike the inevitability of the motion of the Earth's tectonic plates. The degree to which the global economy is integrated virtually guarantees that such a virus mutation will go global. That COVID-19 has redefined the world's steady state, altering our concept of normal in the process, is not in doubt. The complex and outsized eruption of economic and financial volatility after a Wuhan bat flapped its wings was a good illustration of how forces can interact to produce outcomes that appear chaotic and evoke comparisons with black swans. The experience also gave policymakers a taste of the sort of interventions that could be required to deal with future seismic events.

What Central Banks Were Made For

All policymakers were aware of the virus early on, as we had seen the reports from China. My first glimpse of how seriously people were taking the matter was on February 22, 2020, when the G20 finance ministers and governors met personally in Riyadh. Our Chinese colleagues did not travel to Riyadh, but China's ambassador to Saudi Arabia briefed the group in detail. We also heard in-depth analysis from Italy, South Korea, and Singapore, other early victims of the spreading virus. They provided first-hand accounts of how the virus was spreading and affecting health care systems, as well as the scale of policy responses that were under consideration. The tone of the meeting was very subdued, even grave. Discussions about the economic outlook became completely conditional on how COVID-19 might affect things, virtually overnight. I recall coming home from that meeting convinced that serious trouble was on the way.

Global oil prices had already dropped significantly, from around $60 at the start of the year to about $45 in late February, mostly due to an eruption of a competition for market share between U.S. and Saudi Arabian producers. This alone had a significant impact on Canada. Canada produces much more oil than it consumes, so a drop in price means lower national income, less investment in the oil sector, and the immediate loss of jobs in oil-producing regions. These effects spread across the country—when an oil sector worker loses their job in Alberta, they delay their plans to purchase a new vehicle, new clothes, or a new deck for the backyard, affecting jobs in the auto sector, the retail sector, the construction sector, the forestry sector, and so on. At the Bank of Canada, we were already thinking about what interest rate adjustments might be necessary in the event of a sudden negative turn in the economy.

On March 4, very early in the morning, there was an international coordination meeting dedicated solely to COVID-19, hosted by the IMF. It was becoming clear that the virus was spreading like wildfire. Later that morning, the Bank of Canada cut interest rates by fifty basis points; we knew that weak oil prices alone would necessitate a material easing of monetary policy. However, I was already getting the feeling that fifty basis points would prove to be insufficient, given the other effects that COVID-19 might have. This was a challenging analysis given that interest rates were already very low, leaving monetary policy very little room to manoeuvre. I was beginning to suspect that the bank would need to break out some unconventional tools beyond the usual interest rate actions.

The following day, March 5, I travelled to Toronto to deliver the traditional day-after-decision economic update speech at the Royal York Hotel, hosted by Women in Capital Markets. There were six hundred people in attendance. During the pre-lunch cocktail gathering, some people were doing elbow bumps by way of greeting, but most of the people I met that day gave me a warm handshake or a hug. How quickly that would change. I concluded my talk with a few words about what everyone was already talking about—the virus. A lot has changed since then, but I stand by what I said that day. I offered reassurance that the economy was in good shape to deal with whatever arose. This state of readiness for unexpected volatility—resilience—will be key to responding in the higher-risk environment of our future.

Importantly, crises such as COVID-19 do not affect the whole world at the same time or in the same way. Starting conditions matter. When the weather forecaster feeds a litany of starting conditions into their model, just a small error in data entry can produce wildly different forecasts. Economies are the same. In trying to understand how different economies coped with COVID-19, it is helpful to have a good sense of conditions when the virus arrived. If two economies are at different places relative to their steady state, we should not expect them to react to COVID-19 in the same manner.

Canada offers an insightful example. When I returned to the bank as governor in 2013, the Canadian economy was operating well short of its full capacity and inflation was below target—a legacy of the Global Financial Crisis. People were understandably impatient to leave that legacy behind; after all, in 2013 it had already been five years since the Global Financial Crisis, and in many countries the recovery had proved halting, despite continued low interest rates.

I recall being asked repeatedly during 2011–12, when I was still with EDC, why the economy was not recovering from the post-crisis recession in typical fashion. I have always been a big fan of metaphors as they help translate abstract economics into something more memorable that aids the intuition. In a session at the Conférence de Montréal, founded by my good friend Gil Rémillard, I first laid out my spaghetti sauce metaphor, which proved to be quite durable.

The story goes like this. At the time, many were attributing the Global Financial Crisis to the bursting of the real estate bubble in the U.S., and the Great Recession that followed as part of the usual boom-bust-recovery cycle. I explained that the economy has a lot in common with a pot of spaghetti sauce warming on the stove. As it approaches boiling, it begins to form bubbles on the surface. The thicker the spaghetti sauce, the better, but the bigger the bubbles it generates.

Most people have observed that when the bubbles in the spaghetti sauce burst, there is a momentary crater underneath the bubble. How big is the crater? Exactly the same size as the bubble. There is nothing arbitrary about it. The bursting of the U.S. housing bubble had left behind a crater in the economy. How big was the crater? Exactly the same size as the bubble.

I reasoned that the U.S. housing bubble had really begun in the wake of the consumer spending boom that unfolded right after the events on September 11, 2001. If it took six to seven years for the U.S. housing bubble to form, it would probably take six to seven years for us to walk across the bottom of the crater and climb back up the other side. In other words, it would take until 2014–15 for the U.S. economy to return to normal, and in 2012 it was simply too soon to expect a complete recovery. When I gave my first speech as governor in June 2013, I suggested that the economy would take perhaps two more years to find its way back "home." For me and for many other central bankers, "home" lies at the intersection of 2% inflation and full employment. To be honest, though, "home" is more of a neighbourhood than an exact address.

As it turned out, there was another detour on the way home, as energy prices collapsed in 2014. But by the second half of 2019, the economy was operating near its full capacity again, with unemployment at a forty-year low and inflation at target. Home indeed.

And then came COVID-19.

There is never a good time for a global emergency. But there is no better starting point from which to confront a crisis of the magnitude of COVID-19 than a healthy, balanced economy. Just as a healthy, fit individual would be more likely to shake off the virus, so would a healthy Canadian economy. The central bank's job is to maintain that level of health, administering interest rate adjustments from time to time to help offset shocks that are hitting the economy, using inflation as the central guide.

The central bank has another job, however, which in some ways is even more fundamental: to ensure that financial markets continue to function well. To this end, I organized a call on March 6 with the big-six bank CEOs to get their sense of the evolving market situation. This is a group I had been meeting twice a year, along with senior deputy governor (SDG) Carolyn Wilkins. Over the years, this group of eight people had developed a warm and informal relationship, very high on trust. It proved to be very important in the weeks ahead.

Most of us were already splitting our operational teams as a guard against contagion of the virus, and the bankers reported the emergence of some tensions in financial markets. For example, certain borrowers through the commercial paper market—where companies borrow directly from the market by issuing short-term notes in their own name—were struggling to complete their deals, and rates were rising. The bankers had also seen an increase in credit line draws by their own corporate customers. One thing that was on my mind was the possibility that a major disruption in the economy would make it difficult for people to meet their mortgage payments. I asked whether they had any contingency plans to defer mortgage payments in the event of a major downturn in the economy, and they told me that they did, but at that point it appeared unlikely that such a tool would be necessary.

I also had a call on March 6 from the deputy minister of finance, Paul Rochon, who was already sketching out actions that the government might consider taking to support the economy. Later that day, I also had a call from the prime minister, who wanted to compare notes. It was very clear from these conversations that fiscal policy would need to be the tool of choice in the circumstances. However, there was a lot of discussion of the various options available to the government for channelling financial support to the economy. We discussed early examples from affected countries such as Italy and Japan, where wage subsidies flowing directly to companies from the tax authorities were the main tool. Remarkably, only thirteen days had passed since the G20 meeting in Riyadh.

At a special virtual meeting of major central bank governors hosted by the Bank for International Settlements (BIS) two days later, on Sunday, March 8, we heard first-hand from our colleagues in China, Italy, and South Korea. The situation had clearly worsened, and economic activity would need to be curtailed dramatically to manage the virus. The reader will by now begin to appreciate the relentless daily pace of events. Most of the meetings were international in nature, often at odd hours, and there was considerable sharing of experience and plans. Of course, there was no unified response by policymakers. Countries were fighting fires in their own backyards for the most part using fiscal policy tools. While there was a certain commonality in approach, the details varied from one country to another. Nevertheless, there was a high level of international coordination during those early days, in terms of sharing developments in real time and discussing the pros and cons of various policy options. The gatherings worked as intended—in normal times, these meetings are informative but can be quite dull; in a crisis, they serve an essential purpose.

Later that same Sunday, I attended a memorial service for a close friend who had died after a long battle with liver cancer. That was my last social activity before we moved to a new footing as a society. I will always associate my dear friend Jim's memorial service with the day the COVID-19 penny truly dropped.

Over the next few days, the economic and financial situation seemed to deteriorate hourly. The Bank of Canada's governing council (myself,

SDG Wilkins, and deputy governors Lane, Schembri, Beaudry, and Gravelle) was meeting virtually multiple times per day. Other central banks were cutting rates to soften the blow to their economies, as well as releasing bank capital buffers, which gives banks more capacity to increase lending to their customers. I was staying in close contact with Jay Powell at the Federal Reserve, Mark Carney at the Bank of England, Finance Minister Morneau and his deputy Paul Rochon, Superintendent of Financial Institutions Jeremy Rudin, the big-six bank CEOs, the eight top pension CEOs, and the heads of Canada's capital market agencies. Taking account of all this market intelligence, we talked internally about a menu of measures to ensure continued financial market functioning. We had shifted frames from monetary policymaking—which is about managing the economy to keep inflation on track—to pure central banking, which is about maintaining orderly financial markets.

On March 13, we held a Special Advisory Committee (SAC) meeting. Chaired by the deputy minister of finance, this committee includes the governor, the superintendent of financial institutions and the heads of the Canada Deposit Insurance Corporation, and the Financial Consumer Agency of Canada. SAC is designed to provide a flow of advice to the minister of finance, who holds ultimate responsibility for the financial system itself. We also held a meeting with the big-six bank CEOs to get a market intelligence update. Soon after, the minister asked if the superintendent and I would join a press conference with him that afternoon when he announced new fiscal measures to support the economy, thinking that a team-based message would help buttress Canadians' confidence in the future.

The notion of confidence is a very important one. When something happens to the economy that causes people to lose their jobs, those people obviously reduce their spending, which causes those job losses to affect jobs in other sectors. But what about people who believe their jobs are secure? If they remain confident, they will go about their business and spend money more or less as they were before. If they worry that the problem is spreading and they might also lose their jobs, they will cut spending, which compounds the original impact on the economy. This is how an economy falls into a recession from which it is hard to exit. Efforts to maintain confidence are intended to minimize the damage.

I was supportive of demonstrating that policymakers were working together to get the economy through the pandemic. However, I was mindful of what appearing with the minister might symbolize in terms of central bank independence. Would financial markets observe the central bank working closely with the government and worry about higher inflation in the future? Before agreeing to appear with the minister, I consulted with governing council and we decided that visible coordination would be a source of reassurance for markets. We also returned to the question of cutting interest rates again, rather than waiting for our next official decision date, which was four weeks away. We concluded that cutting rates at the same time that the minister of finance made his fiscal announcement could provide quite a powerful signal to financial markets. We were also expecting the U.S. Federal Reserve to cut rates again the following week. Accordingly, we agreed to cut rates by a further fifty basis points later that day, March 13, and to announce it at the same time as the press conference organized by the minister. Meanwhile, over at the Office of the Superintendent of Financial Institutions (OSFI), they were considering cutting the domestic stability buffer, an extra layer of reserves required to be held by Canadian banks. OSFI decided to do so, thereby freeing up as much as $300 billion in additional lending capacity for the banks. The superintendent made the announcement at that same press conference—a three-fer, you might say.

There were meetings between various federal partners and bilateral meetings with several bank CEOs all weekend long. Sunday afternoon, March 15, the Fed made its big move, taking its rate down to the effective lower bound and launching an array of measures aimed at supporting financial market functioning. One key component of its announcement was a facility to purchase commercial paper in the open market. This is a critical financial channel for firms. It matters to the banks, too, as many of them have committed credit lines with the same firms. If for some reason the commercial paper market were to get jammed up—in which case firms could not replace maturing commercial paper with a new issuance—firms would be forced to draw heavily on their bank credit lines and the banks themselves would face the funding pressure. Over the next few days, we became convinced that Canada, too, needed a commercial paper purchase facility, where the central bank would offer to buy commercial paper at market rates to backstop the market.

Minister Morneau again asked me to appear with him before the media three days later, on Wednesday, March 18; he planned to release further details of the government's fiscal package. When notification of the upcoming press conference was posted, indicating that I would be present, markets and the media went into a frenzy speculating that there would be another surprise interest rate cut at the same time. We took the unusual step of preannouncing that there would be no new measures taken by the bank later that day.

Nevertheless, we were being briefed in the background by bank staff—given the further decline in oil prices and the other likely hits to the economy, it seemed likely we would need to deliver all of the monetary stimulus we had available. But we felt that further monetary policy moves could wait while we focused on ensuring good financial market functioning. Ideally, we would wait until we had a new economic analysis and could publish our next *Monetary Policy Report*, scheduled for April 15.

What followed in the next several days was a series of adjustments to our market actions designed to meet financial market challenges as they arose. Eventually, these included a provincial bond purchase program, which meant announcing that we would purchase a portion of each new bond issue from a provincial borrower. It also included a commercial paper purchase program and a corporate bond purchase program, both of which implied lending directly to corporate borrowers. Each of these actions meant an increase in the central bank's balance sheet—when the central bank acquires an asset, such as a corporate bond, it creates new liquidity on the liability side. This is essentially creating money out of thin air; the underlying reason to do so is that borrowers need to be more liquid to feel assured that they can meet their day-to-day obligations without defaulting. It is not at all the same as creating new money out of thin air and then forcing it into the economy so that there is too much money chasing too few goods. When liquidity demands jump during a period of market tensions, the risk is that there will be too *little* money chasing too many goods.

Some might wonder why we would not go full throttle on all these programs at the flip of a switch. There are a few reasons. First, as central bankers, we would very much prefer that markets work these things out on their own. It is not the central bank's job to short-circuit the natural credit process, so it is important to give markets at least the opportunity to function on their own.

Second, some of these intervention tools had never been used before. These programs opened up the ability to convert a wider array of assets into cash than had been done in past liquidity operations, in order to ensure that no pockets of market dislocation remained. Although they all lie within the central bank's legal purview, in most cases they broke new ground for our traders and for our back-office staff.

Running a new program means announcing that on, say, next Wednesday, the central bank will be accepting bids from the market to sell a certain class of assets (e.g., commercial paper) with a list of quality criteria for a particular term, in exchange for cash, and with a volume limit for the auction. The price of liquidity emerges through the auction process itself. The criteria need to be developed and published in advance, the bid process needs to be managed, settlement carried out, and so on. In some cases, the mere announcement that the bank would be backstopping a particular market segment would calm the situation: the additional reassurance allowed the market to function on its own, and there was modest take-up for some of the programs.

Third, some of these programs imply that the central bank is taking credit risk. For example, when the bank accepts some commercial paper or a corporate bond issued by a Canadian corporation, it is taking on the risk that the company will be downgraded or even go bankrupt, in which case the central bank experiences a credit loss. To avoid that, it is traditional for governments to indemnify their central banks from potential credit losses. Although the central bank's balance sheet is ultimately the government's own, the separation is important, as it is one of the foundations of central bank independence. What this meant in practical terms was that some of the new market-functioning programs required full, formalized co-operation from the Department of Finance and the minister.

Fourth, some of the programs were sufficiently outside the bank's expertise that we decided to get outside help to develop and execute them. This required that we entertain proposals from various interested financial firms and choose between them on the basis of their past experience, proposed service levels, and pricing. That took time.

It is also important to understand what was going on in the business world at this time. Companies were drawing heavily on their credit lines with their banks—to pay staff, for more general working capital, and in some cases as a purely precautionary measure, seeking comfort in a time of extreme uncertainty. While some would question a company's action to hoard cash during a financial crisis, it is a perfectly natural risk management tool, and various boards of directors were undoubtedly instructing management to do exactly that. People might be surprised at how little liquidity many large companies carry on their balance sheets. Minimizing cash is, of course, consistent with the efficient deployment of capital, but in a volatile world it is possible that cash demands will rise unexpectedly, and credit lines can freeze up. This is what happened in 2008, and corporations were undoubtedly concerned this would happen again in 2020. Happily, there was no credit squeeze.

When companies draw their lines with their banks, banks must source the funds from somewhere. Normally, they increase their own issuance of bonds in the marketplace, but with bond markets practically frozen, banks turned to the Bank of Canada for funding, pledging collateral through repurchase agreements. Instead of selling an asset in the marketplace, it is offered to the Bank of Canada as collateral in return for immediate cash, and the bank agrees to buy the collateral back on a specified date. The Bank of Canada made a number of adjustments to its collateral guidelines during the stress period, thereby ensuring that the system had all the liquidity it needed through these repo operations. The result, of course, was that the central bank balance sheet ballooned. A contributing factor was that the commercial paper market jammed, and firms that usually use that market also turned to their bank lines. By offering easy liquidity access to the banks and standing as buyer of last resort of commercial paper, the Bank of Canada can relieve market pressures in more than one dimension and across different players.

Meanwhile, the international situation had not stood still. A number of central banks, including the Bank of Canada, came together to enhance the provision of U.S. dollar liquidity to global markets on March 20. Then, on March 24, the G7 finance ministers and central bank governors issued a joint statement underscoring that we were meeting weekly and would "do whatever is necessary to restore confidence and economic growth and to protect jobs, businesses, and the resilience of the financial system." A number of central banks had already moved interest rates to their effective lower bound, including the Federal Reserve, but Canada had not. This was giving rise to an odd distortion at the front end of our money market: because market pressures had taken short-term interest rates below the Bank of Canada overnight rate, market dealers were paying more to finance their inventories of government debt than they were earning on the debt itself. Governing council therefore decided that the system could not wait for April 15 and that we should cut our rate to the effective lower bound of 0.25%. We had our eye on March 27, the following Friday.

In addition to the various liquidity programs already mentioned, we made a commitment to underpin system-wide liquidity by purchasing Government of Canada bonds at the rate of at least $5 billion per week. We believed that the term "at least" in this program was essential in light of the past experience of other central banks, where use of the term "up to" had led to a rush on liquidity as the market worried whether more capacity would be available. Ceilings on market intervention always seem to run into this problem, so we adopted the notion of "at least" and did not put a cap on the program. Rather, we said that the bond purchases would continue at that rate at least until such time as the economic recovery was well underway. Accordingly, these large-scale asset purchases (LSAPs) served as the bridge from our focus on market function to a renewed focus on monetary policy once the market dislocations had dissipated.

Meanwhile, the minister of finance was preparing to lay out additional fiscal details and was again seeking a joint press conference with me. Governing council debated the issue once again, very conscious of the possibility that people might see these joint press conferences as eroding the independence of monetary policy. Because central banks have the power to lend, but not the power to spend, the power of their tools is built on that foundation of independence. The Canadian government has always been unwavering in its commitment to central bank independence, even if it is not actually written in the Bank of Canada Act, and we again saw the merits in emphasizing domestic policy coordination.

Since we already had the wheels in motion for an interest rate announcement, we stuck to our schedule and made our announcement independently on the morning of March 27. In the afternoon, I joined the minister for his press conference and took some additional questions. One exchange with a journalist was particularly memorable for me. Because we had announced government debt purchases of at least $5 billion per week, I was asked if I had an upper limit in mind. I replied bluntly that the program would be unlimited. In follow-up, the reporter asked if I might be overdoing it a little. My response would cement my reputation as a lover of metaphors: "A firefighter has never been criticized for using too much water." Fortunately, in the coming days, the calm kept spreading and spreading; the crisis had been defused.

Looking back, it is clear that there were a number of important factors that helped to limit the financial crisis that erupted due to the spread of COVID-19. These lessons will prove useful in the future as the tectonic forces produce more frequent economic and financial earthquakes. First, it was helpful that the economy was already "home"—in a resilient position when the shock happened. Second, coordination with other countries was very important, not so much in terms of mimicking policies but in terms of comparing policy options, learning from one another, and honing communications. Third, deploying crisis-management tools quickly and at scale, rather than sequentially as in 2008, helped to defuse the crisis rapidly. These ingredients were essential to move from crisis management to the business of fostering an economic recovery.

Setting the Stage for Recovery

One issue that came up as the crisis-management tools were unveiled is that commentators began referring to the bank's large-scale asset purchases (LSAPs) of Government of Canada bonds as "quantitative easing" (QE). While LSAPs are operationally identical to QE, I resisted use of the term "QE" during the crisis because the objective behind the LSAPs was limited to ensuring good market function. In effect, we were making certain the ship could survive the storm rather than debating the direction in which the ship should be sailing. LSAPs are a market function tool, while QE is a monetary policy tool aimed at influencing interest rates when markets are functioning well. Our plan was to switch to the term "QE" once market functioning was restored and the central bank's attention could shift from market intervention back to monetary policymaking.

The distinction between LSAPs and QE may seem to be one of form over substance, but it is a distinction that matters, at least to me. LSAPs aimed at ensuring good market function can increase or decrease as necessary, depending on the market stresses that arise. QE is not about market function; it is about monetary policy. It is about using extraordinary tools to get more monetary stimulus into the economy by extending the effect of lower interest rates from over-night rates to longer-term interest rates farther out the yield curve. Accordingly, QE is generally expressed in terms of a target for a longer-term interest rate. When overnight rates are effectively at zero, chances are that longer-term interest rates have been pulled down to their theoretical minimum, too, with rates rising gradually the longer the maturity of the bond. A QE program could be aimed at reducing, say, five-year bond yields a little bit more, given their importance in driving five-year mortgage rates in Canada, which in turn are a critical part of the monetary policy transmission mechanism. For example, cutting overnight rates by 150 basis points might only lead to a reduction of five-year mortgage rates by fifty or seventy-five, and getting even more of that interest rate relief to households can be facilitated by the deployment of QE.

Ultimately, QE may be aimed at "yield curve control"—in effect, managing where the entire yield curve is at a point in time. This would be achieved by spreading QE purchases across all maturities of government debt. QE is generally accompanied by "forward guidance" statements around how big the operations will be and for how long. Such commitments describe the future pace of debt purchases, expressed either as a specific time frame or as contingent on specific economic or inflation outcomes. In these circumstances, on March 27, we said that our weekly government debt purchases of $5 billion per week would continue "until the recovery was well underway."

This gave the market confidence that we would not arbitrarily stop providing stimulus but would openly discuss how the economy was evolving and continuously review the program.

The following two weeks were fully occupied with preparation of the April *Monetary Policy Report*. There was no interest rate move to decide, since we had made it clear that 0.25% was the effective lower bound and we had no intentions of taking rates negative. With fiscal policy taking the lead in stabilizing the economy, I was confident that we would not need to resort to negative interest rates to put a bottom under the economy; negative rates would be reserved as a last-resort measure. Staff updated us on their views for the economy, drawing on a variety of newly developed economic models based on high-frequency data sources and constructing alternative economic scenarios for governing council to consider. Because economic activities had been shut down to contain COVID-19 transmission, typical measures of the economy were likely to plunge in ways never experienced before. When restrictions were eased, we knew we would see a bounce, but the actual recovery would depend on how long the shutdowns lasted and whether the effects on economic confidence spread beyond the closed sectors. We decided at an early stage not to try to pull precise forecasts out of this analysis but instead to offer one scenario where the shutdowns were short, and another where they extended for several months. This approach gave a wide range of possibilities for the next two years, rather than a set of forecast numbers. It was a controversial decision, as the bank has always provided point forecasts for the economy and inflation over the policy horizon (two years), and markets and commentators were looking forward to those numbers.

There was no shortage of economic forecasts from other sources, and they became more negative daily, progressing from "worse than the Global Financial Crisis" to "the biggest downturn since World

War II" to "the biggest decline in the economy since the Great Depression." This reporting made me uncomfortable, as consumer and business confidence can be fragile things.

In my view, these comparisons with past episodes were totally unhelpful, as they were based on arithmetic rather than underlying causes. There is no point comparing apples and oranges. No one needed an economist to tell them that we were looking at a massive drop-off in economic activity. But a recession is conventionally defined as at least two successive quarters of negative economic growth. It was not evident that this criterion would be met in 2020. More importantly, that definition says nothing about the underlying conditions in the economy. A recession is a dynamic phenomenon, where demand declines for some reason, firms lay off workers, confidence declines, people cut back on purchases, more firms lay off more workers in a self-reinforcing negative cycle that takes time and healing to reverse. A depression is even worse: it is deeper, longer, and happens because deflation interacts with debt to create widespread defaults of companies and even financial institutions. Neither recessions nor depressions lend themselves to a simple numerical standard. Neither term applied to an economy where there had been a mechanical shutdown—an attempt to stop the clock, as it were—to be followed by a restart. No one had ever tried to stop the clock before. Rather than being described as "the biggest downturn since the Great Depression," the pandemic downturn should perhaps be described as "the shortest recession in history." In most advanced economies, the economy shrank during March and April and began to grow again in May. Economic activity was back to 97% or more of pre-COVID-19 levels by late 2020.

The COVID-19 downturn is unique in history, not only because of its underlying nature but because of the immediate and forceful fiscal response that was rolled out. In Canada, most of the support was aimed at individuals and had the effect of preventing the negative contagion that creates a true recession. These fiscal measures were designed to be elastic—to expand or contract depending on the scale of the ultimate shock to the economy. This elasticity is what makes simple numerical measures of them so inappropriate—the amount of government spending depends on how much trauma the economy endures. This feature also means it is unnecessary to turn off the measures, for they turn themselves off gradually as the economy returns to a more normal growth track. In addition, the wage subsidy was intended to maintain the connection between employees and their employers, allowing for a rapid rebound in activity once containment measures were removed. Canada's major banks played a central role in the delivery of stabilization measures, allowing loan and mortgage deferrals, expanding credit dramatically for existing clients, and creating new loans for small businesses.

The situation could hardly be more different from the Great Depression, to which policymakers offered very little response. Some governments even worsened the situation by enacting protectionist international trade policies. In my opinion, the COVID-19 event is much more like a natural disaster than a typical economic recession, and recoveries from natural disasters are usually quite rapid and robust. Certainly, most economies have demonstrated a better ability to bounce back from the shutdowns than economists expected.

Post-Pandemic Considerations

The pandemic has left scars. Extended periods out of work led to a deterioration of workers' skills. Companies have disappeared. Shopping habits have changed. Travel will never be the same, as the power of virtual meetings has been experienced. Working from home will become a much more significant element of many people's lives.

A K-shaped, or two-track, economy emerged that is likely to remain for years, with sectors that have been damaged permanently lingering in the bottom part of the K. For example, e-retail has exploded higher, creating many jobs in e-fulfillment centres and delivery services, for which workers who held in-person retail jobs are equally qualified. Canada lost nearly 120,000 companies during the early months of the pandemic, a drop of 13% in the population of firms. However, new company creation began to outpace company exits by the summer of 2020, and by the end of the year, the number of firms had recovered by some 85,000, to a level less than 3% lower than the year before. This company dynamism is Schumpeter's process of creative destruction in action and is testament to the underlying resilience of the economy. Few people realize that the Canadian economy destroys and creates something like 40,000 companies every month. The healing process after a major disruption can appear surprisingly fast.

Even so, there is a strong sense that COVID-19 has accelerated some of our tectonic forces, which will test the elasticity of the economy in the years ahead. First, debt accumulation, particularly by governments, has risen to levels not experienced since the mid-1940s. Second, the deployment of new technology is visibly picking up speed. One contributing factor has been the need to create more separation between production workers, which makes it an opportune time to introduce more robotics on the factory floor. This faster deployment will mean more worker displacement, sending even more workers into the bottom part of the K-shaped economy. Third, these developments will magnify concerns about inequality in the economy, and it is already clear that COVID-19 has exacted its greatest toll on the bottom end of the income scale, especially on women. Fourth, many governments have stated that they will endeavour to orchestrate a green pivot during the rebuilding phase—never waste a good crisis, use it to do some fundamental good. Finally, anecdotal evidence suggests that fertility rates may have dropped during the pandemic, perhaps due to an increase in uncertainty about future economic prospects. If this effect is not reversed by a mini post-COVID-19 baby boom, it is possible that population aging will also have been accelerated by the pandemic.

There will be many more lessons learned from the impact of COVID-19. It has been a very demanding test for policymaking organizations. The importance of diversity in senior teams was demonstrated over and over, as people drew from their past experiences and their own networks while operating in the fog of war. A deep bench of succession candidates was crucial, not least because it was always possible that one or more of us would fall ill. The relentless pace of the crisis was also exhausting, especially when operating from home, some of us with young families. Being able to spread the work across a diverse team was invaluable. At the same time, it was essential to stay in touch with the rest of the staff, who were keeping all the typical operations on track from their home offices while we fought financial market fires. I was ever so glad that our technology team had previously persuaded us to overinvest in our technological capacity. On any given day, we had more than 1,500 people connected remotely, often in video meetings, and we barely exceeded 50% of our capacity. Just as the lessons from 2008 helped in managing the COVID-19 crisis, future periods of instability will benefit from the lessons learned in 2020–21.

Investments in resilience will probably become increasingly commonplace. The distant future is more uncertain today because the COVID-19 pandemic happened. Even as COVID-19 recedes in the rear-view mirror, our five tectonic forces will come again to the fore and affect everyday economic life in myriad ways. To look ahead, I will begin with the central banker's favourite subject: the future of inflation.

9

THE FUTURE OF INFLATION

Reflections: Personal Inflation Experience

I didn't think about inflation much until I was a teenager. It was in the early 1970s when I first heard reference to "the cost of living" around the dinner table. Looking back on this as an economist, I realize that inflation was a revelation for my parents at the time. They had grown up during the deflation of the 1930s; had seen scarcity, rising prices, and rationing coupons during the war years; but had experienced nothing except very low inflation and rising prosperity in the period since.

By the time I was studying economics in the mid-1970s, inflation had become public enemy number one. I wrote a major project paper in 1976 on the efficacy of wage and price controls for one of my economics classes. Later, I became especially interested in understanding how much money individuals were holding in the form of cash or in their bank account relative to their income and the rate of interest. This was seen as a crucial piece of the framework designed to get inflation under control, based on the monetarism of Milton Friedman. Understanding how much money people wished to hold would allow the central bank to supply the appropriate amount without adding to inflationary pressures. For a given rate of inflation, money holdings would exhibit a predictable growth rate; gradually slowing the rate of growth in the money supply below that level would bring inflation down.

A formal framework based on this thinking was deployed at the Bank of Canada in 1976, at about the same time as the Pierre Trudeau government put in place wage and price controls. The policies were intended to complement one another and reduce the disruption to the economy of adjusting to a lower inflation rate. Unfortunately, the framework stumbled almost immediately on an emerging disconnect between money holdings and economic growth and inflation. Central bank and academic researchers were highly engaged in this issue.

My undergraduate thesis at Queen's in 1978 entailed using an experimental statistical technique to understand it better. It was this work that opened the door for a summer job at the Bank of Canada. While there, I learned that the practicalities of money targeting are far more subtle than Friedman's simple correlation would suggest. Data on the money supply were published every week—several months sooner than data on the economy. If the money supply were to decline unexpectedly for a few weeks in a row, it could be a signal that economic growth had slowed, inflation had slowed, or perhaps something else entirely. The central bank needed to understand the underlying reason for the slowdown in order to decide whether interest rates should be adjusted. Only several months later, once the economic data were all published, could the researchers use their models to reconcile the behaviour of money with the rest of the economy. When they did, they discovered that money growth was slowing for no apparent reason.

This was not just a Canadian phenomenon. Almost from the day central banks began to target money growth, researchers began having difficulty explaining the behaviour of money holdings, which tended to be less than the models predicted.

After working at the bank for the summer of 1978, I went to Western to pursue my MA and PhD, and I continued to think about the problem. My PhD thesis explored one possible explanation: that exchange rate movements might affect money holdings by households and firms. The idea was based on the observation that more and more households and firms had begun to make use of both Canadian and U.S. dollars. This started in the wake of the big exchange rate movements in late 1976 in reaction to the election of a separatist government in the province of Quebec. I hypothesized that people might be shifting their cash holdings back and forth across currencies in order to take advantage of, or protect themselves from, the likely next movement in the exchange rate. This hypothesis was known as "currency substitution," and I was able to find empirical evidence in support of the idea.

I returned to the bank in 1981 to work full-time, and I was highly committed to the monetarists' explanation of inflation and to monetary targets aimed at controlling it. It was like a dream come true for me to help reconfigure the bank's monetary control framework in order to allow for additional elements such as currency substitution and new types of bank accounts, thereby ensuring that money remained at the centre of policy deliberations and actions.

Alas, my well-intended research proved fatal to the bank's monetary targeting framework. When I presented solid statistical proof that the underlying demand for money—measured as cash plus conventional chequing accounts, or "M1"—had shifted, Bank of Canada management concluded that the future relationship between money and inflation could not be relied upon sufficiently to warrant continued use of monetary targets. Governor Bouey famously said at the time, "We didn't abandon M1; M1 abandoned us."

Over the next decade, bank researchers looked for an alternative framework to guide monetary policy, and direct inflation targeting emerged the winner. The bank has pursued direct inflation targets since 1991, under a series of formal agreements with the Government of Canada.

Direct Inflation Targets Have Worked Well

As a researcher who studied direct inflation targeting long before it was practised, I find it remarkable how successful it has been. There is such a complex chain of economic linkages between central bank interest rates and inflation eighteen to twenty-four months ahead that I was skeptical that inflation was controllable at all, except over very long time horizons.

As explained earlier, real interest rates are expected to remain low on average for the next generation, for demographic reasons. What that means is that central banks will have even less room to cut interest rates when the economy contracts in the future. This loss of flexibility is asymmetric. If the economy booms and threatens higher inflation, central banks will have no problem getting the situation under control by raising interest rates, for there is no upside limit. But if the economy slows abruptly, risking a decline of inflation below target, there is limited space to cut interest rates to get inflation back on track. All other things equal, we can expect there to be somewhat less success in keeping inflation on target in the future.

The challenge of targeting inflation will be made even greater as the tectonic forces produce more volatility. Since central banks can only influence inflation in the future, their policies in the present are framed by their forecasts. Making reliable economic forecasts will become much more difficult in the next age of uncertainty. The practicalities of central banking suggest that we will experience even more volatility in inflation rates in the future.

It is one thing for inflation to become more variable because of the tectonic forces. Although higher uncertainty will be unwelcome, it is possible for people to see through it. But it is quite another thing for the average rate of inflation to rise to a higher level, for people cannot see through that. Even today, many people find it difficult to believe that inflation targets have been successful at all, because the 2% reported figure does not seem to carry over to personal experience. They point to high prices for houses or cars, for example, as evidence. In general, there is a striking gap between perception and reality with respect to measured inflation.

Inflation is a measure of average price performance over literally everything we purchase, and people tend to forget that many items they regularly buy have declined in price over the years. Their focus instead is mainly on things that have risen in price. Furthermore, they focus on the level of prices, remembering a specific price for, say, milk or gasoline from many years ago, and comparing it to today to create their impression of inflation. They focus on items that they buy frequently, like gas for their car, as opposed to things they buy only occasionally, like cars. In addition, few appreciate that the statistician is trying to adjust for quality improvements in the background— when quality of an item rises and its price stays the same, its price is deemed by the statistician to have fallen.

To illustrate, consider the purchase of an automobile. We were a one-car family for a very long time, from the mid-1970s until the late 1990s. My first car was a lovely four-year-old 1968 Chevrolet Impala, at a cost of $1,600. Six people could sit in it comfortably, and it had an enormous trunk, besides. In my days as a disc jockey, I loaded that car with gigantic speakers, a console with two turntables, amplifiers, and hundreds of vinyl records, both 45s and LPs. I purchased a new car for my own personal use in 1999, a Toyota Corolla, for just under $18,000. Some fourteen years later, my daughter bought her first car, and I guided her to the Corolla, given my experience and having noticed that—although I had traded mine in long before—the same model as my original Corolla from fourteen years earlier could still be seen on the road. Imagine my surprise when the new Toyota Corolla was basically the same price as in 1999, despite vast improvements in the meantime! In 2020, another seven years down the road, the Corolla could still be purchased for about $19,000, once again with significant improvements in technology.

These observations suggest that the purchase price of a basic entry-level car has hardly changed at all in the past twenty years. We can confirm this with official data from Statistics Canada. The total consumer basket of goods and services has risen by close to 40% in that time, almost exactly 2% per year as intended by the Bank of Canada. In contrast, the price index for purchasing a new car has risen by only 7% altogether over the same twenty-year time frame, less than 0.4% per year. The price of leasing a new car has risen only 1% in this same period, or less than 0.1% per year. This is true despite the fact that almost everyone you talk to would say that the cost of vehicle ownership has risen a lot over that time period.

Since the quality of a basic entry-level car has increased tremendously, its price index has actually declined over the last two decades. However, a country's price index attempts to capture the average car purchased by its citizens, which is a combination of various vehicles. The price of certain types of vehicles—SUVs and pickup trucks, in particular—has risen more than others, and their share of total vehicle purchases has also increased. These are the higher-margin vehicles in dealers' portfolios.

Another common deflationary example that many tend to forget is computer equipment and other digital devices. According to the same official statistics, the price of a computer has fallen by over 90% in the past twenty years. Most people would probably say that the cost of replacing their computer has not really changed much over the years. However, the capability of the home computers we buy has increased dramatically over this time period, and these quality improvements mean that for $500 you get a lot more computer than you did in the past. Therefore, the implicit price has fallen, and this is what goes into the inflation index.

And then there is my favourite example: televisions. I can recall vividly the purchase of our first colour television in 1978. It was an Electrohome television, assembled in Kitchener, Ontario, but by then it contained mostly Japanese parts made by JVC. That television was $549 and had a nineteen-inch screen. If television prices had kept pace with inflation, that television would now cost around $2,000. Instead, we can purchase a fifty-five-inch flat-screen television for around $500, assembled in Mexico using components sourced from several different countries, mostly in Asia. Official statistics show that video equipment that cost $100 in 2000 would cost only about $21 in 2020. This is how globalization can boost consumer purchasing power by reducing inflation, a factor that is not widely appreciated. We can spend $500 instead of $2,000 on a television and that allows us to spend the other $1,500 on whatever we want. This extra $1,500, a gift to us consumers due to globalization, supports jobs across the entire economy.

Where do perceptions of high inflation originate? According to Statistics Canada, key categories contributing to higher inflation include food, especially meat, the price of which has risen nearly twice as fast as average inflation. Another is insurance, as well as the water bill and the hydro bill—but not the gas bill or the phone bill. Financial services. Public transit and parking. Reading material and tuition. Cigarettes. But not alcoholic beverages from stores, for they have risen more slowly than average inflation. Categories such as clothing, household appliances, furniture, exercise equipment, and toys have all experienced deflation on average over the last two decades, also primarily due to globalization.

We have to appreciate that inflation targets are about an average inflation performance across the entire bundle of goods and services purchased by Canadians, and this captures a mixture of inflating and deflating prices. Each individual price behaves in its own way, and it seems that people rarely notice deflation when it happens. On average, for nearly thirty years, inflation in Canada has remained very close to 2%, after allowing for the occasional deviation, such as big movements in energy prices or perhaps the exchange rate. Expectations of Canadians have become firmly anchored around the 2% target when it comes to negotiating pay rises. This is ironic given that casual observation points to inflation being much higher than this.

This anchoring of inflation expectations has some profound consequences for the economy. Among other things, if inflation deviates from this target in either direction, it has increasingly been met with indifference by casual observers, for they have a strong expectation that in the background the central bank will be taking decisive action to ensure that it returns to 2% over a reasonable time frame. The central bank has a lot of room to manoeuvre when the economy does go off track—it can put in place aggressive policies to correct the situation, relying on the faith of its constituents that it will not put inflation targets at risk.

This situation differs markedly from that of the 1970s. In those days, were the central bank to react to a disturbance in the economy in a manner that might appear to increase future inflation risk, observers would ratchet up their inflation expectations right away. Attempts by the central bank to boost growth in the economy were almost certainly frustrated, because inflation would accelerate immediately.

So why worry? In a word, politics.

The Debt-Inflation Interaction

The long history of the relationship between government debt and inflation is pretty clear: large build-ups in government debt have historically been followed by outbreaks of inflation. Obvious examples of the relationship can be seen in individual countries, such as Germany in the 1920s or Argentina in the early 1980s. The intimate relationship between a government and its central bank always raises concerns at such times. A central bank is the banker for its government and has the power to create new money. Central banks create new money all the time, by buying newly issued government debt and giving the new money to the government to spend. Provided this is done in pace with the rate of economic growth, inflation will remain low and stable. But if the government is issuing debt at a rate faster than financial markets believe is sustainable, markets can get indigestion, interest rates rise, and the government can hit the wall at some point and be unable to sell more debt to the market. If the central bank relieves this constraint by purchasing a rising share of new government debt, the creation of new money can easily outpace the economy's need for it. If this happens, Milton Friedman's parable of "too much money chasing too few goods" plays out, and inflation rises.

This intimacy of the relationship between a government and its central bank is necessary: the government owns the central bank, the central bank is the banker for the government, and their balance sheets are intertwined. To create new money for the economy, the central bank must purchase government debt—that is how its balance sheet balances. But the potential for danger in this relationship arises not only when government debt is rising unsustainably. Governments are always looking ahead to re-election, and happy voters tend to keep incumbents in office. What makes voters happiest is a strong economy, where jobs are plentiful and wages are rising. This gives governments an incentive to try to boost the economy with extra spending in the period leading up to an election. If the stimulus is too great, and inflationary pressures rise, chances are the voters will not know until after the election.

This tension is why central banks in most advanced countries are given operational independence to pursue targets for inflation. As an extra safeguard, the terms of central bank governors are generally independent of the electoral cycle. If a government stimulates the economy excessively just before an election, an independent central bank with its eye on future inflation pressures will raise interest rates, keep economic growth steady, and essentially offset the government's efforts. Governments are generally accepting of this system of checks and balances—but not always and definitely not everywhere.

As discussed in chapter 5, global government debt has been rising steadily in the last twenty years and ballooned during the COVID-19 crisis. Central banks worked closely with their governments during the crisis, often purchasing extraordinary amounts of government debt in order to stabilize financial markets and counter the collapse in economic growth. The unprecedented situation, with a very high level of fiscal and monetary policy coordination, gave rise to doubts in some quarters about central bank independence and the consequences for future inflation. These concerns have been fuelled by the emergence of some unconventional thinking around government debt, which its proponents have labelled "modern monetary theory." Non-specialized readers can be forgiven for believing that this new thinking gives us a way to relieve the debt burden that advanced economy governments face in the post-pandemic world.

The leading advocate of this thinking is Stephanie Kelton, whose 2020 book *The Deficit Myth* sets out the argument that angst over government deficits is misplaced because governments have the power of the money printing press. A government that has control over the national currency can never go bankrupt, she argues, because it can always print more money to cover its obligations. Unfortunately, many media reports on this idea stop there, missing important details and leaving the impression that the proverbial free lunch is available to governments. The most important of these missing details is that proponents of modern monetary theory acknowledge that governments must stop issuing new money if the economy reaches its capacity limits, for going further than that will mean an inflationary outbreak. In other words, governments should pay their bills by issuing new money only until they begin to see inflation picking up—after that, they need to pay their bills in the old-fashioned way, borrowing from investors rather than from their central bank.

With that additional detail, one can see that modern monetary theory was almost fully anticipated by John Maynard Keynes in 1936. In his foundational book, Keynes was attempting to explain what would happen in an economy where monetary policy had reached its natural limits—that is, when interest rates could go no lower, as was the case during the Great Depression when Keynes was writing. This is where the world landed in the wake of COVID-19. Keynes argued that in this situation monetary policy would set interest rates as low as possible and exhaust its ability to boost economic growth. He called the situation a "liquidity trap," because if the central bank kept adding even more liquidity to the monetary system, it would just sit there. Households and firms would not be motivated to borrow the money or spend it. In this situation, he argued, the only way to help the economy find its way back toward full employment would be to use deficit spending by governments.

Advocates of modern monetary theory suggest exactly the same thing: when interest rates hit rock bottom, governments should spend their way to an economic recovery, borrowing newly created money from the central bank and spending it in the economy. Modern monetary theory is not modern. Nor is it monetary, as the envisioned stimulus to the economy comes from government spending, regardless of how it may be financed. There is also very little by way of theory in the framework: it is based on accounting, which connects the standard process of new money creation to the government balance sheet.

In practical terms, when pressed, modern monetary theory advocates recommend that central banks create just as much new money as necessary to achieve their inflation targets, and no more. By that standard, central banks have been doing exactly this for about thirty years now, though this is not how monetary policy is usually described. Rather, the central bank chooses a rate of interest consistent with the economic outlook that will maintain inflation at its target. That narrative has a mirror image in the central bank's balance sheet and the rate at which new money is created. That creation of new money, in turn, is directly linked to direct purchases of government debt, as described earlier, and therefore puts new spending power into the hands of the government. It is simple accounting. One could say that "modern monetary theory" and "conventional wisdom" have identical practical implications for monetary and fiscal policy. But notably modern monetary theory does not offer a way out if markets begin to balk at financing the government's deficits.

There was one important historical episode, however, when it was decided to try what modern monetary theorists recommend doing today. In the late 1960s, the burden of financing the war in Vietnam was straining government finances in the U.S. The result of that fiscal-monetary experiment was the global Great Inflation of the 1970s, which took nearly twenty years to rectify.

The Great Inflation is so labelled because the inflation went global. The 1950s and 1960s saw low and stable inflation in most advanced economies. In this era, many economists believed that there existed a trade-off between inflation and unemployment: by allowing a little bit of inflation, a country could run the economy hotter and achieve a slightly lower unemployment rate. However, inflation for the major economies after World War II was essentially being controlled by the United States, as the major economies were tied together by the Bretton Woods exchange rate system. Under this arrangement, most major currencies were tied to the U.S. dollar, which in turn was tied to the price of gold—if prices went up in one country, they tended to go up in all the others.

This system was brought under strain in the mid-1960s as the U.S. struggled to finance the war in Vietnam. Big increases in military spending led to ballooning government deficits, excess demand in the economy, and rising inflation. The U.S. Federal Reserve raised interest rates in late 1965 to contain inflation pressures, prompting a showdown with President Johnson, who wanted the Fed to keep rates low. The chair of the Federal Reserve, William McChesney Martin, insisted on policy independence and raised interest rates in defiance of the Johnson administration. The outlook for inflation was hotly debated at the time, not least because of an important tectonic force: the global population was steadily getting younger, and the baby boomers were beginning to enter the workforce. The net result of this inflation debate within the Federal Reserve was that interest rates rose only modestly, monetary expansion remained rapid, and inflation pressures continued to build in the economy. Those pressures really gained traction beginning in 1970 under Martin's successor, Arthur Burns, who was known to be more sympathetic to the fiscal stresses that the war was creating for the Nixon administration. Essentially, war-related government deficits were partially financed through new money creation by the Federal Reserve in the context of an already hot economy.

This combination produced a surge in U.S. inflation to over 6%, which was automatically exported to countries maintaining a fixed exchange rate with the U.S. The exchange rate system collapsed under the strain, but not before global inflation rose everywhere, albeit more in some countries than in others. Inflation pressures were compounded by big hikes in oil prices in the early 1970s in the wake of the Arab oil embargo. Unemployment was rising in most countries at the same time. This combination of rising unemployment and rising inflation had not been witnessed previously and was at odds with mainstream economic models, making it extremely challenging for policymakers to understand what was going on, let alone get inflation pressures under control. They were contemplating raising interest rates to reduce inflation just as rising unemployment suggested they should do the opposite.

It took more than a decade for central banks to rectify this situation. The effort was led by Paul Volcker, who was appointed chair of the U.S. Federal Reserve by President Jimmy Carter in 1979 with a clear mandate to get inflation under control. Grinding inflation expectations back down to a reasonable level required extremely high interest rates, recessions, high unemployment, and years of lost national income. The political pressures on Volcker were extreme in those years, and the situation was made doubly uncomfortable given that his predecessor—G. William Miller, who replaced Arthur Burns in 1978—had become President Carter's treasury secretary after running the Federal Reserve for less than two years.

The very steep economic costs associated with bringing inflation back under control were judged to be worth paying, since there were also economic costs associated with ongoing high inflation. Economies with high and variable inflation are inefficient, as individuals and firms alike make ill-informed decisions, both economic and financial. In that state, the economy produces less national income every day than it would with lower inflation. Inflation acts like a tax on economic growth, and that tax can cumulate to a lot of lost income over a lifetime. Lower and more stable inflation since the early 1990s has given us lower and more stable unemployment rates at the same time.

Nevertheless, it needs to be recognized that the Great Inflation of the 1970s represented a financial gift to indebted households, which came in two forms. First, real estate prices rose significantly. Using Toronto as an example, the average single detached home rose in price by about 150% between 1970 and 1980. Second, a mortgage taken out in 1970 effectively fell to less than half its original value by 1980, measured in 1970 dollars. This combination was therefore very profitable for typical homeowners, especially those carrying a mortgage. People without debt fared much less well. Stocks and especially bonds delivered very poor returns; sophisticated investors paid a very high price through unexpectedly higher inflation, whereas less wealthy households whose primary assets were in real estate made out very well.

What about the experience of governments? With cumulative inflation of more than 100% over the 1970s, the real value of outstanding government debt was cut by more than half. During the 1980s, inflation averaged nearly 8% a year, further eroding the value of outstanding government debt. Since the 1990s, however, inflation has averaged very close to 2% per year. While this still represents a gradual erosion in value, through most of that time, bondholders were compensated with interest rates well above the rate of inflation.

In short, the inflation of the 1970s and 1980s represented a significant transfer of wealth from investors to governments and to indebted households. It is not hard to see why both governments and large voter constituencies might prefer to lean in the direction of higher inflation.

A Dangerous Cocktail of Inflation Risk

Governments did not set out in the late 1960s to create faster inflation or to confiscate investor wealth to reduce their fiscal debt burdens. The dominant economic models of the era did not envisage the events of the 1970s, which is what prompted John Kenneth Galbraith to write *The New Age of Uncertainty*. The Great Inflation was the result of a policy mistake, one of the gravest on record, made in a highly unusual context. Several tectonic forces were in motion that confused policymakers and upended their economic models: the workforce was getting younger, technological progress had slowed compared to the early postwar period, and government debt was setting new records. On top of this, the world needed to cope with expensive oil and the breakdown of the gold-based international monetary system. There is little to suggest that governments wish to revisit the trauma of the 1970s in the wake of the COVID-19 pandemic. However, the tectonic forces identified earlier, combined with the fallout from the COVID-19 pandemic, present a dangerous cocktail of inflation risk—an environment made for policy mistakes—that investors should take very seriously.

At the root of this risk is the Fourth Industrial Revolution, which appears to be picking up pace in the wake of the pandemic. Industrial revolutions have historically been accompanied by falling prices, and this should be equally true now. However, as we saw during the Third Industrial Revolution, inflation targeting by central banks can be expected to prevent a technology-led generalized deflation. In the near future, accelerated technological progress should translate into enhanced economic capacity—in effect, a pickup in inflation-free economic growth through rising productivity. The constraint on this will be a pronounced slowdown in global labour force growth as a result of an aging population. Therefore, the more significant consequence of technological progress will be the displacement of workers and rising income inequality. Together, these can be expected to become top-line issues for politicians.

Of course, there are government policy options that could deal with these stresses. Flexible income redistribution programs, universal basic income programs, or enhanced unemployment safety nets are the most obvious. Minimum wage increases might fall into the same set. Such policies can have unintended consequences, too, including lower labour force participation, elevated unemployment, and increased costs for employers. Such social programs are rarely simple to deploy politically, as competing interests and ambiguous economic analysis drive a wedge between constituencies. Moreover, there is a further constraint operating: the tectonic force of rising indebtedness across the economy, especially on the part of governments. The post-COVID-19 fiscal situation will make new social programs quite challenging to implement. The argument may simply come down to perceived fiscal cost, regardless of what the long-term economic benefits might be.

It is impossible to predict how these political stresses will be resolved, but the situation does point to a higher risk that we will end up adopting policy options that are politically palatable rather than ones that actually work. Those options almost certainly would include placing more restrictions on international trade to buttress incomes at the lower end of the scale. Unfortunately, as discussed earlier, deglobalization is not only a policy with potentially inflationary consequences but one that would also lead to lower national income and more job losses across the entire economy. These arguments may fall on deaf ears as they have in the past. The risk of deglobalization must appear as a risk to higher inflation in the future.

Indeed, Charles Goodhart and Manoj Pradhan argue in their 2020 book *The Great Demographic Reversal* that this ship has already sailed. They point out that the world benefited from a prolonged disinflationary trend over the past twenty-five years, driven by the opening up of China and globalization. A side effect was that many manufacturing workers in advanced economies lost much of their bargaining power, since they could not compete with the wages paid in China or other emerging markets. This took away a traditional source of upward pressure on costs and inflation. This combination of forces, Goodhart and Pradhan contend, deserves much of the credit for central banks' success in controlling inflation over the past twenty years. Now, those forces are stalling and might easily go into reverse if the deglobalization trend gains traction.

Given all these constraints and political polarization, would it be a stretch for some politicians to campaign on the promise of a higher rate of inflation, thinking it would help to eradicate a significant portion of today's public debt? Would it be a stretch for a government to override its independent central bank to ensure that inflation would go above target for a period of time? Would it be a stretch for a government to succumb to the superficial allure of modern monetary theory and give it a try? Would it be a stretch for heavily indebted households to agree with, and vote for, exactly this policy?

I think not. Although I have a deep faith that both central banks and the general public have not forgotten the inflationary lessons of the 1970s, politics is the art of the possible, and it is too unpredictable for us to dismiss the possibility of higher inflation without another thought. Setting aside politics, the potential interactions between our tectonic forces will create an environment in which even the most independent and well-intentioned central bank can make a policy error, as happened in the late 1960s.

Central Bank Independence

An important mitigant to future inflation risk is an independent central bank. But central bank independence is more ambiguous in practice than it sounds, and we are seeing a gradual evolution in central bank mandates that is likely to add to future inflation risk at the margin.

Formal central bank independence is not universal, and in some countries, it is quite a recent phenomenon. In the U.S., political independence of the Federal Reserve is essentially presumed, because its decisions do not require any governmental approval and it does not rely on the government to fund its day-to-day operations. The European Central Bank has the clearest independent mandate, a product of modern-day thinking behind its creation in 1998. The Bank of England was given statutory independence around the same time.

The Bank of Canada offers a unique take on independence. It does not have statutory independence, but its inflation targeting framework provides a reasonable substitute. The Bank of Canada Act states that the government of the day can issue a directive to the Bank of Canada in case there is a serious disagreement over policy, thereby overriding the bank's policy. However, the minister of finance would have to publish the reasons for their dissatisfaction and dictate exactly what the bank must do. It is generally agreed that, following the use of such a directive, the governor would resign, so this arrangement creates a delicate balance of power between the two. This mechanism was created in the mid-1960s after a messy disagreement between the government and former governor James Coyne, who resisted government demands for the central bank to cut interest rates. Today, monetary policy in Canada is anchored by an inflation target, which is the subject of an agreement between the Bank of Canada and the federal government, reviewed and renewed every five years. The bank pursues this target with "operational independence" for the subsequent five-year period. If the government of the day preferred that the central bank target a lower unemployment rate for the next five years, instead of the inflation rate, it could force the issue, which would likely result in a major reaction in financial markets.

Whether central bank independence is statutory or not, the Global Financial Crisis and the subsequent Great Recession greatly enhanced the reputations of the major central banks. People on Main Street probably give too much credit to central banks for that positive outcome and may expect too much of central banks as a consequence. The risk that people will ascribe excessive responsibility to their central bank for economic outcomes is well recognized by many, and active steps have been taken to mitigate that risk, including increased central bank transparency. More frequent press conferences, minutes of meetings, published forecasts, forward guidance for markets, public consultations on major issues, and so on, have been deployed to enhance accountability while at the same time demonstrating that central banks deal with competing objectives.

One concrete manifestation has been the U.S. Federal Reserve's decision in early 2020 to pursue an enhanced policy objective. The Fed has always had what is referred to as a "dual mandate": 2% inflation and "maximum employment." In the future, it will put even more weight on maximum employment and take account of the quality of employment by probing the limits of the economy until inflation has moved above 2%, and only then tightening monetary policy to guide inflation back to 2%. In the past, the Fed would act in a pre-emptive manner to keep inflation from breaching 2%, so this outcomes-based approach will mean a higher average rate of inflation in the future for the U.S. Beyond taking even more responsibility for economic outcomes, this move is premised on a good bit of technical control over the inflation rate.

Whether this refinement of monetary policy objectives will spread to other countries remains to be seen. But given the importance of the U.S. to the world economy and financial markets, and the intellectual reach of its central bank, these considerations add further upside risk to global inflation. Importantly, the presumed ability to control inflation closely has yet to be demonstrated, as central banks have struggled to get inflation up to their targets in the past decade. Control of inflation depends on a virtuous circle: stable inflation means anchored inflation expectations, which in turn create maximum room to manoeuvre for the central bank. Provided that virtuous circle remains a reliable one, this is the natural direction to take monetary policy. If inflation expectations show signs of de-anchoring, however, the central bank's ability to control inflation could erode, opening the door to larger policy errors. Before asking central banks to pursue more ambitious policy objectives, it may be advisable for countries that have not already done so to make explicit the statutory independence of their central bank.

The COVID-19 pandemic has brought the issues of central bank independence closer to home. With interest rates around the world about as low as they can go, it was up to governments to use fiscal spending to help stabilize economies when COVID-19 hit. This necessarily created a much more explicit partnership between fiscal and monetary authorities. Governments issued huge quantities of debt, large swaths of which were scooped up by central banks to keep the system liquid, and governments reassured markets that debt service would remain manageable because interest rates would remain low. This delicate balance could easily be upset as economies and interest rates normalize. This tension has the potential to result in "fiscal dominance" of monetary policy—a situation where it is relatively easy for governments to lean on their central banks to keep interest rates low for longer, thereby allowing inflation to rise above target and ease public debt burdens. In these circumstances, governments have a strong incentive to be clear about central bank independence; if they fail to do so, inflation expectations will rise, push up interest rates, and render their fiscal plan unsustainable.

The confluence of tectonic forces is destined to bring greater variability and unpredictability to inflation, even if the most likely outcome remains a return to average inflation of around 2%. Investors need to acknowledge that the tectonic forces present a potentially dangerous cocktail of inflation risk, especially as those conditions will bring polarized politics into the mix. Accordingly, it is appropriate for individuals, companies, and investors to plan for 2% inflation in the future but to be prepared to deal with higher inflation variability, acknowledging that the risk that global inflation will ratchet up is greater than it has been in a generation. This is particularly the case for certain emerging markets, where fiscal and institutional capacity has been put under enormous strain by the pandemic.

The inflation outlook will be made doubly uncertain by the consequences of the Fourth Industrial Revolution, as well as by the reoptimization of workforce arrangements in the post-pandemic economy. Technological progress will lead to a tendency for inflation to decline, as occurred in the 1990s. Similarly, the work-at-home experience during the pandemic is leading to hybrid arrangements in which employers and employees alike have more choice, which is almost certain to boost productivity and lower inflation further. Neither of these effects are quantifiable, however, leaving central banks to judge the complex array of forces impacting inflation.

Governments that explicitly endorse central bank independence and support continued low inflation will reap the dividends of calm financial markets and continued low interest rates. The latter are crucial to the sustainability of the fiscal plans of highly indebted governments, not to mention households with mortgages and companies carrying debt in their capital structure. Investor sentiment around inflation risk and its consequences for interest rates are not to be taken lightly. Anti-inflation credibility proved very hard to earn during the 1980s and may be comparatively easy to lose. If inflation is allowed to break out, a renewed political consensus will be needed to rein it in, and the return to low inflation will be very costly in terms of lost employment and incomes. The laws of economics have not been rewritten.

The post-pandemic environment is seeing renewed interest in the inflation outlook, for the reasons discussed above. This is probably one of the reasons for widening interest in Bitcoin, the scarcity of which could theoretically protect investors from future inflation. More conventional inflation hedges like gold and real estate have also been in high demand in the wake of the pandemic—and at least they have the advantage of having demonstrated their usefulness as inflation hedges for centuries, unlike Bitcoin.

Even a fully independent and well-intentioned central bank pursuing a 2% inflation target will be more prone to making policy errors in the uncertain environment that the tectonic forces will deliver in the future. Major policy mistakes were made in the late 1960s and early 1970s because economic models were incomplete and invisible tectonic forces were upending conventional wisdom the very same tectonic forces that are operating today. It can happen again. And the most personal place where those chickens can come home to roost is in the jobs market.

THE FUTURE OF JOBS

Reflections: Convocations

One of the biggest preoccupations of parents is the future employment of their children. What will they do for a living? What should they study in school? How do they maximize their future options? What jobs will be available when they are ready to work? Parents think a lot about these things, while their kids seem not to think about them at all. Parental advice is often met with indifference, sometimes with hostility.

Nowhere is this issue more apparent than at university convocation ceremonies. Proud parents watch as the embodiment of their many years of commitment and financial investment walks across the stage and emerges as a graduate. The question of what the graduate will make of all that investment hangs in the air like the odour from a landfill site on a hot June afternoon.

I have been fortunate to have been awarded two honorary degrees in recent years. Trent University conferred on me an honorary doctor of laws in 2017. I had no connection with the school, except to have admired the campus when visiting Peterborough. The motivation behind the degree was unique, however: Trent has a substantial campus in Oshawa, and the administration wanted someone from Oshawa who had "made good" to talk to the graduates from Trent's Durham campus. The pre-convocation dinner on the main campus in Peterborough was particularly interesting, as we met several prominent past graduates of Trent. I had a great conversation with Keith Knott, a First Nations leader from nearby Curve Lake, who also was receiving an honorary degree. My wife and I had visited Curve Lake often in the past, as it was not far from her family cottage, and we enjoyed browsing the art and other unique items in the shop there. Trent has an extensive Indigenous studies program.

I was also granted an honorary degree from the University of Western Ontario in 2019. The motivation was similar, with the important addition that my PhD in economics was earned at Western, nearly forty years earlier. I can remember my first glimpse of Western's campus back in 1978 like it was yesterday. Driving up Richmond and through those stately gates, with the view all the way up the hill to the original buildings, still gives me a thrill. It is quite a contrast to Queen's University, architecturally speaking, to which I will always carry a strong attachment. I suppose this happens to most people with a place where they spend four undergraduate years, which seem to be life-changing. Frankly, of all the places I have lived, Kingston remains my favourite. I can still recall the first time my father drove me to Queen's, and we weren't sure we had arrived. The reason? The university has no gates—you simply arrive and begin to notice those lovely old limestone buildings.

I struggled with my message to these proud Western graduates, who were absolutely brimming with possibility. I was reminded of my graduation from high school in Oshawa in 1974, when the economy was particularly strained. John Kenneth Galbraith was working on his series *The Age of Uncertainty* for the BBC at the time. As it turned out, my valedictory message to my fellow high-school graduates, including my future spouse, was about the economics of the era. Without even a glimmer of true understanding of economics, I suggested to them that the difficult economic situation would not endure, as there were forces at work that would bring things around. It turned out to be true . . . eventually.

Fast-forward to the late 2010s and I found myself back at Western having similar thoughts, now magnified and perhaps clarified by my training and my own experience. I tried to help the graduates shift their frame from "What do I know, and how will I use it?" to "Now that I have learned how to learn, what do I need to learn next?" After years of memorization, this is a difficult shift to make, but in today's rapidly changing world, those who have learned how to learn will surely succeed and leave others behind. These graduates would need to adapt to economic change and job disruption more often than I did in my career. Make learning a habit, I advised. Learn how to learn from others, as that is far more efficient than learning by yourself— face it, you can learn more in a thirty-minute conversation with a practitioner than by reading many books on a subject.

At Western's convocation, I was especially fortunate to be addressing the graduating class of engineers. As a lifelong fan and student of science fiction, I knew that these graduates had nothing to worry about. In *Star Trek*, no matter what problem pops up, no matter how much intellectual horsepower is at play among all the central characters, in the end it always comes down to Scotty or Geordi or Miles or one of a long line of Starfleet engineers who are adept at learning something new and applying it in real time. I told them, and their proud parents, as much. I'm sure this was not what they expected to hear from the governor of the central bank in such a formal setting.

Jobs will be the most important and most personal point of intersection of our five tectonic forces, because the labour market connects
to everything. Literally no one will be left untouched by the five
forces and the associated volatility, as uncertainty about the future
will be seriously magnified compared to the past.

The labour market never seems to be blessed with balance and
tranquility for any length of time, as there is always something going
on to make its bobblehead wobble. Think of labour market stress as
arising through two distinct channels: volatility in the economy that
impacts the job market often but temporarily, and disruption stem-
ming from structural or permanent changes in the economy. In the
real world, of course, the two happen at the same time, and from the
ground level it may be impossible to distinguish between them. The
main difference is that volatility is generally short term, with both ups
and downs, whereas disruption implies permanent job losses in a
transforming economy. Tectonic forces can operate through both
channels—interacting forces will generate a higher level of general
economic volatility, while technological progress will destroy some
jobs permanently while creating completely different new jobs.

Job Volatility

The central inference of this book is that the five interacting tectonic
forces will cause the economy to be subjected to bigger and more
frequent disturbances in the future. By definition, such volatility will
be two-sided, meaning individuals can experience both the good and
bad. Every disturbance will be felt in the labour market. From the
ground level, volatility will manifest as more frequent periods during
which workers are laid off, punctuated by periods where companies

are scrambling to hire workers. These episodes will probably affect most sectors of the economy at the same time, as the volatility I have in mind will be macroeconomic.

As a point of reference, we have been experiencing cyclical downturns quite regularly, roughly every ten years or so—1974, 1981, 1991, 1998, 2008, 2020. Each of these episodes had different drivers, so it is not possible to predict the sort of frequency that the tectonic forces might deliver. However, we do know that such economic cycles will occur more frequently and with greater effects.

When there is a macroeconomic event, whether positive or negative, there will also be policy responses from governments and/or central banks. What is observed in the world, and experienced by an individual, is the net effect of the event and the partially offsetting effects of the policy responses. In theory, it is possible to design a policy that offsets perfectly the macroeconomic event, leaving the economy unaffected on a net basis. This perfection is never achieved, and the higher volatility environment that the tectonic forces produce will place heavier demands on government programs. This issue is taken up in chapter 12, but for the purposes of this chapter I will work with the assumption that the net volatility on the ground will be greater than in the past.

Firms will experience the increase in volatility along with their employees, as firms make the painful decisions to cut staff when the economy is weak, and they scramble to compete with other firms to rehire workers when conditions improve. Even if volatility is perfectly symmetric over time, increased job churn is not innocent, for it is costly to both employees and employers. There are always frictions in the labour market, based mainly on the costs associated with searching for a job or searching for an employee, and these frictions will be higher in a more volatile world.

To illustrate, a company lays off workers when its business softens, those workers search for and find other employment, and then the firm has trouble finding new workers with the appropriate experience when business picks up. These frictions can be expected to lead to a higher level of unemployment at any point in time, regardless of economic conditions. This level of unemployment, which economists sometimes refer to as the natural rate of unemployment, is also thought of as the lowest it can go without creating inflationary pressures.

We have seen this before. For the U.S. economy, it is widely believed that the natural rate of unemployment is around 4%. This view was given substance during 2019 when unemployment fell to what seemed like unusually low levels without creating inflation. Back in the 1950s and 1960s, that rate was considered to be around 5%, but during the stagflationary 1970s, when economic and financial volatility was exceptionally elevated, the natural rate of unemployment rose well above 6%. It has been declining very gradually for nearly forty years as inflation fell and labour markets became increasingly efficient. A very important consequence of the higher volatility coming from the five tectonic forces will be higher frictional unemployment—the natural rate of unemployment will rise globally.

The upshot is that much of the predicted increase in business volatility is likely to land on workers. Even if wages are quite flexible during periods of strong economic growth, they presumably would also be flexible during downturns. Moreover, if increased economic volatility means more frictional unemployment and a higher natural unemployment rate, then individuals will on average spend more of their lives unemployed than in the past. Even if average incomes turned out to be the same as in a less volatile economy—and that is a big if—workers would feel less well off than in the past because of the increased uncertainty about their employment and income.

Volatility will have concrete costs well beyond a dwindling sense of security. As the level of household indebtedness rises, the consequences of a spell of unemployment go up. A household that dedicates, say, 40% of their income to servicing their mortgage is more likely to lose their home during a spell of unemployment than one dedicating half as much to debt service.

No doubt, individuals will see this burden of extra economic uncertainty as unfair. As we know, many workers already feel that income is being distributed unfairly, and income inequality appears destined to continue rising as the Fourth Industrial Revolution unfolds. When incentives change, behaviour changes. How will people adapt to this more challenging employment environment?

One possible response is that workers may remain in the workforce until a more advanced age. The aging population will mean slower growth in the workforce, perhaps making it difficult for firms to maintain appropriate staffing with the right skills. Accordingly, they may adjust compensation systems to encourage workers to remain longer. Households that face increased economic uncertainty may feel insecure about the future as normal retirement age approaches. They may have experienced sufficient negative volatility that they have fallen short of their savings target for retirement. In other words, people may find it necessary to work deeper into their lifetimes.

Another possible response from workers is that they will try to negotiate better terms with employers, such as higher wages or job security. Examples from the 1970s and 1980s include arrangements between North American auto manufacturers and their unions, according to which laid-off workers received partial incomes as well as government-provided unemployment insurance. This kept the skilled, laid-off auto workers on standby and prevented them from seeking employment elsewhere, which saved the manufacturers time and effort when they ramped up production again. I will return to this idea in chapter 13.

Unionization has been declining in the advanced economies for many years, although the experience varies widely. Some thirty years ago, unionization density in the U.S. was around 20% of the workforce, and today it is around half that. Unionization in Germany has fallen from close to 30% to around 17%, and in the U.K. from around 30% to just over 20%. Even in heavily unionized Sweden, unionization has fallen from over 90% to just over 60%. These declines have been driven by many factors, including the shrinkage of the manufacturing sector as a share of total economies and a general perception in the 1990s that rising prosperity made trade unions less necessary.

In recent years, workers' share of total income in the economy has been declining steadily. In advanced economies, that share has gone from around 55% in the 1970s to around 50% recently. In the U.S., the share was steady in the mid-sixties range during the 1980s and 1990s, but it started declining in the 2000s to the mid-fifties range. As discussed earlier, this has been mostly due to technological progress and the associated phenomenon of winner takes all, reinforced by globalization. It is also related to the rising share of finance employment in the total economy, as incomes in the finance sector are highly skewed to the top. From the ground level, the trend manifests itself as wages rising more slowly than workers' productivity.

This analysis presents a strong impetus toward a resurgence of workers' interest in unionization. It is no wonder that we are seeing attempts to organize in diverse parts of the economy, including certain Amazon workers and gig workers such as Uber drivers. This is not the same as predicting that unions will actually see a renaissance, however. The actual outcomes will depend on the give and take between workers and companies. Companies that proactively manage these stresses for their workers can avoid unionization. What matters is that the nature of the employer-employee contract will change as the tectonic forces generate more economic volatility.

Job Disruption

The second effect of the tectonic forces on jobs is structural disruption. The continuous impact of technological progress will make disruption a permanent condition in the coming decades. Structural change is another name for creative destruction—the process by which part of the economy heads for the sunset, while another part gets started. The impact is direct and immediate, as new technology displaces jobs, changes the nature of jobs, and tilts the growth path of the economy. Among our tectonic forces, technological progress due to the Fourth Industrial Revolution and the energy transition dictated by climate change will have significant and permanent disruptive effects.

The economy almost always has two tracks—a slow track for the sectors being restructured, and a fast track for the new arrivals—which economists represent with a K. Any structural change that disrupts jobs puts some people in the bottom of the K, and retraining or perhaps geographic relocation could move them back into the top of the K. The confluence of tectonic forces may mean that a larger share of the workforce will find itself in the bottom part of the K at any given moment. The permanent nature of the Fourth Industrial Revolution means that individuals may live in the bottom part of the K for a long time, and some may never make it into the top part.

A particularly useful study on how the global labour market is likely to adapt to the Fourth Industrial Revolution was conducted by the World Economic Forum (WEF) in 2020. The study builds on a comprehensive survey of 291 unique global companies, representing some 7.7 million employees worldwide and covering sectors and countries representing around 80% of the global economy. It finds that technology-driven job creation is still expected to outpace job destruction over the next five years—even though job destruction is being accelerated by the impact of COVID-19. The study concludes that this acceleration in the deployment of new technology raises the risk of a repeat of the jobless recovery of the 1990s in the post-pandemic period. By 2025, around 15% of global workers will be at risk of disruption, and 6% fully displaced by new technology. Estimates indicate about 85 million jobs may be displaced by machines by 2025.

The good news is that these same corporate leaders expect that upwards of 97 million new jobs will be created. These will be different jobs, of course—in the creative side of creative destruction—but both sides of the equation will be seen within the same firms. Fully 84% of employers see major opportunities to digitalize work processes. They also see significant opportunities to allow for remote work or hybrid work models.

The authors of the study highlight job categories that will be hard hit, which include computer operators, administrative assistants, filing clerks, and data entry and payroll personnel. Those on a growth track are in areas such as cloud computing, AI, data science, encryption, robotics, e-commerce, and personal care. Interestingly, twentieth on the list of occupations that will see increasing demand is risk management specialists, which is heartening, given the central conclusion of this book. The WEF study offers granular insight into what is coming for individuals. However, less attention is paid to the dynamics of adjustment that will be playing out at the aggregate, or macro, level.

As discussed earlier, there are three channels of adjustment to a technological advance. First, the new technology disrupts or destroys existing jobs. Second, it creates jobs never seen before. Third, the new technology creates incomes that did not exist before, while rendering many products in the economy less expensive and creating new purchasing power for everyone.

The job destruction effect attracts most of the attention in real time, unsurprisingly. The creation of new jobs is visible but plays less well in the media. These new jobs are often portrayed as geeky or completely beyond the skill level of those workers displaced by the new technology. But it is the third effect that is by far the most important economically. It receives almost no attention, for it is invisible and its existence is very hard to prove. The new incomes generated by the new technology and the increase in generalized purchasing power through falling prices create increased demand across the entire economy. Demand expands across the economy because the new technology increases general purchasing power. Thus, jobs are created across the entire spectrum—the demand for workers increases in all sectors, in all skill levels, in both goods and services sectors.

The more traditional way to think of the economic effect of new technology is that it displaces workers embedded in an old way of doing things, while creating jobs in the new tech sector. The problem we face, as eloquently described by the WEF study, is that few of the displaced are qualified to work in the newly created jobs. A displaced fifty-year-old manufacturing worker cannot suddenly begin writing code for a living. While a useful observation, it only considers half of the problem; it ignores the third and most important effect of technological progress.

We can illustrate by means of a real-world example that has been widely studied, namely the Third Industrial Revolution. Consider the latter half of Alan Greenspan's reign as chair of the U.S. Federal Reserve. What Greenspan encountered was a jobless economic recovery following the 1990–92 downturn, characterized by solid economic growth and lower than expected inflation. Given the monetary policy framework in place, interest rates were kept low for much longer than previously expected. We know now that this policy allowed financial vulnerabilities to build, and these manifested in the Global Financial Crisis and the Great Recession that followed, but we will set that aside for the moment.

As aptly described by Federal Reserve chair Jay Powell in his address at Jackson Hole, Wyoming, in late summer, 2018, U.S. monetary policy was managing through a period of elevated uncertainty during the mid-1990s. Chair Greenspan and his colleagues were finding it exceptionally difficult to estimate the maximum growth capacity of the U.S. economy. At the time, many commentators felt that Greenspan was taking a significant risk of allowing inflation to increase, as the economy seemed to be pushing against its limits. As Greenspan shared in his 2007 book *The Age of Turbulence*, even then-president Bill Clinton was fully aware of the debate among economists around the maximum rate of inflation-free growth. The president raised the issue in public at the time of Greenspan's reappointment in early 1996, an act that many found surprising from a political perspective, but not surprising given the chair's performance in the job. According to Greenspan, with the economy entering its sixth year of expansion, the president was motivated to see what the economy could achieve in terms of faster growth, higher wages, and new jobs.

The next few years would prove to be very lucky indeed. The economy continued its expansion and inflation remained low. Greenspan surmised that the economy was beginning to generate higher productivity through the widespread deployment of computer technology. This translated into persistently low inflation even as the economy churned out new growth and new jobs, reducing unemployment to what many feared might be inflationary levels. By maintaining his focus on inflation performance and little else, Greenspan saw no reason to raise interest rates, which would have halted the expansion, even though economic models suggested that he should. This proved fortuitous, because the economy's transition to a new technology was much smoother than was observed through the First and Second Industrial Revolutions, when policy was dictated by the far stricter gold standard.

With the benefit of hindsight, we know that technological progress led to a significant increase in capacity in the U.S. economy beginning around 1995. By 2005, the deployment of new technology had increased the level of national income by more than ten percentage points relative to the level that had been anticipated by economists ten years earlier. However, it was not until around 2000 that the importance of this phenomenon entered forecasters' outlooks, as they repeatedly underestimated economic growth during the late 1990s. As economic growth kept exceeding their forecasts, and inflation failed to increase, they upgraded their estimates of capacity in the economy, as that was the only way to square the circle. We now know that long-run potential growth for the U.S. economy was being underestimated by a margin of about 1.25% per year, on average, through this period. Greenspan was probing the economy's new limits intuitively, without the benefit of a model and a coherent economic forecast.

It is clear now that the jobless nature of the economic recovery after the 1990–92 recession was the result of the deployment of computer technology, and the 10% upgrade in the level of potential output over a period of ten years is a good summary measure of the societal benefits of that deployment. To ordinary consumers, this would appear in two forms. First, higher productivity would be associated with higher wage gains, although we know the spoils tended to be gathered by technology companies and the globalization of production at that time.

Second, the spread of technology lowered costs and prices throughout the economy, which meant higher purchasing power for all consumers. Both are dynamic processes that take time, possibly a long time. The creation of new jobs lags the immediate destruction of jobs due to technology and makes the recovery phase seem jobless.

The crucial benefits of the new technology came in the second phase, when low inflation allowed the Federal Reserve to maintain low interest rates for much longer than anyone expected. The economic expansion grew on itself—companies faced with strong growth and low interest rates invest in new capacity, raising the overall capability of the economy over time. The underlying force causing this is invisible to most observers, and certainly not measurable in real time, much like the theorized existence of dark matter in the universe. In the 2000s, the U.S. economy set new records for low unemployment and still saw below target inflation performance as the full and complete benefits of the Third Industrial Revolution were realized.

From the ground level, economists observed a K-shaped expansion during the Third Industrial Revolution. The top track showed strong growth in both output and employment. The bottom track showed companies struggling to deploy new technology and cutting workers, and those workers finding themselves without the necessary skills to transition to the new economy. However, the broader, macroeconomic benefits from new technology measured at least ten percentage points of national income, a huge upgrade in future economic prospects. Total income in the economy was 10% higher than previously thought possible, not just in 2005 but in every year since. For the U.S. economy alone, this amounts to over $2 trillion of additional spending power, every single year, forever.

That extra $2 trillion was spent and is still being spent across the entire economy—on houses, on home renovations, on motor vehicles, on clothing, on vacations, on restaurant meals, and so on—thereby creating increased employment in all sectors, in addition to the brand-new jobs created in the IT and IT services sectors.

Exactly the same thing was happening in other economies during 1995 to 2005, as the new technology was deployed worldwide. The implication is that each wave of technological progress can be expected to produce underperformance of inflation relative to target, expanding real incomes, higher consumption, and eventually more than enough job creation to move most individuals from the slow track of economic growth to the faster track. This experience was very different from the first two industrial revolutions because economies have been running monetary policies based on inflation targets, rather than the gold standard.

Looking ahead to the Fourth Industrial Revolution, an oft-cited prediction is the displacement of truck drivers, as driverless vehicles are expected to become the norm. This structural change is often described as if it will occur all on one weekend. But transport trucks are built to last for many years, and the economics of replacing a truck with a driverless vehicle will depend on the cost of that new driverless truck, how long the replacement will take to pay for itself given that the driver loses their job, and so on. Driverless vehicles will also need to be built, monitored, managed, and maintained; in other words, automated vehicles will be supervised by people. This infrastructure and its associated services will not be costless to the truck owner and will create many new jobs that do not yet exist. It could take decades to replace the trucks on the road today with driverless vehicles. It is even conceivable that this will happen in pace with the rate of retirement of truck drivers, which would make the adjustment by current drivers very manageable.

Even so, it is worth considering what the displaced truck drivers of the future might do next. The answer will depend on what the creators, manufacturers, programmers, monitors, and maintainers of driverless trucks do with their new incomes. For one thing, those people in the newly created jobs related to driverless vehicles might buy houses, and this would create jobs for people who build and renovate houses, maintain furnaces, make furniture, and so on. This is only a glimpse of the broad macroeconomic effect of an increase in total income that comes from a new technology. Jobs are created across the entire spectrum of the economy, not only in the new technology sector, providing a wide range of opportunities for the displaced truck driver. The upskilling required for a truck driver to become a furnace technician, an electrician, a drywall installer, a roof installer, or some other construction tradesperson does not appear insurmountable. Unfortunately, this crucial job-creating growth effect is never credited to the original technological advance—people just see it as normal economic growth.

This is exactly what has occurred in the wake of every industrial revolution in the past, but what the above in-depth analysis demonstrates is that policymakers are getting better at managing such disruption over time. This suggests to me that the pervasive gloom about the potential job-displacement effects of the Fourth Industrial Revolution is misplaced. This is not to say that it will be painless, for extended periods spent in the bottom part of the K will be very difficult for many families, especially those carrying high debt loads. However, if the Fourth Industrial Revolution is managed well by policymakers, a bright future is within our grasp.

Population Aging and Future Work Arrangements

Another important finding of the WEF study on the future of work is the growing importance of personal care workers in the future. Charles Goodhart and Manoj Pradhan offer a unique analysis of this issue in *The Great Demographic Reversal.* As the baby boomers age, the old age dependency ratio will rise, meaning that the elderly will have fewer young people to depend upon for care. They argue that rising old age dependency will mean a rising proportion of people living with various forms of dementia, requiring far higher levels of personal care than needed in the past. Although this implies growing demand for professional caregivers, in many families this may mean an individual shifting their energy from the labour force to unpaid support of an elderly relative. In either case, this will constitute a headwind to economic growth, as more people will be working in a sector in which there will be no productivity growth. Furthermore, the overall shortage of workers could be severe, unless there is a meaningful increase in immigration.

The WHO estimated in 2018 that the global cost of caring for people with dementia was around $1 trillion, and that this amount could double by 2030. This is a gigantic emerging issue for the world. Of course, the ideal solution would be a medical treatment for dementia, but society should be prepared for the scenario where such a treatment does not arise in time.

It is interesting to speculate on how society might adapt to these stresses. Not only will many more caregivers be needed than exist today, but because of the nature of dementia, those caregivers will ideally bring significant emotional loyalty to the job. One possible outcome would see caregivers spending a portion of each day with each client, the amount of time spent being proportional to the severity of their case. Some people will require full-time care, which brings to mind some sort of institutional living, a system that may require significant public investment in the years ahead.

Interacting tectonic forces will bring a new normal with greater economic and financial volatility to the post-pandemic world. What makes this abstract concept personal is that every fluctuation in the macroeconomy touches the labour market. The tectonic forces will mean increased personal uncertainty, which translates to greater risk in personal decisions. Volatility means a mix of bad luck and good luck and a reasonable outcome on average, but it is the uncertainty around the outcome that weighs on people—you can drown crossing a stream with an average depth of six inches.

Individuals, companies, and governments will all change their behaviour in the new riskier environment. People will lose their jobs more often, get new jobs more often, and spend more time in the process of switching jobs, boosting the natural rate of unemployment. Absent a change in the behaviour of companies or the policies of governments, higher job risk will figure into important family decisions, such as purchasing a home, taking on debt, and what level of savings to maintain. In other words, people will become more fiscally conservative in the riskier new normal and look to governments and employers to help them manage higher risk. Governments will adjust policies in response, a subject taken up in chapter 12. Companies will adjust their behaviour, too, and we will come to that in chapter 13.

Before examining how governments and companies will adapt to the next age of uncertainty, we turn to the other central preoccupation of individuals and families: housing. Is it possible that the rising population of elderly persons, persistent job market disruption, and the rising cost of home ownership will foster a return to the work-life arrangements of a bygone era, the live-in help model? One pictures the loyalty of the folks who worked downstairs in *Downton Abbey* with three generations of Crawleys living upstairs and a fourth generation just down the road. Toward the end of the series, the downstairs folks were showing signs of discontent, driven by income inequality and the ever-tightening finances of the estate. Is it possible that an arrangement similar to that of *Downton Abbey*, but with a more modern and sophisticated compensation system, could solve two of society's problems at once? This question touches directly on housing, which is the subject of the next chapter.

11

THE FUTURE OF HOUSING

Reflections: The Family Home

For my parents, the only asset worth having was real estate. They had no material financial savings and no pensions at work. There was never a discussion of the stock market at our dinner table, except in a derisive "That's not for us" tone. And much of the savings they built came in the form of sweat equity aimed at improving our home.

They had overextended themselves in 1960 to build their dream home out in the country. The process consisted of selling the house on Grierson Street, arranging a new-build mortgage with a bank, hiring a contractor, and then building the house according to plan. My father did a lot of the work himself. I can recall that the sunken living room—a prized feature in my mother's mind—still had a ply-wood floor when we left seven years later, as the budget had run out.

Giving up that home at the end of a long period of unemployment was a major financial setback, and there were insufficient proceeds to start again with a home of scale. However, my parents again demon-strated their real estate bias by investing some of the money from the sale of the dream house and quite a lot of sweat equity into my grandparents' home while we lived there. Also, before long, they were making a down payment on a modest cottage in the Kawartha Lakes region. Owning a vacation property was quite inexpensive back then, unlike today. I remember that my parents needed to borrow to buy it, but the amount was small enough that the seller agreed to hold the mortgage privately. The proclivity for investing sweat equity then shifted to that property.

After my grandparents both passed, the old family home was sold and the proceeds divided, and my parents bought another property; later they moved to another larger one. They also sold their first cottage and bought another with a bit more room. After my father retired, they moved house again to be closer to their first grandchild in Ottawa. The cottage was sold, and over the years my father downsized once, after my mother passed. When he died, he left a modest legacy, almost entirely in the form of real estate.

It should be obvious that this was not a coherent master plan but a series of optimizations taken in light of circumstances. Peak holdings of real estate were around the age of fifty, with a lovely home and a very well-appointed cottage on a lake, both owned outright. That holding declined by one major property when my father was just over sixty years of age, then real estate holdings were halved again after my mother passed and he downsized. My father never worked for an employer that offered a pension plan. His financial plan was simple: maximize exposure to real estate and accumulate just enough savings to supplement the government pensions that would come their way. Living in seven different houses and two cottages over the years provided sufficient capital growth to manage a comfortable retirement with resources to spare.

If rising economic and financial volatility will be felt first in the job market, it will be felt second in the housing market. Fluctuations in the housing market affect everyone, whether they are working or not. Economic instability will spill over into both housing sector activity—buying, selling, and building—and house prices, too.

People in my age group have mainly experienced rising house prices, just as my parents did. There have been a few setbacks when house prices declined—during the 1990–92 recession and during the Global Financial Crisis, for example—but these memories tend to fade against the glow of a perpetual uptrend in house prices. There will be two important differences between these past experiences and the future: first, housing market fluctuations will be bigger, and second, they will be more frequent. Expectations of ever-rising house prices will be upended, as periods of declining prices will be more noticeable and more memorable. There will be obvious implications for people's attitudes toward housing.

Volatility in housing and house prices is one thing; housing bubbles are another. The level of angst around housing has risen steeply in recent years, and especially during the pandemic, as the price ascent has been picking up speed. It is natural to worry that house prices are in a bubble that could collapse at any moment and to blame the situation on central banks for keeping interest rates so low for so long.

The situation is far more complex than that. For one thing, to conclude that house prices are in a bubble that could collapse at any time, one needs a concrete understanding of what the price of the house should be, given everything else that is going on. For this, the analyst would need a model that predicts where prices would be in the absence of speculation or irrational exuberance, but as discussed earlier, economic models are rarely so reliable that they can support such a conclusion. And models are very prone to failure when tectonic forces are operating, which is the case today. As with other parts of the economy, understanding housing requires understanding the dynamics of the tectonic forces, but the goal is not to forecast what happens next but to be prepared to manage higher risks in the future.

Home Ownership Is a Cornerstone

Home ownership is a cornerstone of life in much of the developed world. Most major economies have home ownership rates in the 60% to 70% range, including the U.S., Japan, the U.K., France, Italy, Mexico, Korea, Australia, and Canada. Across the OECD, only two countries have a majority of renters over owners: Switzerland and Germany, where around 40% own their homes either outright or through a mortgage. There are some outliers where home owner-ship rates are extremely high, including India at over 80%, China at around 90%, and Romania at around 95%. These differences are cultural in some instances or due to tax systems that favour either home ownership or tenancy. In countries formerly part of the Soviet Union, a high rate of home ownership is the result of state-owned housing being taken over by the occupant on favourable terms. In any case, housing markets matter to just about everyone, either because they are owners now or because they are renters and wish to be owners someday.

My own impression is that a human preference for ownership as opposed to tenancy comes from the desire to feather one's own nest, a deep driver instilled in all species by Mother Nature herself. Landlords often recognize this desire and allow tenants to feather their nest, some-times even sharing in the cost of such projects if they believe that the improvement will add to the market value of the rented home. Of course, the renter might enjoy the feathering, but the benefits may accrue mainly to the owner, if the plan is to move on soon.

The feathering instinct is most natural with an owned residence, for then the feathering improves the occupant's experience and represents accumulating equity that may be passed on to future generations. My father's financial plan, which was dominated by real estate and sweat equity, was not a unique one. He earned a far higher return by maximizing his exposure to real estate—supplementing that return using his own sweat to add incremental value—than he would have by banking his savings. Exposure to the stock market was a relatively exotic phenomenon in those days, particularly for very small investors.

In other words, the desire for home ownership primarily has natural drivers—it is not the brainchild of governments. And yet through history, governments have frequently tapped into this fundamental desire for political reasons, facilitating or otherwise encouraging home ownership and claiming credit for helping people to advance their dreams. This is why, for example, governments in countries as different as the U.S., the Netherlands, and India treat mortgage interest as a tax deduction. According to the OECD, the most generous tax relief schemes of this nature are offered in Norway, the U.K., the Netherlands, and Sweden, followed by the U.S., Belgium, and Canada.

Canada has a long history of political support for the housing sector. The creation of the Canada Mortgage and Housing Corporation (CMHC) after World War II had its roots in the desire to stimulate the economy and help returning war veterans move into decent housing. My grandparents lived in a wartime house in Oshawa built under that program. Subsequent policy changes were designed to encourage home ownership even more. The ability to insure mortgages with CMHC meant that banks were more willing to grant mortgages, as overall risks were lower. Over time, the required down payment for house purchases was reduced to open the door to home ownership even wider.

Historically, housing investment has represented about 5% of a typical economy. Since the financial crisis, housing's share of the economy has been closer to 7% or 8% in most major economies. Low-for-long interest rate policies have made housing purchases more accessible and increased participation in the market. The analysis of population aging suggests that this condition is likely to persist, probably for a generation or more.

People in their sixties today can only marvel at how low an interest rate their children are paying to own a home. However, this does not mean that young people today are paying less interest than their parents did, for the rise in the price of housing has essentially offset the benefit of a low rate of interest. Indeed, mortgage payments as a share of total disposable income—or so-called debt service ratios—have changed little over the years. This suggests that households tend to purchase as much housing as their circumstances allow, regardless of what the rate of interest may be. In other words, the constraint is not the size of the mortgage but the size of the monthly payment relative to income.

House Price Fundamentals

The purchase of a home delivers two things: housing services extending long into the future and an asset for lifetime accumulation of equity, just like the earnings being delivered by a company through ownership of its stock. Importantly, the value today of that future stream of housing services is greater the lower the rate of interest on the mortgage, just as a company's stock price is higher for a given stream of earnings when interest rates are low. Accordingly, low interest rates have two separate effects: they make it easier to carry a mortgage, thereby boosting the demand for housing, and they boost house prices through the asset valuation channel. This interaction between interest rates and house prices is known as the interest capitalization effect. In theory, assuming interest rates remain constant, building new housing at the rate at which the population is growing would leave house prices roughly unchanged—subject to two caveats, both having to do with geography.

The first caveat is that land to accommodate new housing may be scarce, in which case a growing population puts upward pressure on housing prices through higher land costs. Obvious examples are Hong Kong and Vancouver, where natural geographical constraints contribute to higher house prices. The second caveat is that even if land is plentiful, conveniently located land is always scarce and becomes more scarce as a city grows. Historically, individuals have been willing to pay more to live closer to a city's centre, thereby saving time and money in commuting. As cities grow larger at their frontier, existing house prices rise, and they rise more the closer to the centre the house is situated. This price effect happens irrespective of geography, the price of virgin land, the supply of new houses, or the level of interest rates.

This point is underappreciated. Suppose we were to start a new city from scratch in a wide-open part of the country. Suppose we located all businesses in the centre and issued housing permits in rings radiating out from the centre. As more people were attracted to this new city, the demand for operational business space in the downtown core would grow. People building homes in the outer rings of the suburban area would pay lower prices for land but face a longer daily commute to work. Those living in a future outer ring would face an even longer commute, so people would be willing to pay more to be in a closer ring than in that furthest ring. As a city grows, the cost of getting to work in the core from the outskirts continually rises—not just in the cost of public transit (which may be fixed regardless of how far one travels on the system) but also in the time cost of getting to work, which can be significant. The longer one must travel in order to get to work, the more one is willing to pay to live closer to work. Cities exist in order to capitalize on the synergies created when people work together in the centre, so their very nature dictates that a lot of daily activity will take place in the city core. Hence, many people must travel there every day.

This logic leads to tall, dense buildings in the city core and a rising profile of house prices from the outskirts in. This is what economists refer to as the "rent curve": a chart of housing prices starting from the outskirts of a city and ending at its centre. The rent curves of all cities rise steadily until we get to the centre. The larger the city, the longer the commuting times, and the higher the rent curve becomes in the centre, regardless of what may be happening to inflation or interest rates in the rest of the economy.

Even if population is constant, we can get significant movements in house prices in reaction to interest rate fluctuations. If we lower interest rates in this imaginary world, people who are planning to purchase a house someday have a reason to buy sooner. But the capitalization effect causes the price of existing houses to rise at the same time. The present value of the future stream of housing services goes up as interest rates go down.

This process of house price revaluation can easily become disorderly. Lower interest rates also boost demand, so prices can be bid up even more than the capitalization effect. People who plan to buy a house someday but who cannot yet qualify for a mortgage see their dream slipping away as prices rise; the fear of missing out sets in. The supply of new houses may not keep up with increased demand, either because of construction lags or, as is most commonly the case in Canada, because municipalities are slow to release new land for housing and to install water, sewers, gas, and electricity. In this case, house prices often

get bid up more than can be explained by these simple models of housing prices. These big price moves attract speculators—people who buy
unbuilt homes with the intention of selling them at a profit when they
are completed, or who buy homes just to flip them a few months later.
House prices can rise abruptly and unsustainably, making them vulnerable to a decline later—bad news for a recent homebuyer with a large
mortgage, possibly larger than the value of the house after prices drop.

In the real world, both sets of dynamics often happen together,
compounding the price action. The COVID-19 pandemic provided a
good illustration of how housing market volatility relates to tectonic
forces. Interest rates fell to historic lows, raising house prices through
the capitalization channel and boosting home buying, which pushed
house prices even higher. Meanwhile, there was a massive shift of work
activities from the office to the home and a shift in housing demand in
favour of suburban or rural properties. As a result, house prices have
risen overall, but rent curves have flattened, as prices in the outer regions
of cities have risen faster than those downtown. Companies and
employees have discovered that things worked pretty well using virtual
platforms, so some of this shift will become permanent. Although the
situation will vary, a consensus is emerging that we are heading for a
hybrid work model, where a typical employee will work in the office a
certain number of days per week and from home the rest of the time.
The tectonic forces churning beneath the surface promise to transform
our views on real estate even more significantly in the future.

Tectonic Housing Volatility

For a few generations, it has seemed as though nothing could slow
rising house prices. Part of this had to do with population growth,

especially in cities, and the inability of municipalities and builders to build sufficient supply. Moving forward, the demographic assumptions will shift, but more importantly, the five tectonic forces acting in combination will bring a new level of volatility to the housing market. Shocks that affect economic growth and employment will impact the pace of activity and prices in the housing market. Interest rate fluctuations will lead to ebbs and flows in house prices through the capitalization effect. In short, we can expect that rising volatility will prove that house prices can go down as well as up, and they will do so more often.

This higher volatility environment will naturally lead to shifts in household behaviour. In general, housing will be seen as a riskier investment than in the past, because of a growing perception that house prices are more volatile, in both directions. Because owning a house is usually accompanied by a mortgage that must be renewed from time to time, increased volatility in interest rates will add to the risks around home ownership. In short, it is quite possible that a more volatile environment will lead to a shift in preferences toward renting over owning, leaving landlords bearing the higher level of risk instead of households.

This logic comes up against Mother Nature's preference for home ownership. This preference is being reinforced by the trend toward lower real rates of interest due to population aging. In the absence of the other tectonic forces, population aging would mean a continued increase in rates of home ownership and in the share of the economy devoted to home construction, maintenance, and renovations. It would also mean a rising price trend for existing houses, as population growth will continue even as the population ages and keeps real interest rates low.

However, the interactions between the tectonic forces will lead to greater volatility in housing sales, prices, and interest rates, thereby adding to the risks associated with home ownership and potentially reducing the demand for houses. The net outcome of these contrary factors affecting the home ownership decision will depend on how people manage higher risk. Some households with no intention of moving will be able to "see through" house price volatility, for example. The risk of being forced to renew a mortgage at a suddenly higher rate of interest can be managed by taking a short-term renewal and locking in a lower rate later. Income gaps caused by more frequent bouts of unemployment may be managed by carrying a higher level of savings. Those locked out of home ownership because of sky-high prices may exercise patience, waiting until Mom and Dad are finished with the family home (if there is one).

Household Debt and the Depression Mentality

Now, this may all sound fine to some, but others are disturbed by the entire saga. As governments encourage people to own houses, they implicitly also encourage them to take on a lot of debt, particularly in markets where housing scarcity has significantly boosted the relative value of housing. As a result, household debt relative to disposable income has reached very high levels in many advanced economies. The highest debt-income ratios exceed 200%, in countries such as Denmark, Norway, the Netherlands, Switzerland, and Australia. Such countries as Canada, the U.K., Sweden, and Korea generally exceed 150%, while countries like the U.S. and Japan are more in the 100% range. Notably, the U.S. debt ratio was well above 150% just before the Global Financial Crisis, which had at its core major convulsions in the U.S. housing market and a period of household deleveraging.

These household debt levels are absolutely horrifying for people who grew up during the Great Depression, like my parents, and remain quite concerning for those in the next generation who still hold those learnings dear. Importantly, such summary measures of household debt represent an average for all households. Since many households have no debt at all, the average level of debt for indebted households is far higher. Critics have suggested that governments should further restrict household borrowing to prevent a future calamity. The precise nature of this calamity is not always clear, but it usually depicts a household that has borrowed too much, cannot make its payments, loses its house, and is then destitute forever. The financial system is deemed to be vulnerable to this day of reckoning. As with all such issues, there is more than one way to look at it, and looking at it in different ways can add important perspective.

Critics of household debt appear to have in mind a standard life plan with roots nearly a century old. The life plan is as follows: a household is formed; children arrive; the household needs expanded housing well before they can save enough to purchase it; they borrow to buy the home, pay for the mortgage over a period of twenty-five to thirty years, and become mortgage-free prior to retirement. The family then has a stock of savings in the form of real estate that, if necessary, can be drawn upon to supplement income during the retirement years. Perhaps they downsize their home after their children leave, or perhaps they become renters during their retirement years and use the proceeds of their home sale to supplement other sources of retirement income.

Renting versus Buying

As it turns out, this standard life plan will not work for everyone. Average house prices in some cities—such as London, Paris, Sydney,

Vancouver, or Hong Kong, for example—have gone beyond the level where an ordinary citizen with an average income can accumulate a down payment and then qualify for a mortgage to achieve home ownership. According to conservative observers, the solution is to rent rather than purchase housing. This requires finding the right accommodation for the family, finding the right landlord, and paying rent for their entire lives. If they expect to need additional monies to supplement their income during retirement, they need an independent stream of savings along the way to prepare for that day. In the end, they remain renters and live on their retirement income supplemented by savings they can accumulate through their lives.

It is interesting to look at how conventional thinking around mortgages affects these two life plans. Suppose that one family grew up, works, and lives in an attractive but small city, like Moncton, and follows the standard life plan with home ownership to the letter. Another family grew up, works, and lives in Vancouver. The Vancouver family finds that the conventional requirement that the mortgage be amortized over twenty-five or perhaps thirty years is a brick wall given their incomes, so they choose to rent instead of purchasing a home. To end up in the same financial place at retirement as the Moncton family, the Vancouver family must save over and above their rent so that they will have a financial nest egg equivalent to the accumulated equity in the Moncton family's home. Supposing they achieve this, then the two families have reached the same destination by two different routes. Unfortunately, the Vancouver family never experienced the joy of home ownership or the ability to feather their own nest.

Imagine what happens when we drop the convention that the mortgage must be amortized over twenty-five or thirty years. Suppose it can be forty or fifty years. Indeed, suppose it need never be paid off at all, so that the Vancouver family is able to enter into home ownership. The Vancouver family no longer pays rent to a landlord for their entire lives but instead pays interest to a bank. By paying down some of the principal each month, they accumulate an amount of equity in the home similar to what they might have saved while renting. They remain free to sell the home at retirement, pay off the remaining mortgage with the proceeds, extract their accumulated equity in the process, become renters, and use the recovered equity from the home sale to supplement their retirement income. Or they could instead remain in their home until they pass away, at which point the house can be sold, the remaining mortgage extinguished, and the accumulated equity in the home disbursed to their estate.

There are only two real differences for the Vancouver family between this plan and the plan where they rent for their entire lives. First, they pay "rent" in the form of interest to a bank rather than to a landlord; second, they own an appreciating asset, thereby adding capital gains to their nest egg at the end of their working lives. Indeed, in many countries, including Canada, the tax system is designed to favour home ownership over renting. On an after-tax basis, the life plan based on renting is more expensive than buying. The Vancouver family that carries a mortgage their entire lives are essentially co-owners of the home, partnered with a bank, except that all the market appreciation (or depreciation) of the house falls to the family, not the bank.

By eliminating conservative biases around debt, one can efficiently separate the housing decision from the investment decision. To remove emotion from the analysis, one would need to construct two life plans, one based on renting and accumulating financial assets, and the other based on home ownership, where the accumulation of equity is assumed to be equal to the renter's accumulation of financial assets, regardless of the original purchase price of the house. That analysis needs to be done on an after-tax basis, because in some countries tax systems favour home ownership, while others favour renting.

Maintaining such constraints around borrowing in our highly efficient banking system amounts to imposing yesterday's morals on today's borrowers and lenders. A mortgage is an affair between the borrower and the lender. Even if a household remains in a too expensive house, carrying a mortgage until death, the household's children will inherit the equity in the house that remains after the mortgage has been paid out to the bank.

Another way to look at the housing-mortgage dilemma is to ask not what is going on with debt relative to income, but debt relative to assets. Debt relative to income is an attempt to get at the ability to service debt, where a more appropriate metric would be the debt service ratio—how much income must be allocated each year in order to service the mortgage. Surely today's sophisticated banks are very capable of deciding whether a given household is able to service the debt they are about to take on. If they are wrong, they are big enough to absorb any losses that arise. Ultimately, the mortgage agreement is between the borrower and the lender. Why should the government or a regulatory authority impose its values—which, by the way, are based on very old thinking developed during the Great Depression—on this arrangement?

It is interesting to compare this analysis to life's other big financial transaction: the purchase of a motor vehicle. As with houses, it is possible to think of a car as providing transportation services and a real asset. The main difference is that cars are depreciating assets, whereas houses (if properly maintained, an activity that offsets depreciation) generally are appreciating assets. One individual chooses to purchase the car outright, extracts the desired transportation services, and watches the value of the car decline steadily to zero. A second individual borrows to buy the car, makes regular monthly payments, and finishes paying for the car at around the same time its value approaches zero. A third individual leases the car, also making regular monthly payments. These payments essentially rent the transportation services for the life of the lease; the cost of leasing is the interest on the entire value of the car plus the depreciation in the value of the car. At the end of the lease, the car is turned in and the process repeats.

What is the difference between these three scenarios? All three individuals pay for the depreciation of the car. The first one pays up front. The second pays over time, including interest. The third also pays interest but never owns the car. The stock of savings they would have had to hand over to own the car (whether immediately or over time) can instead be invested somewhere else, presumably in an appreciating asset. What the leasing option does is to create a clear distinction between transportation services and the asset that delivers them. The point is, there is no actual difference between these three plans—if there were, people would shift to the best option and forces of competition would make them the same again.

Why then do experts lament the debt load that households are carrying in order to drive a vehicle, when all they are doing is using an efficient financial system to optimize their personal preferences? The same anti-debt morals are at play in automobile markets as they are in housing.

Since real rates of interest seem destined to remain low for a very long time, households will be able to service more debt than in the past. Should there be rules that prevent people from doing so? Only if it is believed that borrowing behaviour is putting the entire financial system at risk should this be a consideration, in which case the authorities should adjust the regulatory parameters around lending. This could include ensuring that the financial system and the borrowing households have financial buffers that enable them to manage higher risks associated with fluctuations in employment, interest rates, and house prices. But once those prudential parameters are set, it is wrong to make a moral argument against debt, regardless of where people are in their life cycle.

There is very little reason why it should not be almost as simple to lease the home of your dreams as it is to lease the vehicle of your dreams. It is basic arithmetic to add the gradual accumulation of home ownership to a leasing structure—in effect, a co-ownership model, where the renter contributes a stream of principal payments as well. Sharing the capital gains on the property between the occupant and the financial institution that owns a significant portion of the home is also simple to do. Home improvements and sweat equity contributed by the occupant would not be difficult to track. In today's modern financial systems, there is little place for attitudes toward debt that were formed during the 1930s.

The Debt-Equity Framework

The most telling way to examine debt is to compare apples to apples, which means judging indebtedness against the stock of assets. For a household considering the purchase of a home and qualifying for a mortgage, they generally need to come up with at least a 10% to 20% down payment. Taking a house valued at $500,000, 20% equity means a down payment of $100,000 and a mortgage of $400,000. Assuming this is all the household has at that point in time, what is their debt-to-equity ratio? Some would say that it is 4:1, and a 10% down payment would mean 9:1. However, that ignores that the household now owns a significant asset valued at $500,000. The actual debt-equity ratio, therefore, is 0.8:1 or 0.9:1, and this is only for the new homebuyers.

As mentioned, in Canada, household debt to disposable income is running at close to 170%. However, the debt service burden is running at around 15% of income, which is roughly what it has been for many years. But consider the asset side of the balance sheet. Canadian households have some $14 trillion in assets, roughly half financial and half non-financial, and only about $2 trillion in financial liabilities. Net worth therefore is on the order of $12 trillion, which is around five times total income in the economy. Of the $12 trillion, real estate constitutes $6 trillion, against which mortgages outstanding are $1.5 trillion and other loans of around $0.8 trillion. The aggregate debt-equity ratio in Canadian household real estate is about 1:4, or 0.25:1.

In the business sector, there is a much more logical approach to debt than for households. A typical structure for a project being financed by a company is 60% debt and 40% equity, for a debt-equity ratio of 1.5:1. To support an ongoing business, companies almost always use a combination of both debt and equity, since having some leverage in the company boosts the return on invested capital. Debt-equity ratios vary by industry and by firm. The economy-wide average in Canada is around 1:1, but something between 1:1 and 1.5:1 is very common. And what is the preferred debt-equity ratio for households according to the prudent debt critics? That ratio, it seems, should be 0:1 and preferably well before retirement!

There is yet another factor that many choose to ignore when criticizing household debt, and that is the legacy effect. The outstanding stock of personal real estate in Canada is approximately $6 trillion, which is on the order of $170,000 per person, or $125,000 per person after accounting for outstanding mortgages. This per capita figure includes all individuals, even small children. When a person dies, this stock of wealth is not destroyed and much of it is not even taxed. It is passed on. Surely young people taking on large mortgages are aware that their parents may one day leave them a legacy. Of course, they do not know how much equity might be left when their parents die, or when that might be. But the real estate is owned by someone, and its value will be passed on. This effect is hard to calculate, but we all know it affects the behaviour of young people—as well it should.

In their 2014 book *House of Debt*, Atif Mian and Amir Sufi undertook a painstaking analysis of the U.S. housing market, broken down by Zip code. They showed that during the U.S. housing collapse of 2008–09, people whose homes declined in value below the mortgage outstanding (called going underwater) cut back on their consumer spending, even when they had no intention of selling their home. Obviously, people who were forced to sell their homes ended up with less than their original loan, but people who had every intention of remaining in their home, and who eventually saw their house price recover and move above the original purchase price again, cut their regular spending, independently of their level of income or interest rates. As a consequence, the U.S. recession was deeper and more prolonged than it otherwise would have been—not because incomes were lower, but simply because some households perceived that their wealth had declined. This is exactly as if there had been a tightening of monetary policy during an economic downturn.

In order to reduce the vulnerability of the economy to housing price risk, Mian and Sufi advocated the development of a shared-responsibility mortgage (SRM). The idea is to share a mortgage's risks differently between lender and borrower. In a normal mortgage, all the risk is borne by the borrower—risks related to fluctuating interest rates, losing one's job, or falling house prices. The lender can evict the borrower and sell the house should anything go wrong. Lenders are far better placed than borrowers to carry such risk, since they have considerable scope to diversify their risks, whereas households have little.

Under an SRM, the bank would offer a degree of downside protection to the borrower, and the borrower would promise a share of any capital gains from owning the house to the bank. The property is essentially co-owned, with the share owned by the bank declining over time. Under such an arrangement, when house prices in a certain area fall, the monthly mortgage payment would also fall by the same percentage. In the background, the principal amount owing on the mortgage would also be falling, as the bank would absorb the risk of falling house prices. The buyer's share of equity in the (now lower-priced) home would remain unchanged. However, when house prices recover, so does the mortgage payment and the principal amount outstanding.

The mortgage lender would want to charge more than usual for this rearrangement of risk. The additional cost would depend on expectations around house prices and their typical amount of volatility. This is a complex calculation, but it is easily calibrated by adjusting the share of any future capital gains on the house that would go to the lender. According to Mian and Sufi's analysis, which was based on the history of the U.S. housing market, allocating 5% of any future capital gains to the lender, and 95% to the household, would more than compensate lenders for the downside risk protection they would be providing in an SRM. To illustrate, if the homeowner someday sells their home for a capital gain of $100,000, $5,000 of that gain is the bank's; this seems like a small price to pay for protection against all those potential downside risks.

There is little doubt co-ownership models that make mortgages more like equity and less like pure debt would mean a more stable economy and financial system. For one thing, mortgage lenders would be much less likely to facilitate the creation of housing price bubbles if they were sharing in any future downside risk. For another, fewer homebuyers would overextend themselves because of fear of missing out, so there would be less fragility in household finances. But most importantly, house price risk would no longer play a significant role in the prolongation of fluctuations in the economy—in either direction. The rising tide of risk we are predicting due to our five tectonic forces would be less likely to have as many profound effects on the housing market in the future, besides.

The housing market stresses that will emerge as the tectonic forces interact in the future could make such ideas a much more popular form of risk management. A shared-responsibility or shared-equity mortgage model would seem to be a natural for community-based financial institutions, such as credit unions. It should also be attractive for Canada's large banks, which would benefit from a more stable financial system and a less vulnerable economy.

Objective analysis of housing is difficult since it is such a personal and emotional matter. Two housing propositions that are identical in cost may be perceived very differently by two different households. This is what makes the housing market so special, and so important to policymakers.

The tectonic forces will bring new uncertainties into housing markets. If the post-pandemic rent curve is flatter for most major cities, that does not mean that house prices will stop rising. Net population growth will continue, even if population aging means that it will be slower than in the past. Net migration to advanced economies is likely to increase, both because of lower workforce growth and climate change stresses in developing countries. A typical city's rent curve, now flatter because of less commuting, will resume its inevitable rise as cities get larger, even if municipalities step up the development of virgin land at the frontier. Immigrants are drawn mainly to major cities because, in an increasingly service-oriented economy, new businesses can begin there in an already scaled market to support them. As cities become even larger, existing home prices will again rise even faster than new home prices. Inflation-adjusted interest rates are likely to remain very low for the foreseeable future, putting a strong foundation under the housing story globally. Even so, outsized economic fluctuations and interest rate volatility will affect homeowners, for better or worse.

A cynic would perhaps see home ownership rates in most countries as excessive, having been distorted by a history of ownership-promoting government policies. A high home ownership rate usually means a high level of household debt, and this makes the economy vulnerable to interest rate or economic fluctuations. Dedicating a high share of the economy to housing also means less capacity for business investment and lower productivity growth for the overall economy. All true. But pity the poor politician who decides that they know what is best for households and tries to change all this. Policymakers would be better to encourage more financial innovation around what is by far the biggest decision of most people's lives. The result would be improved risk management from which there would be significant macroeconomic benefits.

Policymakers routinely face demands that they address problems in the housing sector, along with everything else that impinges on society's well-being. How the tectonic forces will affect government and central bank policies is the subject to which I now turn.

12

RISING RISK WILL TAX
POLICYMAKERS

Reflections: Passion for Policy

Getting into the business of making policy was the whole motivation behind my entry into the field of economics. The possibility of making lives better en masse through the practice of economic policy held a strong attraction for me. My work at the Bank of Canada always had this feeling of significance to it, given its lofty purpose. The feeling was palpable in the office of governor. Awesome in the true sense of the word.

One of the best parts of the role is the collaboration with other central bank governors. There were meetings every second month at the Bank for International Settlements in Basel, Switzerland. Layered on top of this regular schedule were usually two to three meetings per year of the G20 finance ministers and central bank governors, a couple of G7 meetings, the twice-annual meetings hosted by the IMF, and the annual summer conference hosted by the Federal Reserve Bank of Kansas City at Jackson Hole, Wyoming. On most of these occasions, the smaller group of governors constituting the BIS economic consultative committee—U.S., European Central Bank, Japan, Germany, France, U.K.,

Italy, Canada, Sweden, Belgium, China, Brazil, India, and Mexico—would get together, along with the general manager of the BIS, the managing director of the IMF, and the secretary-general of the OECD.

The meetings at the BIS were easily the most productive, it seemed to me. G20 meetings were the least productive, albeit highly informative. No doubt the productivity scale is mostly about the size of the meetings. The G20 table has more than sixty participants around it, each seat with a backbencher. People tend to offer scripted interventions rather than interacting in real time. Still, strong relationships build up over time in the corridors. The G7 meetings are much more like a real conversation. But the BIS meetings, both in the large room (around eighty governors) and the smaller intimate dinner Sunday evening (the fifteen members of the Economic Consultative Committee) made for true international policy coordination. The code has always been: what happens in Basel stays in Basel.

I remember well my first BIS dinner as governor, only a couple of weeks after taking office. When I arrived on the top floor of the BIS tower, the first person I saw was Federal Reserve chair Ben Bernanke. "Mr. Chairman," I said, extending my hand, "I'm Steve Poloz from the Bank of Canada."

The chairman shook hands with me politely and said quietly, "Steve, I know who you are . . . and around here, everybody calls me Ben."

That simple exchange set the tone. We talked briefly about how it felt to be a rookie governor. Then Mervyn King, governor of the Bank of England and chair of the economic consultative committee, and therefore the host of this dinner, approached us and said, "Steve! Great to see you again, congratulations on your appointment, and welcome to the BIS. Since this is my last dinner and your first, come and sit with me and Ben." Truthfully, I kept pinching myself.

Over the years, I would develop close relationships with many other governors. I had the pleasure to work with Ben Bernanke, Janet Yellen, who followed Ben as Fed chair, and Jay Powell, and for all three the special relationship with Canada was abundantly clear. Every meeting included a catch-up with Christine Lagarde, first in her role as managing director of the IMF, then as head of the European Central Bank. Christine, as is her nature, always asks after my wife, Valerie; the two of them came to know one another during a G7 gathering in Whistler, British Columbia. The meetings also gave me a chance to stay in close touch with my predecessor, Mark Carney, who had been a "rookie governor" twice over and liked to follow developments in Canada very closely. One year, Governor Stefan Ingves of the Swedish Riksbank invited Valerie and me to attend the Nobel Prize ceremonies in Stockholm, which was truly memorable. I still have the white tie and tails in case I am ever invited to dine at *Downton Abbey*.

The BIS dinner table is round, symbolizing a dinner among equals. It proved to be the most informative channel of communication available to me as governor. It was a place where we could brainstorm, share good and bad stories, laugh a little, and build relationships. The seating arrangement varied each time. One night I was seated between Jens Weidmann from Germany and Klaas Knot from the Netherlands, another night between Mario Draghi from the ECB and Alejandro Díaz de León from Mexico, and so on, but the conversation jumped back and forth across the table until the chair brought order and organized a discussion on a specific topic. The next day, we would be in the larger Global Economy Meeting, where there were many more central banks represented. Many of those relationships blossomed, too.

I have always believed and hoped that central banking would be carried out mostly behind the scenes. Of course, I believe strongly in active communications and transparent public accountability for the central bank. But if the world were to remain tranquil for an extended period, steadied by good policymaking, people could forget all about their central bank—to me, this would be a sign of success.

I had watched my predecessor manage through the stress of the Global Financial Crisis and become a household name in the process. When I became governor in 2013, I hoped for none of that during my tenure. Near anonymity would be fine with me. I thought my plan was coming together in 2014. I was on yet another evening flight from Toronto to Zurich for the regular meetings in Basel. The flight attendant came by to offer me a beverage and recognized me from a previous flight.

"What brings you to Zurich so frequently?" she asked. Obviously, she had recognized me as a frequent flyer but not as governor of the Bank of Canada.

"Oh, I have regular meetings up in Basel," I replied cryptically.

"Are you a banker?"

"Well, yes . . . actually, a central banker." Cryptic again.

"Oh my goodness! Do you know Mark Carney by any chance?"

"Well yes, as a matter of fact, I do."

"Cool! Is he as terrific in person as he seems on television? He saved us during the crisis!"

"Well, yes, he is a special fellow. As a matter of fact, I am having dinner with him tomorrow evening."

"Oh, good for you! He's fantastic . . . they even recruited him to head up the Bank of England . . . say, who was it who replaced him, anyway?"

I hesitated and then said, "Well, that would be me."

It is fair to say that she felt terrible for not recognizing me, but I reassured her that this was exactly as it should be—no crisis, no notoriety for the central bank, no worries.

Later that year, however, the Bank of Canada was thrust back into the headlines as oil prices collapsed and the economy experienced a significant setback. The bank cut interest rates in January 2015 and again a few months later to cushion the blow. By responding early and forcibly, the bank was able to limit the damage to the economy. It progressed on two tracks for the next year or so but found its way back home relatively quickly.

As challenging and controversial as that episode was, it pales compared to the arrival of COVID-19. Relationships with other governors proved hugely beneficial when the COVID-19 crisis hit, even though our BIS meetings became virtual by necessity. Jay Powell became the chair of the BIS global economy meeting in the middle of the pandemic, after Mark Carney retired. At my last virtual BIS meeting in June 2020, Jay said some very nice things about me, most of them true, and then commanded that all microphones be opened simultaneously for the applause. It was a touching moment—not quite like the more traditional parting of ways of a group of close friends, but very nice all the same. And many of those relationships remain active even today.

Policymakers around the world certainly did their jobs in response to COVID-19. It was quite remarkable just how aggressive the response was. Most importantly, the consensus that had developed during 2018–20—that monetary policy tools were nearly exhausted, so that any major downturn in the global economy would require fiscal policy to do the heavy lifting—was embraced globally with relatively little debate.

The question addressed in this chapter is about the future of fiscal and monetary policymaking in the post-pandemic economy. This must take account of the large increase in government debt from the pandemic and ask what stresses policymakers will be dealing with in the future. In the aftermath of the pandemic, some have legitimately asked whether policymakers have sufficient capacity to deal with a second one in the near future. To put the question another way, if governments knew that they would face similar episodes in future years, would they have used their tools so aggressively in 2020–21, or would they have held some fiscal resources in reserve? Most observers seem to think that the extraordinary demands placed on policymakers during the pandemic have been unique, never to be repeated, except perhaps at time of war, which thankfully is rare. However, it is my contention that the confluence of the five tectonic forces will push policymakers to their limits regularly in the future.

There are two levels on which to consider the challenges policymakers will face. The first is structural: the tectonic forces will place growing baseline demands on government programs, from health care to seniors' pensions to programs for the unemployed and disadvantaged. The second level concerns rising volatility and risk: the tectonic forces will reinforce one another and combine with politics to create more frequent outbreaks of economic and financial volatility, during which citizens will naturally look to governments for protection, drawing deeply on support programs. Since the economic environment will become much harder to understand and to forecast, everyday decisions by individuals and companies will become much riskier. Individuals and companies alike will look to their governments and central banks to manage this rising tide of risk. Even more policy capacity will need to be kept in reserve and used only when necessary, after which the reserve capacity would need to be rebuilt for the next rainy day. All of this starting from a fiscal plan that has been upended by the pandemic.

The question is whether governments and central banks have the capacity to deal with both the structural stresses coming from the tectonic forces and the volatility they will generate as well. The short answer is that the coming stresses are likely to prove too much for existing policy tools.

Tectonic Forces Mean Rising Fiscal Burdens

The five tectonic forces will mean a growing financial burden on governments, quite apart from the anticipated rising tide of economic and financial risk. It is a core role of government to provide public goods such as a military for national defence, policing, and lighthouses. These are goods that private markets will almost never deliver on their own. This is why infrastructure investment generally falls to governments. Another typical role for government is to protect the welfare of society, providing for education, medical care, and care for the elderly, as well as redistributing national income to those most in need.

An aging population and a steady increase in longevity will create exceptional fiscal stress through medical care systems in most countries. We can illustrate this basic point using Canada's system of medical care as an example. According to the Canadian Institute for Health Information, national health spending has risen steadily for the past forty years, from around 7% of national income during the 1970s to around 12% today. Unsurprisingly, seniors absorb a disproportionate share of these dollars, some 44%, while they represent under 20% of the population. This bulge in costs will continue to grow for the next twenty to thirty years as the baby boomers age and require more care. Although the allocation of spending across demographic groups does not vary much over time, the rising share of seniors in the population will strain the system in the years ahead.

A related issue is government pension schemes, whether for their workers or for the general population, which will also be strained for the next thirty years or so. In addition to the sheer number of pension participants, the low real rates of interest make it more difficult to generate the safe returns needed to underwrite most public pension schemes. The present value of government pension obligations extending into the future is much higher than it would be at higher rates of interest.

All of this will be happening as population aging leads to a gradual slowdown in economic growth. Once rates of taxation are set—whether those rates are applied to business or personal income—government revenues will see headline growth roughly equal to economic growth, measured in current dollars. Government revenue growth is boosted by inflation. For example, if inflation is 2% and real economic growth is 1%, government revenues will grow by around 3% per year. Absent an increase in inflation, government revenue growth will be slowing due to an aging population, while the demand for government services rises.

Meanwhile, the Fourth Industrial Revolution is gathering momentum and will generate waves of worker displacement. Even though the future benefits will eventually create work for everyone, a K-shaped economy with growing weight in the bottom will mean persistent unemployment and a perpetual draw on government income support programs. Income inequality—already elevated in many parts of the world—will continue to rise. Demands for a more equitable income distribution became very loud during the pandemic, and a major wave of technological change is just around the corner that will add to the urgency.

As if this is not enough to look forward to, most governments used much of their spare fiscal capacity during the pandemic. Global government debt rose by more than 20% of global income during 2020–21. Some countries have little fiscal or institutional capacity remaining. Fortunately, the most fiscally constrained countries are also those with relatively young populations—they will see less fiscal drag from the tectonic forces than the advanced economies.

Accordingly, governments will face considerable growth in the structural demand for their financial support in the years ahead. At the same time, government revenue growth will be very modest at current tax rates, given the moderating trend in global economic growth. Borrowing to meet these demands will shift today's burden onto future generations, which many will see as unacceptable. Presenting a credible fiscal plan that embraces the coming stresses is crucial, for otherwise bond investors will demand higher real interest rates on government debt and make it even more difficult for governments to service their existing debt load over the next ten to twenty years.

One way or another, governments will need more revenue to manage these rising structural demands and to maintain a credible long-term fiscal plan. Basically, two channels are available to them.

New Taxes versus Economic Growth

Addressing the global government revenue shortfall can be reduced to two basic choices: raise taxes directly, or use policies to boost economic growth, thereby generating more government tax revenue indirectly at current tax rates.

It goes without saying that no one wants to pay more taxes. But there is more at stake than personal preferences, for many taxes impede economic growth. Higher taxes on companies reduce the incentive for them to innovate or to invest in new growth and make it less attractive to start a new company in the first place. Higher income taxes on individuals discourage them from working. Either way, lower economic growth means slower growth in government revenues, which can mean that higher taxes actually lead to lower government revenues. This argument has some merit, even if the situation is far more complex than it sounds.

If it was difficult to raise taxes in the past, today's political climate makes it close to impossible. Any major fiscal initiative these days incites a cacophony of contrarian debate, amplified by news media and social media, in the context of which political consensus can be a very rare bird. The fractured state of politics suggests that a more nuanced, or balanced, approach will be needed to develop future fiscal plans. The emergence of an international consensus around preventing tax shifting and a minimum rate of corporate taxation offers some promise in this regard. However, even if these proposed global tax adjustments are fully deployed, they will not produce a major increase in government tax revenue.

Future fiscal plans will need to put more emphasis on fostering faster economic growth, thereby increasing government revenues without a significant increase in tax burdens. The irony is that this has always been a desirable approach to fiscal policy. Perhaps in the past there was always enough baseline economic growth that governments could deploy multiple taxes aimed at pleasing special interests, and the attendant loss of economic growth was not all that noticeable. But with economic growth now slowing as baby boomers exit the workforce, every decimal point of economic growth seems more meaningful, even in the face of polarized politics.

Most observers underestimate the importance of the overall structure of tax systems in determining, or holding back, economic growth. Tax systems are complicated. One tax promotes this, another promotes that, and there can be vigorous debates about each individual proposal and the various unintended consequences it might cause. However, the interaction of the various parts of the tax system—and whether something simpler might raise the same amount of revenue to give us more economic growth left over—is rarely considered.

For example, taxation of incomes is known to be a disincentive to work and therefore represents a headwind to economic growth. Labour force participation would be higher, and economic growth higher, if we did not tax the returns from work as highly as we do in most countries today. In addition to taxing personal incomes, we impose a variety of payroll taxes on firms, which discourages the creation of new companies and new jobs.

The preferred form of taxation from an efficiency and growth point of view is to tax consumer spending, not income, using sales taxes. Taxing spending, instead of income, causes people to work more and save more, which provides more capacity for investment by firms in future economic growth. Taxing spending has the added benefit of applying equally to retired individuals, which makes it a more sustainable form of taxation in an aging society. Despite these attractive features, many argue that consumption taxation is "regressive"—that it worsens the after-tax income distribution because low-income individuals spend their entire income, whereas high-income individuals spend only a part of theirs. Income taxes normally do not have this problem, as they are "progressive"—the percentage paid rises as income rises. But it is easy to introduce consumption tax rebates at the low end of the income scale to adjust for this issue, thereby negating the objection. Canada has such a consumption tax rebate system. Even so, consumption taxes are often seen as politically difficult to implement, because consumers see the tax every time they buy something and are reminded too often who imposed the tax on them.

The economic calculus is much simpler than the political: removing income and payroll taxes and instead generating the same level of revenue by taxing consumer spending would result in an economy with higher growth and more income overall. Consider a thought experiment. Suppose that a government were to simplify the currently complex tax structure by calculating the sales tax rate that would need to be deployed to replace all other taxes and keep government revenues unchanged. The simplest possible example would be to eliminate income taxes and various corporate taxes altogether, except perhaps on the highest incomes, and raise the sales tax to keep government revenues the same. If these two changes were made on the same day, leaving everyone as well off as before, would that be politically impossible? My guess is that most people would shrug and carry on, as there would be no change in the money in their pocket. But from a macroeconomic point of view, the result would be a far more efficient economy with a faster trend growth rate and higher fiscal revenues as a result. This is essentially what New Zealand did when it first deployed a national sales tax in the mid-1980s, a tax reform that is still delivering efficiency benefits today.

Introducing tax reforms that move the burden from working to spending might even be politically attractive in the post-pandemic context. There is a widespread expectation that tax burdens on companies and individuals alike need to increase significantly in order to repair the fiscal damage done by COVID-19. Consider a second thought experiment. Suppose everyone is dreading higher taxes to pay for the debt incurred during the pandemic, and instead governments announce that they are reforming current tax policies in such a way that no taxes rise, economic growth increases, and government revenues go up automatically. The political mileage to gain from the collective relief is incalculable. Making such an initiative politically palatable, however, would require considering it as a balanced, all-or-nothing package—since all the pieces interact with one another, debating and compromising on the individual changes would erode the benefits and take it to certain political defeat.

A tax reform that leaves tax rates unchanged while boosting economic growth would give a highly indebted government considerable fiscal flexibility. Higher economic growth would mean that the ratio of government debt to national income would be falling, reassuring markets and the general population that government capacity was being built up to prepare for the next crisis. The decline in the debt-income ratio could be accelerated, if preferred, by allocating some or all of the new growth in government revenue to a faster retirement of debt.

However, it is worth asking whether the government debt incurred while dealing with the pandemic ever needs to be repaid. It is rare for governments to pay off their debt. Instead, they get their spending under control, balance their budgets, and then economic growth and inflation reduce the magnitude of the debt burden over time. For centuries, government borrowing has been based solely on its ability to service debt, not the ability to pay it off. From a societal point of view, government debt is better thought of in the way we think of equity in a company. The government's ability to borrow depends on its entire franchise, which comes from its ability to collect taxes and service its debts forever. A history of honouring debts and offering clear guidance as to how that debt will be serviced in the future is generally sufficient to reassure borrowers. This is a very old idea, with its origins in late-seventeenth-century England.

A sustainable fiscal plan is one in which government debt relative to national income is stable or falling. If it is rising, perhaps because of a major downturn in the economy, then there needs to be a plan to restore sustainability after the episode is over. In a world of fractured politics and low economic growth, fiscal sustainability will depend more on trend economic growth than it has in the past. And no opportunity to boost that trend can be ignored.

The most important source of new economic growth in the post-pandemic economy will be technological progress, our second tectonic force. Judging from past industrial revolutions led by general-purpose technologies—the steam engine, electricity, and the computer chip—the digitalization of the global economy, the associated spread of artificial intelligence, and biotechnological advances could raise the level of global income per person significantly. This is not the same as raising trend economic growth permanently. An increase in the level of national income of, say, 10% spread over a decade would boost economic growth by about 1% annually. The growth trend would ease again once the technology had been widely deployed. As discussed earlier, this is roughly what happened between 1995 and 2005, and arguably the benefits of the computer chip are still accumulating. That seems to be the minimum of what can be expected over the next decade due to the Fourth Industrial Revolution. Governments will automatically receive a significant share of this growth without raising taxes.

Since technological progress has also usually meant an increasingly unequal distribution of income—a situation that has been worsened by the pandemic—it is very likely that governments will need to address income distribution issues as they tackle their debt overhang. Otherwise, they will face electoral defeat from those who believe they have been left behind.

The optimal distribution of income is an elusive concept, especially as perceptions play such an important role. At a basic level, it is widely believed that the more income that goes to the rich, the slower economic growth will be. The rich spend less of each additional dollar of income than do lower-income families, who may spend it in its entirety. A more nuanced analysis would acknowledge that economic growth comes from innovation, entrepreneurialism, and risk taking, all motivated by the financial rewards that technological success brings. This suggests that economic growth is actually supported by an income distribution skewed toward the wealthy. To overtax the gains from entrepreneurial behaviour is to frustrate it, and to encourage businesses to take their ideas, capital, and enthusiasm to a lower-tax environment. Reducing overall tax burdens by taking advantage of cross-country differences in tax regimes is commonplace for wealthy individuals and multinational corporations alike. The fact that policymakers have been working for years toward international agreements to level the taxation playing field only underscores the point that the underlying tensions between innovation, economic growth, and taxes are real. Those who advocate changes to the domestic tax system to alter the post-tax distribution of income must acknowledge both sides of the argument—a more equal distribution of income could boost growth or it might reduce it.

One does not need to choose sides in this debate to appreciate that income distribution discontent is helping to support polarization in politics. This discontent has real roots, as documented in chapter 4, but few individuals would know about or understand the Gini coefficient for their country. The mere perception that the rich are getting richer while you are losing out is sufficient to foster discontent, even anger. Some taxation systems seem to be designed to confuse rather than clarify this issue. For example, in Canada, lower-income individuals have income tax deducted from their pay but then receive regular family benefits, a sales tax rebate, and a carbon tax rebate. There is also a plethora of social support programs, all transferring money to lower-income families. What this results in is a highly progressive net income tax system, but those at the lower end still pay income taxes, and that is what they remember when they hear of wealthy individuals who pay little or no income tax.

This undercurrent of income distribution discontent makes it increasingly difficult to form a consensus in policymaking. It might make sense to set aside the endless debate about what is optimal with respect to income distribution and simply adjust distributional parameters in the direction of increased equality, by enough to create the buy-in necessary to make progress on other policies. The situation in the U.S. comes immediately to mind, where income distribution is the most unequal of the advanced economies, and politics the most fractious. Making income redistribution more progressive does not require radical shifts in the tax system—it does not require wealth taxes, for instance—but could be achieved with an earlier and steeper tax rate on income, while tightening the definition of "income" for those at the top.

Supposing that this is politically plausible, the next question would be, How does one redistribute the money after the tax revenues flow in? Governments generally have multiple channels, program after program, all run by earnest and under-resourced bureaucrats. Ironically, the boldest of redistributive frameworks is also one of the oldest ideas: the universal basic income (UBI).

This idea has been subjected to vigorous debate for decades and even experimented with in small jurisdictions. The core issue is that if you give someone an income that satisfies basic life needs, you provide them a disincentive to work. This is true, all other things being equal, but all things are never equal. Those who argue against the provision of a UBI stand idly by as governments instead assemble a patchwork system of supports to protect the disadvantaged that often costs more to manage than the amount of money it delivers. Replacing such bureaucratically complex programs with simple ones can free up fiscal resources for investments in higher economic growth. The UBI idea is simplicity itself: every individual has an account with the tax agency, and each month a minimum basic income is deposited in each bank account. Those who are earning more than the minimum face a carefully calibrated progressive tax rate that recovers the UBI and, toward the top, takes sufficient revenue to pay for the program. As was discovered in many countries during the pandemic, such a system can be set up with a few strokes on a keyboard. The administrative costs are negligible, a stark contrast with all the other expensive social safety net programs that suffer from layers of red tape and administrative delay. A lot of government spending could be saved through such a simplification, and those savings could be invested in long-term economic growth.

The debate about UBI always goes next to the disincentive effects on workers: if those barely scratching out a living can get free income from the government, then they will drop out of the workforce. This is an obvious point, but one that can be easily managed by ensuring that the system retains an incentive to earn more income on top of the UBI. If some individuals drop out of the workforce, it would not upend all the other positives of UBI. Currently, those individuals are turning to far less efficient programs for various bits of uncoordinated support, which all still costs money.

The fact remains that the most important ingredient in economic growth is people, so the plethora of government policies that impact labour force participation need to be considered together, not just one such as UBI. For example, allowing more immigration is one of the most important things governments can do to boost economic growth, as it spreads government debt loads across more people and more incomes. But more importantly, immigrants are well known to have higher rates of entrepreneurialism and contribute more to economic growth than a homegrown labour force participant. The tension that arises around immigration is more on the political side; domestic workers who have been displaced from their jobs by technological change may see immigrants as scooping up the jobs that they hoped to get, thereby reinforcing income inequality and discontent.

Boosting domestic labour force participation should be a top priority for all governments. The biggest source of untapped labour force participation is women, and many connect this to what is perhaps the world's most significant social infrastructure gap—the scarcity of childcare services. Certainly, this is the case in Canada. The price index for childcare and housekeeping services in Canada has risen by around 80% over the last two decades, while the overall consumer price index has risen by half as much. Labour force participation by women is generally less than it could be, as a consequence.

To see the power of investing in daycare infrastructure, one need only consider the system created in Quebec over twenty years ago, which fostered a significant increase in female labour force participation. This single element deserves much of the credit for improved relative economic and fiscal performance in the province during the last decade. Twenty years ago, the labour force participation rate for prime-age women in Quebec was about 74%, far below the participation rate for men. The provincial government identified barriers keeping women out of the workforce and decided to reduce them, primarily by lowering the cost of childcare and extending parental leave provisions. As a result, the percentage of female labour force participation rose to the high eighties.

If similar policies were deployed Canada-wide, and the national female labour force participation rate could be boosted to near that

for men, total income in the economy could be raised significantly—
by 2% easily but possibly far more. This potential gain and the associated new tax revenues need to be considered when deciding whether
additional government investment in childcare is economically sensible. Calibrated properly, a program like this can essentially pay for
itself, given the additional revenues generated by the higher potential
output. Unfortunately, government spending on social infrastructure
is usually regarded as a fiscal outlay, not an investment. In Canada,
we have a growing number of seniors who expect to live far longer and
want to extend their participation in the workforce, and the need for
more and more care workers in the workforce, for children and for the
elderly. This combination could be turned to our advantage.

Structural government policies can very often be self-financing in
this sense, as the benefits to the macroeconomy will mean higher
growth, a bigger tax base, and increased government revenues. Rarely
is the proposition for a change in government policy put this way,
however. Often such structural changes are described as "politically
impossible"; examples from Canada include reforming supply management systems for dairy products, eggs, or chicken and liberalizing
international or interprovincial trade. This political impossibility
arises essentially because those who perceive that they would lose as a
result of the change have their voices magnified by news media and
social media and create serious political fallout for the government.
But if governments are confident that the policies would improve
economic growth, the change would create a fiscal dividend, along
with being a positive for the majority of Canadians. It is a simple
exercise to estimate those fiscal benefits and allocate some (or even all)
of them in advance to those most likely to be negatively affected,
thereby compensating those who will lose and winning the macro
argument at the political level.

A favourite area for policymakers looking to boost economic growth is to increase public investment in infrastructure. It is hard to argue with this proposition. Prioritizing these investments to add the most to economic growth is the hard part. A good guide for prioritization is to follow the flow of immigrants, investing in more infrastructure wherever the immigrants go (which is to wherever the jobs are) and to capitalize on new business opportunities, which is major urban areas. Rather than trying to persuade immigrants to locate outside of cities where there are fewer job opportunities, no diaspora, or more risk for their business idea, governments should focus their infrastructure investments in areas where the strains are showing up. By all means, invest heavily in digital infrastructure so that businesses that do not rely on agglomeration to succeed have the freedom to locate wherever they want. However, when agglomeration is important to success, government should facilitate it, not resist it.

A lot of infrastructure investments are growth enhancing and therefore have a self-financing dimension that is rarely promoted by governments. Workers who spend less time in traffic jams are more productive; firms that have access to excellent roads, ports, airports, pipelines, reliable power, and telecommunications have higher productivity than those that do not. It is rare for governments to put up these economic gains beside their infrastructure program proposals. As a result, many commentators simply criticize excessive government "spending."

As a case study, consider that it took building the Canadian Pacific Railway to create what we call Canada today. It cost approximately $140 million to build the CPR in the early 1880s, which was equal to about 25% of Canada's national income in 1885, a gargantuan investment. That cost is equivalent to around $4 billion in 2019, but as a share of the Canadian economy, 25% today would be over $500 billion.

As to the benefits of this investment, the railway was foundational to the deals struck between the colonies to create Canada in the wake of a breakdown in U.S.-Canada trade relations in 1866. In the absence of that Confederation agreement, the natural north-south business linkages would probably have seen what is known as Canada today gradually be incorporated into the United States. Evaluating the costs and benefits of that one cross-Canada infrastructure project would need to reckon with the incalculable costs associated with never forming a country.

Policymakers can also boost productivity growth by promoting basic research and the commercialization of innovation. R&D enjoys economies of scale—more technological progress is made by pooling innovations, which efforts such as organizing and backing sectoral clusters are intended to achieve. Even during the Great Depression, some important innovations had long-term effects on our economy; companies like Dupont and GE demonstrated that maintaining investment in R&D is critical to long-term business performance. Rather than attempting to choose winners and losers in their economies, governments could make a better contribution by eliminating or lessening barriers to innovation and economic growth. This would include simplifying and clarifying land-use permitting and environmental requirements, reducing red tape, making early stage financing more available to young companies, and minimizing other legal restrictions. And, as discussed in Chapter 4, the past gains from international trade cannot be taken for granted. With every decimal point of economic growth mattering so much more than in the past, no growth-enhancing policy can be left untapped, and imposing new trade restrictions would constitute swimming against the current.

The bottom line is that governments face enormous structural challenges in the coming years, and they begin the post-pandemic period in a precarious financial position. Although it may be possible to simply service the high stock of debt and watch the ratio of debt to national income decline slowly, many governments will want to do better than this—to rebuild fiscal capacity to prepare for future demands. I believe that those demands will be sizeable, and every effort to boost economic growth will need to be made, whether politically challenging or not.

Dealing with Rising Risk

The foregoing discussion has been about the structural demands that will be placed on governments in the future, and how governments might respond. I now turn to a different issue, but one that is no less challenging: the episodic demands for support that governments will face in response to the rising tide of risk that will be thrown up by the tectonic forces. When major economic convulsions occur—as seen during the pandemic—it falls to governments and central banks to cushion the blow for individuals and companies. This is a form of insurance that uses resources, too.

The history of using government stabilization policies to iron out fluctuations in the economy when it is disturbed is relatively short. This part of economics was advanced first by John Maynard Keynes during the Great Depression and put into regular practice after World War II. Accordingly, the entire history of stabilization policies overlaps with the postwar baby boom. What this means is that governments and central banks have almost always been able to rely upon new economic growth, fuelled by a growing workforce from below, to resume after a recession.

In that very basic sense, the next age of uncertainty may prove to be especially fraught for policymakers because there will be more and larger fluctuations in the economy to iron out, along with the rising fiscal burdens described in the previous section.

As policymakers have learned, some past crises have led to the reinvention of economics itself, such as when both unemployment and inflation rose simultaneously in the 1970s. The lessons from the Global Financial Crisis were applied very well during the COVID-19 crisis. There were some lessons learned from this crisis, too, that no doubt will carry forward into the post-pandemic world.

One key lesson from the COVID-19 episode is that fiscal policy is more effective when it kicks in automatically, instead of the usual long implementation lag. In the U.S., there were hot debates in both houses of Congress about how fiscal tools should be deployed during the pandemic, leaving the Federal Reserve to shoulder much of the stabilization burden in the early months of the crisis. Canada performed relatively well in this sense, but there were still meaningful lags in implementation of support programs. Importantly, the design of Canada's main fiscal tools during the pandemic—making them elastic, or responsive, to the underlying conditions—was a major step forward in fiscal effectiveness. Employment insurance was always intended to be an automatic stabilizer in this sense, although it operates with more of a lag than some of the programs put in place during the pandemic. In contrast, in the U.S., as the second wave of COVID-19 hit the economy, there was a completely new political cycle of debate before a second wave of government support could be rolled out. Maintaining a higher degree of automaticity in future fiscal frameworks would reduce the load on monetary policy over time.

Another key fiscal learning from the pandemic is that even though an emergency may dictate that the standard fiscal accountability framework around debt and deficit objectives be set aside temporarily, there is still a fundamental need for one. Governments need to offer continuous insight into the fiscal future to help markets form expectations. After all, governments are asking investors to finance expenditures of previously unimagined scale. At a minimum, governments must lay out a credible fiscal plan, showing the likely paths for government indebtedness and how it will be financed, regardless of how bad the situation may look. Offering good and bad scenarios to complement the base scenario is also good practice. Given this framework, the minimum requirement for fiscal sustainability is to make a commitment to stabilizing the ratio of debt to national income or gradually lowering it from its peak as economic growth picks up. This commitment would translate into near-term objectives for government spending and the fiscal deficit.

In terms of monetary policy, the lessons from the Global Financial Crisis played a key role in defusing the COVID-19 economic crisis quickly. Central banks deployed their full array of market intervention tools rapidly and in force, whereas during 2008 the response was more sequential. Further, many countries made use of negative interest rates. Prior to the 2007–08 Global Financial Crisis, it was widely believed that the lower bound for interest rates was zero, or even slightly above zero. However, central banks in many countries have pushed short-term interest rates below zero, and rates on government bonds have followed, shattering this previously held view. The concept of paying interest in order to borrow is so deeply ingrained in us that many find it hard to wrap their minds around a negative rate of interest. There is nothing natural about a negative rate, as the underlying natural rate of interest is a measure of impatience, which remains a human characteristic. But in extraordinary conditions, moving rates below zero can provide more stimulus to the economy. Because banks borrow and lend long, what matters most to the functioning of the financial system and the supply of credit is the spread between the rates at which banks borrow and lend. Provided that there is a reasonable spread, banks continue to do the job. Moving central bank rates below zero pulls lending rates down even further and encourages households and firms to borrow and spend, thereby helping the economy climb out of a recession.

Nowadays, it is understood that the effective lower bound for interest rates is related to the cost of managing cash balances—secure storage of banknotes and insurance against loss. Someone with money in a bank earning negative interest can move their funds into cash and earn zero interest instead, but needs to store the cash. Taking these storage costs into account, most research puts the effective lower bound for the nominal interest rate at around minus 0.5%, or possibly a little lower.

Regardless of the exact lower bound for rates, it is important to understand that when rates are very low, central banks have much less room to manoeuvre if something goes wrong in the economy. Consider a scenario where there is a shock to the economy, unemployment rises, and inflation appears likely to decline below a central bank's target. The authorities will push rates down to encourage more borrowing and faster growth to offset that shock. If interest rates start at, say, 4%, then the central bank can cut rates by at least four hundred basis points and give the economy a sizeable boost. But if rates start at 2%, cutting interest rates to zero will only do half as much work. The ability to cut rates below zero gives another fifty basis points of manoeuvrability.

It is usual to think of disturbances hitting the economy as symmetric around zero; in other words, over time, good and bad luck tend to average out to no luck at all. The lower interest rates are, the more likely it becomes that central banks will not be able to cut rates by enough to cushion the blow when bad luck happens. However, they have complete freedom to raise interest rates, so good luck can

be absorbed by raising rates as much as necessary. The lower bound
for interest rates introduces an asymmetry into the monetary policy
process, which could mean that the central bank is frequently unable
to achieve its inflation target when the average level of rates is low.
Central banks have other tools in their arsenal that can supplement
interest rate adjustments, such as quantitative easing, but these tools
have only second-order effects on the economy. Economic research
is pointing to a heavier use of fiscal tools to stabilize the economy in
the future, when interest rates are likely to remain low on average.
Essentially the same analysis was offered by John Maynard Keynes
in the 1930s.

Meanwhile, the tectonic force of rising household indebtedness
will continue to pose challenges for monetary policy. A high level of
private sector debt in the economy makes it more vulnerable to
downturns—a company with no debt can ride out a storm of negative
economic volatility, whereas an indebted company may be unable to
service its debt and be forced to close. High debt magnifies the consequences of a disturbance to the economy, which makes it harder for
the central bank to keep it on track. A related complication is that
prolonged low interest rates generally lead to what seems like excessive
risk taking as many actors search for yield. This applies as much to
households as it does to firms. While some cautious firms might see
low yields as a reason to walk away from investment opportunities,
others may find it necessary to reach far outside their risk comfort
zone in order to achieve what they consider to be a reasonable return
on capital. Such risk taking makes the economy highly vulnerable not
only to bad luck but to interest rate increases. The possibility that
even a modest interest rate rise could cause an outsized round of business failures and job losses can severely constrain the central bank's
ability to stick to its inflation targets.

In light of the risks associated with debt, some commentators have recommended that central banks keep interest rates higher on average, so households and firms take on less debt. However, a central bank can really only pursue its inflation objectives, while smoothing out economic fluctuations along the way. Trying to limit the rise in debt at the same time is usually a recipe for underachieving the inflation target. That is why governments and central banks have developed a suite of macroprudential tools, such as mortgage stress tests or maximum loan-to-income guidelines, to limit future vulnerabilities of the financial system and to leave the central bank to pursue its inflation targets. In the limit, a full synthesis of the trade-offs faced by the central bank—one that captures both macroeconomic (output-inflation) risk and financial risk due to debt vulnerabilities, bound together through private sector behaviour—remains an objective of economic modellers. In the meantime, a reasonable approximation can be achieved by capturing financial stability risk within the central bank's objectives, provided it is given additional tools to address them independently.

The ability of central banks to smooth out business cycles will be less in future than in the past, given the tectonic forces acting on the economy. This room to manoeuvre will decline at the same time that the volatility that policymakers need to deal with increases due to the interaction of the tectonic forces. Given this challenging environment, achieving the same degree of macroeconomic stabilization as in the past is likely to prove impossible for the central bank working alone and therefore will require fiscal policy to be unusually flexible. One way to tackle this would be to make fiscal policy more automatic, responding to variability in the economy without the need for new legislation. A universal basic income program could be designed to do exactly this. However, more automatic fiscal tools may run up against the nature of politics, where it is better to get credit for fixing a problem than to see the problem get defused automatically and still have to defend the resultant fiscal deficits. The stresses associated with sharp fluctuations in government deficits—both up and down—are likely to be even more acute given the rising baseline fiscal burden.

Managing Climate Change Risk

As discussed earlier, even if society succeeds in achieving net zero carbon emissions by 2050, climate change will continue for a long time and result in more volatile weather, with important implications for individuals, companies, banks, and insurance companies.

It is widely believed that the frequency of severe flooding events will continue to rise in the future, causing potentially catastrophic losses for individuals. Although flood insurance is available to home-owners, and may become more the norm, the insurance industry will only be able to manage damages associated with moderate flooding. Catastrophic floods will land on governments' doorsteps, which requires that governments build financial capacity for when a catastrophe does strike and they essentially have to backstop the private insurance industry. Flood management infrastructure will also need to be strengthened to mitigate this risk.

An even more profound climate change risk is the possibility of severe water shortages in certain parts of the world. Given the uneven distribution of water on Earth, countries that have the most renewable fresh water per capita could wield disproportionate geopolitical power in the future. Most of the top countries according to this metric are small with small populations, but Canada is the largest, with the largest volume of fresh water in absolute terms of any country. A lot of this water is shared with the U.S., in the Great Lakes and the St. Lawrence basin.

It is worth thinking about the role this massive stock of fresh water might play in a global competition, or even a war, over water. Many consider the stock of water as a natural endowment and are highly protective of it, while others see it as a shared common resource. Setting aside the always contentious stock of water, there is still room to discuss the flow. The St. Lawrence basin alone, which contains the Great Lakes, most of which straddle the Canada-U.S. border, accounts for about 25% of the world's stock of fresh water. Huge amounts of water are drawn from the Great Lakes, but an amount approaching one trillion litres (over 250 billion gallons) of fresh water flushes out the St. Lawrence River into the salty Atlantic Ocean every day. This outflow is wasted, given that it becomes undrinkable the instant it enters the Atlantic. Its use by others ought not to be contentious at all. That flow alone could sustain up to ten billion people at the WHO's minimum daily water requirement. That is the projected population of the world in 2050.

The outflow from the St. Lawrence could decline over the next thirty years as population around the Great Lakes grows. Climate change could also affect the flow, although it is not clear whether it would increase or decrease. In any case, it would be possible to capture the wasted water before it spilled into the Atlantic to make it available for other uses. It could be captured by giant tanker ships that transport it to dry parts of the world, the same way we transport oil today. Alternatively, the water could be captured and fed into a pipeline to irrigate large swaths of farmland that could go dry due to climate change in the Canadian and American Midwest. In practical terms, it would make no difference if the water were piped from Lake Superior to farms and communities to the west and southwest.

Provided that there was still a substantial flow out the St. Lawrence, we would be assured that the stock of fresh water remains intact.

While engineers might be able to manage the water problem, the associated politics could be convulsive. Water shortages are almost certain to arise and could become a catalyst to geopolitical upheaval. Some advance planning should take place in order to mitigate that risk. Making provisions to share the wasted water in the near future is one possible risk mitigant. Another would be for governments to invest heavily in desalination, which is linked to investments in dedicated renewable energy sources. No doubt the cost of desalination will decline over time. Yet another would be to invest heavily in rainfall capture technology, as most of the world's rainfall lands in the ocean and is therefore also wasted. However, as we have seen in other domains, knowing that there are ways to mitigate future risks does not mean that they will actually be deployed. The uncertainty will remain, and all indications are that it will rise.

I believe that the coming tectonic stresses will prove too much for the capacity of existing fiscal and monetary stabilization tools. As a consequence, there will be more volatility in business cycles, even after policymakers have made their best efforts to maintain economic and financial stability. We will experience higher volatility in inflation, unemployment, interest rates, stock markets, and exchange rates than we have seen in the past, even if government stabilization policies can be made more automatic. The result will be an environment in which it is much harder for households and firms alike to plan for the future. They will be shouldering more risk than in the past as they make everyday decisions.

The confluence of the five tectonic forces seems destined to present the most daunting risk environment in policymaking history. It will demand clarity of purpose and much political courage to manage the rising tide of risk. Policy will not be reducible to mechanical processes, whether fiscal or monetary. The critical importance of every decimal point of economic growth will demand serious attention to the structural impediments to growth that have accumulated throughout history.

The practical limitations constraining both fiscal and monetary policy, and the political challenges associated with major changes in them, suggest that policymakers will not be able to absorb all of the increase in risks that the tectonic forces will deliver. Muddling through remains a possibility, of course. But my own sense is that growing pressure from investors, whether domestic or foreign, and from employees will encourage companies to take the lead in helping individuals to cope with increased economic and financial risk when governments are unable to. This process of adaptation to rising risk is the subject of the next chapter.

13

A PRESCRIPTION FOR
THE FUTURE

Reflections: Values-Based Leadership

Soon after I became president and CEO of Export Development Canada in 2011, I was visited by a staffer who was writing an article on me for the staff magazine. They asked me what past leaders I admired and tried to emulate in my career. I have been lucky to work with some extraordinary people over the years, and naming names would run the risk of offence by omission. So in terms of leadership qualities, I had to admit that my favourites were from fictional television series: Captain Jean-Luc Picard from *Star Trek: The Next Generation* and President Jed Bartlet from *The West Wing*.

This response was seen as confirming that the new boss had a sense of humour, a trait I have never tried to suppress. But I was in fact quite serious. Both characters, Picard (played by Sir Patrick Stewart) and Bartlet (Martin Sheen), are extremely well written and possess exceptional leadership qualities. They are deep intellectuals—Bartlet's backstory even includes a Nobel Prize in economics—and face the constant challenge of being the smartest person in the room. Both occasionally fall into the hubris trap, but only temporarily. And both manage extraordinary risks as they go about their daily lives. Picard and Bartlet both wear their values on their sleeves, caring deeply about the greater good and loving their people. In return, their people would lie down in front of a train for them. These leaders bring out the best in their people by connecting with them on a very personal level and tapping into their shared sense of purpose.

The situations in *The West Wing* are rarely well defined, certainly not in a scientific way, so Bartlet tends to act on instinct and let his passions show. When Bartlet allows his frustration to boil over and launches into a tirade, his people let it happen and then speak to power and bring him back. A good example is during the first season when a U.S. military plane carrying the president's personal doctor is shot down in the Middle East. Bartlet is furious and vows to wipe the perpetrators off the face of the Earth. His team recommends a more "proportional response," but he repeatedly demands a dispro-portional one. The episode demonstrates how important it is for a leader to learn from their team and to put loftier values ahead of their own. The learning process requires considerable humility from someone as accomplished as Bartlet, something that the team appre-ciates. The process makes them more committed and loyal in the future, not less.

Captain Picard portrays a much more level-headed individual than President Bartlet, habitually keeping his emotions in check. He is a methodically consultative leader. Even with only thirty seconds before the *Enterprise* or a nearby star will explode (a situation that seems to arise with regularity), Picard polls his colleagues for sug-gestions, sharing the stress of the moment with the entire team. He knows from experience that they all share the same values and will come through for the team. The benefits of team diversity and a leader's ability to tap into that diversity are demonstrated repeatedly in the series. And when Picard hears a suggestion that might work, he does not lift a finger, only says, "Make it so!"

It seems to me that a world of rising risk will need more leaders in business like Bartlet and Picard. More focus on people and values, less on numbers. The tectonic forces mean that companies will be faced with increasingly complex volatility and risk, with direct implications for their employees, and will therefore be forced to make difficult, values-informed choices involving trade-offs. I have always been open about my values so that my leaders can anticipate them, and usually they find that they share them. The values I have tried to lead by are: (1) family first, (2) hard work and excellence for a purpose that matters and makes us proud, (3) teamwork, (4) humility, and (5) always take the high road, as the view is better from up there. When coaching my leaders, I have frequently recommended that they watch *The West Wing* for insights into values-based leadership and read the book *Make It So* by Wess Roberts and Bill Ross, based on the leadership behaviours of Jean-Luc Picard. Another favourite leadership book, also by Wess Roberts, is *Leadership Secrets of Attila the Hun*. But the main thing is just to talk—often.

Business leaders deal with incredible complexity every day. Like a driver on a long trip, their minds are on their destination, and they watch the signposts to monitor their progress, but they spend disproportionate energy on the immediate future—staying on the road, watching their speed, keeping an eye on the rear-view mirror, avoiding sudden obstacles, and so on. They are certainly aware of the five tectonic forces portrayed in this book, all of which have been in the headlines at one time or another in recent years. The purpose of this chapter is to help companies and their shareholders understand the deeper implications of this confluence of forces and how they might adapt to them.

Business Planning Scenarios

Population aging is one of the most visible of the five tectonic forces and also the most ignored. Most company leaders know the average age of their staff, particularly of their leadership group, as succession planning is a key activity of all companies. But demographics are too slow moving to be a key element of the corporation's business plan, except when they are considering investments with an extremely long life. This is unfortunate because demographics are responsible for many of the ingrained assumptions that executives and board members alike bring to the corporate planning discussion. In effect, the demographics we have experienced during our lives are sufficiently slow moving that we come to think of them almost as a constant, when they are not.

In Chapter 2, I explained that trend global economic growth is likely to remain lower than has been experienced in the past, once the contraction and rebuilding due to COVID-19 is behind us. Building a business plan on an assumption of slow future economic growth may prove to be quite contentious during 2021–22. There will be a tendency to extrapolate strong post-pandemic growth into the future, but that would be a risky assumption. A safer business planning assumption will be for a return to slow trend economic growth, with companies thinking about how their business plans can be adjusted in real time should the economy perform better than expected. With respect to inflation, it is natural and appropriate for companies to assume a return to about 2% inflation. However, given the tectonic forces, it would be advisable to also consider ways to adjust the business plan should inflation move to a higher range.

The most important implication of the tectonic forces is that there will be higher economic and financial volatility in the future. Although uncertainty is never welcome, the two-sided nature of volatility is crucial. In any given year, the world could turn out either better or worse than the company expects. Taking this added uncertainty into account is not just about choosing conservative assumptions about economic growth, inflation, or interest rates to build into the business plan. It means building more risk into the business plan from the start.

One of the best corporate tools available to manage future risk is scenario analysis. Companies build a base forecast using their best judgment and then construct alternative scenarios around that forecast. The base scenario would use familiar assumptions, such as a return to average economic growth rates, a return of inflation to 2%, and a return of interest rates to slightly above 2% for short rates, perhaps a percentage point higher than this for long-term interest rates. Alternative scenarios would then be developed around a slower economic growth trend, a recession scenario, stronger growth due to technological change, lower interest rates, higher inflation rates, and so on.

Developing a multiplicity of possible scenarios for the business will generate a range of possible outcomes for sales, prices, the necessary production capacity, employment by the firm, and so on. Plotting these various scenarios on a chart creates a cloud of possibilities fanning out into the future, with the base case scenario running down the centre. Importantly, every forecast is uncertain, but that uncertainty grows the farther into the future the forecast goes; the cloud of possibilities widens the farther into the future we look.

To account for this expanding range of possible outcomes, economists can calculate dynamic forecast errors based on their models. For example, the economist might forecast that economic growth during the next twelve months will be 2%, plus or minus 0.6%, giving a range of possibilities between 1.4% and 2.6% for the year ahead. However, if the company is considering an investment in increased production capacity that takes two years to complete, the company will want to know what economic growth will be over the next two to three years. Using the same statistical model, the economist might forecast that growth will average 2% over the next three years, but given the longer horizon they will be less certain and might provide a confidence interval of, say, plus or minus 1%. This implies a forecast for economic growth somewhere between 1% and 3% per year over the three-year planning horizon. This forecast would translate into a company sales target three years from now that is somewhere between 3% and 9% higher than sales today. Adding these expanding "zones of ignorance" around the company's assumptions for sales and price growth generates even more lines in the cloud of possible planning scenarios.

Building uncertainty into a business plan like this is hard work, and it is only the beginning. The cloud of future possibilities needs to be updated continuously to be effective as a management tool since the economy is always changing. New readings on the economy are always being released, and this has implications for the starting point of the scenarios. The company may find itself only a few months into the planning horizon when something happens to throw one of the central assumptions off track. This may invalidate some scenarios while making others more likely. A new set of scenarios should then be developed, and the business plan tweaked in real time. This update may mean deferring a planned investment, speeding one up, laying off staff, or accelerating a hiring plan. Companies that take planning and risk seriously will need dedicated staff to keep these scenarios up to date and to always be thinking about what might go wrong with them.

It has become standard practice for boards to ask management for alternative planning scenarios in the context of their annual strategic sessions. The natural response from the company is to create a baseline scenario, a "lucky" scenario, and an "unlucky" scenario. There is then a discussion of what the firm would do should either the good or bad scenario arise. This is reasonably good practice. However, it reinforces the standard notion that the range of possible outcomes near the baseline forecast is most likely, and the other possibilities fall around it in a bell curve. Especially when the lucky and unlucky scenarios seem extreme, boards quite reliably fall in love with the baseline scenario. But a central implication of the interaction of tectonic forces is that the range of possible future economic outcomes is likely to be flatter and much less bell-shaped than we have seen in the past. The bad and good scenarios have higher probabilities of occurring than in the past, because the tectonic forces are in motion. As a consequence, falling in love with the baseline scenario will become an increasingly risky strategy for any company.

Hurdle Rates for New Investments

The trajectory of population aging also implies a future with continued low, and possibly declining, risk-free real interest rates. It is astonishing that so few companies have embraced the reality of low-for-long real rates of return when it comes to making investment decisions. I still routinely hear that companies or their boards require the same minimum, risk-adjusted rate of return that they always have, before approving a new investment. This minimum rate of return on a new proposal is commonly referred to as the "hurdle rate," as it represents a barrier that the proposal must exceed to pass muster.

It is a given that investment opportunities with high risk-adjusted returns should be snapped up by a company. Economists believe that the forces of competition in the marketplace will lead a company to exploit all such opportunities; otherwise another firm would do so. What that means is that all the low-hanging fruit in that sector has already been picked. If a firm has capital available for new investments, those investments must compete with the next best place to put the money, including paying down debt or buying back the firm's shares. Hypothetically, if the firm is paying 5% to borrow, whether from the bond market or from a bank, then any new investment opportunity needs to deliver at least 5%—and to do so after adjusting for the risks associated with that new investment—for the project to beat the hurdle rate. Adjusting an investment for risk is a complex task, entailing all the analysis discussed above around the business plan. The firm needs to develop a new plan that incorporates the new investment and captures the potential downside risks that could damage the business case between now and its completion. Supposing that analysis suggests that the new investment should deliver a 10% return, plus or minus 4%, then the worst-case scenario of a 6% return would beat the hurdle rate.

Importantly, the hurdle rate is not the rate of interest that prevails today, but the rate the firm expects to prevail when the project is complete, and on average thereafter. It is a very long-term concept. Managers often use the risk-free rate of interest that has prevailed on average for the last few years as a proxy for the hurdle rate. Others have a hurdle rate that has been the firm's internal standard for a long time.

Looking at today's extremely low interest rates, a company could be forgiven for believing that there will be much higher interest rates three to five years from now. The firm may not be able to find any investment opportunities that meet its criteria. Indeed, in a world of declining real interest rates, a company with a hurdle rate that is too high may hesitate to invest repeatedly, because it assumes that rates of return will recover to historical levels. This can lead a company to dither into irrelevance, as other companies—ones that understand that real interest rates are likely to remain low on average for the next thirty years—snap up those investments and outperform dithering firms. This behaviour has almost certainly contributed to low investment rates in many economies in recent years. Improving our understanding of these fundamentals is crucial to a resumption of business investment and long-term economic growth.

Risk Management: The New Intangible Investment

As the five tectonic forces build and interact, the risks faced by firms will continue to increase. Low real interest rates and the accumulation of debt are reducing the room to manoeuvre for central banks, which will translate into higher variability in economic growth and employment than enjoyed in the last thirty years. Technological progress will be highly disruptive for firms and force a steady flow of individuals to shift occupations, boosting inequality and giving rise to highly unpredictable politics. Green tilts by governments will mean constantly changing business parameters as firms attempt to reposition themselves for a lower-carbon economy. Rising inequality may give rise to continued pressures to deglobalize companies' value chains and to sudden shifts in international trade rules. The combinations that can generate sudden bouts of economic and financial volatility are endless. As argued in the previous chapter, it is unlikely that central banks and governments, especially in light of polarized politics, will be able to shoulder all this additional risk on behalf of companies and their employees.

I believe that much of the burden of higher economic volatility and risk will be borne by companies. Successful companies will need to bring enhanced risk management to the table to survive, maintain jobs for their employees, and deliver superior returns for shareholders. In short, effective risk management will become a key channel of value creation in firms.

Imagine two firms competing with one another, both considering a business expansion in expectation of higher future demand. Both see that the risks in the business environment are higher than in the past, as there has been recent and unusual volatility. Their forecasts of higher demand for their services are more uncertain than they are accustomed to. They both have capital modernization plans in place, but technology is changing daily. Politics have become highly unpredictable.

In this setting, companies and their boards will want to allow for higher risk in the investment proposals they are considering, so will demand a tighter and stronger business case than in the past. The first firm believes that real interest rates will move back up to their average over the last ten years during the life of the project. The second firm understands, however, that aging population effects will keep real interest rates low and rates might even drift lower over the life of the project. The result is that the first firm does not approve the project, while the second goes ahead, and the numbers work out well for the second firm, its employees, and its shareholders.

Consider the same two firms again, but this time suppose they both understand the likely evolution of real interest rates over the life of the project. The first firm has a standard risk management framework, including a chief risk officer who surveys staff each year and provides an annual report to the board demonstrating management's understanding of risks. Board members offer their own perceptions of risks that the chief risk officer may have missed, and all leave satisfied that the corporate plan can withstand the risks that have been identified.

The second firm has made much more significant investments in risk management. They, too, have a chief risk officer, but this one has an entire department of risk experts, and they have worked through the organization to develop a risk culture that makes it resilient and nimble. They have developed the capability to produce rapid and continuously updated scenario planning, they have optimized the firm's liquidity policies, and front-line workers have desktop tools to help them make risk-aware decisions. Every employee takes personal responsibility for managing risk, acting like the shareholders they are, understanding that they represent the first line of defence against all forms of risk to the firm. Unusual risk events are promptly shared at regular team meetings—which always have "risk observations" as the last item on the agenda—and these learnings are sent up the chain to the risk department, which is the second line of defence. The second line shares these insights across the organization and adjusts risk policies, if necessary, to cover the new risk that has popped up. The board has the benefit of in-depth discussions of new and emerging risks with the chief risk officer and the internal auditor, the third line of defence. The internal auditor can rely on this strong risk culture and spends most of their time anticipating future shifts in the firm's risk environment and alerting management and the board to these trends in real time.

Given this accumulated risk expertise, the second firm will be better at managing risks in general, and risky investments in particular. The first firm may look at an investment opportunity and believe it can generate a return of 10%, plus or minus 5%, and decline the opportunity. The second firm, with its superior risk management capability, sees the same opportunity with a likely return of 10%, but plus or minus

3%, and therefore makes the investment because the worst-case scenario still beats their hurdle rate. The second firm grows and delivers better returns to their shareholders. After a few years of this behaviour, the second firm will have established a reputation for turning risk into opportunity, and investors will bid up their value accordingly.

Notice that the money spent on staff involved in risk management by the second company is not classified as investment, even though it generates returns long into the future. Investments in risk management capacity have clear parallels with other forms of investment in successful firms. Companies make incremental investments in their employees and in their computer systems all the time. They build up IT teams to maintain their technology investments, but those teams also spend time developing unique in-house applications of new technology that bring more value to customers and the firm. Employees whose training is constantly being refreshed are nimbler and more productive, which also generates more value for customers and the firm. These benefits extend out long into the future. Although this activity has all the hallmarks of investment, it is usually accounted for as a simple expense.

In their 2018 book *Capitalism without Capital*, Jonathan Haskel and Stian Westlake examine a growing body of evidence on the role of "intangible investment" in delivering value to shareholders. Intangible investment is exactly what it sounds like: investment in the form of knowledge or other soft ingredients of corporate success that pay dividends into the future. These investment streams include research and development, new patents, brand advertising, employee training, and the development of the international relationships that underpin global value chains. My contention is that the next age of uncertainty will come to see investment in risk management as a recognized channel of value creation by firms—the next big important avenue of intangible investment.

Consider a firm that relies on global supply chains for production and distribution of its products. How is this firm to manage the risk of arbitrary trade protectionism that forces it to deglobalize its supply chain? One option is to simply deglobalize as a defensive measure, although it is widely understood that this would significantly increase production costs and prices. Most companies, when forced to reshore their activities to a higher-wage locale, use the opportunity to increase automation, thereby creating far fewer jobs domestically than hoped by the policymakers trying to reshore the activity. Since this is a recipe for a very expensive product, with limited demand, firms are more likely to maintain their global supply chains but take actions to de-risk them. This would include developing redundancies in supply chains, by duplicating suppliers in more than one country, especially in countries with trade agreements in place. Such value chain reoptimization costs money, but it should be viewed as an intangible investment in risk management. Importantly, the optimal response will vary by company—globalization is not an either/or proposition but a full menu of optionality.

Haskel and Westlake show that intangible investment has been growing in importance in the economy, roughly in line with technological progress. For the U.S. economy, for example, ordinary investment in machinery, equipment, and premises has been drifting down as a share of the total economy, while intangible investment has been rising steadily, especially since the late 1990s. In recent years, intangible investment has begun to exceed traditional capital investment. It is normally treated as an expense on the income statement, whereas capital investment is treated as an asset on the balance sheet. Therefore, companies that invest heavily in intangibles will appear to have lower earnings and a lower book value than companies that do not.

Now, consider what happens when one firm takes over another. Suppose a company that has been making years of strategic intangible investments and is perceived in the marketplace to be very valuable is sold to another company. The acquiring firm will pay a premium over book value, with the difference attributed to "goodwill" on the merged entity's balance sheet. It is in the moment of purchase that the market's estimate of the value of accumulated intangible investment is crystallized. In contrast, companies that are quietly investing in intangible capital on their own and are never acquired may perform sufficiently well that it looks like a mystery.

Besides pointing to weakness in some of the typical measures of firm performance favoured by investors, and measures of investment and productivity favoured by national statisticians, these observations point to the difficulty that firms face in coping with new technology. If investors do not recognize intangible investment for what it may be worth to the company, it can be even more difficult for the firm to step up and deploy a new technology. In other words, market focus on short-term earnings results may also be partly responsible for recent low rates of capital investment and a preference for share buy-backs over organic growth. It seems to me that only ultra-transparent, standardized accounting can offset this tendency.

Increasing Scale Is Natural

An important characteristic of intangible capital is that it can benefit large firms disproportionately. This is in contrast to tangible capital, such as machinery, which can only be used in a single plant. A company that invests heavily in its brand, for example, can spread the benefits of that investment across all of its operations anywhere in the world. The same can be said for investment in R&D, patents, and other forms of intellectual property. As argued in the preceding section, this would also apply to investments in risk management capability.

The growing importance of intangible investment is reinforcing the trend toward large-scale companies. This is most obvious in technology companies where a single innovation can cause a firm to explode in scale and in market value. Situations like this can make increasing scale of the firm so natural that it produces a monopoly—a single firm that owns an entire market space. Think of the global reach of Microsoft's operating systems in the vast majority of personal computers.

Historically, firms that grow to dominate their market have attracted one of two policy responses: forced corporate breakups or close regulation. Examples include banking, electricity providers, and telecommunications companies. All of these industries can earn a higher rate of return the bigger they become. When governments force companies to break up or impose regulations around their maximum scale, the result is often a market being divided among a small number of large players, each with a lot of market power. This situation is called an oligopoly, of which the Canadian banking system is an obvious example. Market power means high profitability, and some may argue that such firms should be cut down to size to promote more competition, lower pricing for consumers, and lower profitability. Others value the stability that comes with an oligopoly—if there is a cost to consumers because of a low level of competition, there may also be benefits to the overall economy.

Modern economies are evolving toward a less equal sharing of national income. Growth leadership has gone from the tangible economy to the intangible, from goods to services, and there are natural forces leading to larger firms and higher concentration in their respective markets. This reinforces the likelihood that the next wave of technological progress will benefit the few over the many and worsen income distribution further. This fertile ground for interventionist politics introduces yet another wild card into an already volatile business environment.

If Governments Cannot, Companies Will

It is well within the capability of governments to address the income inequality issue directly. It requires adjusting the income tax system to ensure it is more progressive, or perhaps deploying some form of universal basic income, funded through taxes on the highest income brackets, while allowing large firms to flourish and keep innovating. Political reality often stands in the way, however, and leads to suboptimal policies that address symptoms rather than causes. As politics becomes increasingly polarized, with all sides pumped up by social media, true compromises have become exceedingly rare. Since at a political level all policy alternatives appear unattractive, it seems to me that it will fall to firms to mitigate the risk of rising income inequality.

This could take many forms, but one possible candidate is "stakeholder capitalism," a term coined by the World Economic Forum. The basic notion is that companies take account of the objectives of all their stakeholders, not just their shareholders. The U.S.-based Business Roundtable is a concrete example, representing some two hundred companies employing nearly nineteen million people. The growing importance of environmental, social, and governance (ESG) accountability in the corporate objectives and reporting of all companies reflects these same pressures. This trend has given rise to a debate between those who think society would be better off if corporations continued to operate only for their shareholders, and those who think a broader set of corporate objectives that includes ESG is essential.

I believe that this debate would not even exist in a balanced framework in which ESG was appropriately managed by government as a public good, corporations were dedicated to shareholders only, and shareholders who wanted to do more for society could do so on their own. The growing importance of ESG in the corporate world represents the failure of politics to deliver the right balance of policies. Many companies probably believe that by filling this void, and satisfying the demands of the majority, they can reduce criticism and remove some of the impetus for political leaders to undertake ill-informed or self-destructive policies. In other words, investing in ESG is a form of risk management for firms.

The Edelman Trust Barometer, which measures trust in NGOs, business, government, and media, supports this line of reasoning. It shows that income inequality is reducing trust in our societies, and that the level of distrust is far higher among the mass population than it is among the informed public. There is a far higher level of trust in Canada compared to the U.S., but Canada barely makes it into the neutral zone, nevertheless. Fully 56% of respondents in the world say that capitalism as it exists today does more harm than good. Little wonder then, that firms are embracing wider ESG goals.

Some commentators have sniffed at the ESG trend, arguing that companies should stick to their knitting while governments stick to theirs. This would be fine if governments could get their knitting done and the population could trust them to make coherent judgments, but trusting those outcomes to the cut and thrust of politics seems naive. Companies are reacting in a rational way to pressures that could, if ignored, lead to their destruction. They are evolving in the best interests of their shareholders, not to mention their employees. In short, devoting company resources to ESG goals is not altruism in the end, even if it begins that way.

That is not to say that profitability no longer matters. Indeed, it constitutes table stakes in the broader corporate game. Investor enforcement can be very powerful. Companies that do not meet societal standards on the ESG front will be left out of managed portfolios, their stock prices will fall, and their cost of capital will rise. But the same may be true if a company decides to get too far out in front of society in its ESG commitments. Companies need to balance profitability and ESG responsibilities, with society setting the pace through the market enforcement mechanism.

In this broader framework, employees are a very important group. As discussed earlier, employees are highly vulnerable to the increased economic and financial volatility that is coming. Central banks' ability to smooth out economic fluctuations will certainly be less than in the past. Debt-burdened governments, trying to satisfy everyone but meeting the demands of almost no one, are unlikely to build a social safety net that is up to the task. My contention is, as with the other dimensions of risk set out above, that companies will see it as their business to shoulder much of this burden. There are obvious benefits to the firm, and firms that deal with these issues well should be recognized by investors. Corporate leaders who wear their values on their sleeves—like Jean-Luc Picard and Jed Bartlet—will find it natural to embrace ESG goals for the corporation.

Addressing employees' risks will naturally take the form of an expansion of human capital investments that high-performing firms already have in place. This is intangible capital of the most personal form. But what about the economic and financial volatility that the tectonic forces will deliver to employees? Job insecurity, the declining affordability of homes, volatile interest rates—all things that matter dearly to the well-being of employees—are candidate issues for attention from companies. A company that manages unemployment risk on behalf of its employees—keeping them on and offering retraining if a job is disrupted by technology, for example—will have an obvious recruitment advantage over firms that do not. If labour unions make a comeback, as hypothesized in Chapter 10, firms will feel pressured to reduce the risks their employees face from two directions; even if their employees are not unionized, the firm may wish to act in such a way as to pre-empt union certification. The same argument applies to daycare for children, an infrastructure gap that most governments have done relatively little to close; as childcare is a pressing issue for employees in the most important stage of their career, it seems a natural issue for companies to address.

In an aging society, talented and engaged employees will be scarce, not plentiful, and firms will see it in their interests to retain them, through thick and thin, and shareholders will probably agree, assuming that employee retention translates into better company performance. Balanced values-based management of firms will translate into higher stock prices, the ultimate determinant of success.

Given the importance of housing to employees, and the magnitude of the financial risks related to it, I think it is not a stretch to imagine companies backstopping mortgages for their employees, or even offering those mortgages directly. Backstopping a mortgage would entail the company standing behind its employee and covering their mortgage payments (or equivalently guaranteeing a minimum income) should employment be disrupted. As home ownership becomes increasingly expensive and beyond the reach of more families, companies might even find it advantageous to develop employee housing directly, perhaps even building employee communities. Housing could be part of the pay packet or based on a co-ownership model that allowed the employee to build up equity in their home. After all, a large company is much better placed to absorb interest rate risk and housing price risk

than is an individual. Such a residential plan would represent a form of
golden handcuffs intended to retain employees long-term.

Indeed, labour mobility may already have peaked. Perhaps there
will be a renaissance of the concept of lifetime commitment to one
firm, fostered by a more caring approach to employment by leading
companies. Firms may take responsibility for training and retraining,
and retraining again, through a person's career, tapping into public
programs as appropriate, while absorbing many of the other economic and financial risks faced by their employees.

At a minimum, companies will need to develop fuller transparency around their investments in these various forms of intangible
capital, so that investors can appropriately recognize them. Measures
of ESG performance will need to be constructed, standardized, published, and monitored, and ideally compensation policies should be
based on measured success. In the early stages, companies may be able
to claim to be practising ESG by pointing to charitable giving—a
percentage of profit is set aside for doing public good, and the company seeks recognition for that spending. But this is a long way from
integrating ESG policies and practices into the organization's DNA
and offering measures of performance and compensation incentives
around those practices.

Reporting a carbon footprint is a perfect example of transparency,
and setting out specific plans for reducing that footprint is the next
logical step. This level of transparency needs to rise substantially to
avoid situations where investors can only classify firms as "green" or
"not green." Life is full of shades of green, but it takes too much work
for investors to discern all those shades. Full and standardized reporting of carbon footprints and exposure to climate change risk will be
needed, and the G7 countries are advancing that agenda. As difficult
as that may seem to get right, it will be easy compared to such

governance issues as workplace diversity, embedding environmental criteria in decision-making, and worker and human rights, especially if the company is operating in a foreign country. The company cannot simply state its principles; it needs to measure performance against those standards so that it can be compared to other companies.

In the end, every risk confronted by a publicly traded firm amounts to a reputation risk, since errors are so visible to fast-moving markets. Investors generally trust the CEO to guard the reputation of the firm, to equate it to their own. Developing a rigorous risk management structure means spreading that ownership all the way to the front-line employee. New structures of governance will probably emerge from this line of reasoning. Stakeholder advisory boards, greater involvement of unions, board seats reserved for specific constituencies, and the widespread adoption of values-based leadership are obvious avenues for the future.

Every new element of volatility or risk raised in this book will end up in the corporate boardroom to some degree. It is through the construct of the firm that humans organize themselves around the economy and financial markets. Firms use teamwork to create economic growth and sustain meaningful occupations for people. By extension, every one of those elements matters to the investor.

Managing the increase in economic and financial volatility I am predicting would seem to be the natural province of governments. Through optimal design, governments can do a lot to insure the economy against risk, but it would be fanciful to assume that perfect risk management can emerge from a process as idiosyncratic as politics. The increased risk of the future needs to land somewhere, and it is my contention that firms will need to shoulder it and will see it is in their best interests to do so. Those who do it well will deliver for their shareholders. Just as firms now compete with one another for talent with fancy coffee machines, in-house gyms, and relaxation rooms, the combination of rising risks and a shortage of skilled workers will lead firms to invest more in risk management, not just for themselves but on behalf of their employees.

This may sound feasible for large, multinational companies with big bottom lines but much more of a stretch for smaller companies, which employ the majority of workers in most economies. However, there is little to prevent large insurance companies or other private sector entities from creating risk management umbrellas that smaller companies can operate under, in a manner analogous to how small companies provide health benefits today, working through an insurance company. In short, the situation will demand that companies do more about the S part of ESG. Investors will be the ultimate judge of the outcome.

CONCLUSION

Reflections: Starting a New Era

It was Sunday, July 18, 2004. I headed out early for a round of golf with my good friend Glen. It was a beautiful day, but you could tell it would be a hot one. At around 11:30 a.m., we came to the twelfth hole, which presents as uphill the entire way with a plateau at around the 150 to 200 yard zone. My tee shot landed on the plateau, on the right side; my friend's shot was further up and on the left side.

It was a tough climb up the hill. I was breathing heavily, and as I arrived at my ball, I started to feel dizzy. I sat down on the ground for a moment until the world stopped spinning. I stood up again and as I was reaching for my 5-iron, Glen called over to ask if I was okay. I remember saying no, and that is the last thing I can recall.

Glen was qualified in first aid. By the time he reached me, I was turning grey, and he could detect no heartbeat or breath sounds. He yelled to the group waiting down on the tee box to call for help and began CPR. In less than a minute, I leapt to my feet and reached for my 5-iron again, but golf was done for the day. The course manager collected me in a golf cart, and we waited for the ambulance in the air-conditioned pro shop. The woman working the counter told me how lucky I was, as her husband had died of a heart attack on that same twelfth hole several years prior. For some reason, I did not find this very reassuring.

I had been diagnosed with a bicuspid aortic valve twenty years earlier, and it was being checked annually. A bicuspid valve has two flaps that open and close with every heartbeat, rather than the normal three flaps. It is a congenital defect that develops in the womb; attitudes toward smoking during pregnancy were different in the 1950s, as mentioned in chapter 2. The valve's capacity diminishes over time and eventually can pose a significant risk. I had known about the risk for twenty years and had always considered it to be too low to think about. But a tiny force was raising the risk over time, and it manifested that day when it collided with others—a hill too steep, an especially hot day—and caused a life-changing event.

About eight weeks later, I had a prosthetic stainless steel aortic valve installed, and eight weeks after that, I was back on the chief economist speaking circuit again. People ask if I had a glimpse of the afterlife, or if I saw the legendary lights. I'm afraid not. I have zero memory after my shutdown and only recall the sensation of climbing up out of a very deep sleep and feeling highly energized.

But the event did change me, just as a black swan reframes all subsequent history and alters perceptions of risk. I became less of a perfectionist and more interested in people. I am acutely aware of everything I would have missed were it not for the prompt actions of my friend, and a superb team of doctors—from our kids growing up and partnering up, to the joys of grandchildren, to having my signature on Canada's money, to sitting on the dock with the prime minister at Harrington Lake. Every day since then has felt like a gift, and I find it difficult not to be optimistic about the future. The irony is that it was a major piece of bad luck that helped me frame the future in a more positive way.

I entered a new era that day and it showed. The media called me "Sunny Steve" soon after I became governor. There is no question that I approach economics with a strong faith in Mother Nature, whose forces are always reconstructive, tending to bring the economy back home over time. In a world where economists are prone to emphasizing the negative, I am a nagging contrarian.

I believe that the global economy is also entering a new era, with the separation between the new and the old punctuated by the tragedy of the COVID-19 pandemic. I call it the next age of uncertainty.

The fear we felt when the pandemic struck made other troubles fade into the background, but they have not gone away. Everyone could see that economic instability was already on the rise long before COVID-19 came along. This was due to the growing influence of tectonic forces operating beneath the surface of the global economy, tectonic forces that will interact with and magnify one another in the years ahead. The five forces identified here—population aging, technological progress, growing inequality, rising debt, and climate change—will generate economic and financial earthquakes in the future. The only certainty will be greater uncertainty.

People naturally loathe uncertainty, so this prognosis will sound very negative to many. However, there is considerable room for optimism about the future. We are witnessing tremendous technological progress that will increase longevity, improve living standards, and mitigate climate change. Life will get better, as it did for this generation and the ones that came before.

Pessimists will disagree, for history has demonstrated repeatedly that human progress is never shared equally. It is true that the spoils first go to the inventors, their companies, and their investors. Only in the second round, when those income gains are spent on all the usual things, is there a general rise in prosperity, a tide that lifts all boats. History demonstrates that this always happens eventually. It also demonstrates that it happened more quickly in the Second Industrial Revolution than in the first, and even more quickly in the third. Good policymaking should make the Fourth Industrial Revolution go even better, if politics permits. Certainly, there is considerable room for hope.

Even so, the five tectonic forces are growing in strength and will interact in unpredictable ways in the coming age. Life will become riskier, as economic and financial volatility will be higher, adding new layers of uncertainty to daily decisions. This means that although life will keep getting better, it will be improving only on average because economic and financial volatility will intrude more often and at greater scale. Knowing that the average individual is enjoying improvements in living standards is of little consolation if you happen to be one of the unlucky ones, helping to offset the experience of the lucky ones.

Driven by inexorable long-term natural forces acting in combination, this increase in economic risk cannot simply be erased or wished away. Understanding the five tectonic forces helps provide more coherent explanations for some important chaotic events of the past. These include the Victorian depression of the late 1800s, the Great Depression of the 1930s, the stagflation of the 1970s, the Asian financial crisis of 1997, and the Global Financial Crisis of 2008. Each of these events has been blamed on various drivers, many of them proximate and relatively superficial. The deeper explanation offered here, based on a common set of tectonic forces, means that stresses can build for a long time before a minor event catalyzes a cascade of economic and financial volatility. It is normal to blame a crisis on the catalyst rather than the underlying natural forces.

This new interpretation of history also means that is probably not possible to prevent future crises by correcting one or two factors that contributed to past ones. Other tectonic forces will still be acting beneath the surface, and their confluence will still have chaotic potential. However, history shows that policymakers can at least learn from each major economic episode and become better at their craft. Fixing elements that contributed to past crises is unlikely to prevent future ones, but there is hope that crisis management will continue to improve. To complete the metaphor, we can construct buildings that are more resilient to earthquakes and have contingency plans in place, but we cannot prevent earthquakes from happening.

The rising tide of risk will have significant consequences for people, upending their financial decisions. Both central banks and governments will face tighter constraints on their ability to manage economic fluctuations. For central banks, the persistence of low interest rates will limit their room to manoeuvre. For governments, the rising fiscal burdens associated with an aging population, combined with the massive debts incurred while fighting the global pandemic, will mean a tighter scope for stabilization policies. And yet the economic fluctuations they regularly face will be more frequent and larger than in the past.

In this context, everyone needs to think more about the future of inflation. There is every reason to expect major central banks to remain committed to controlling inflation, but there is a greater risk of politics intruding on that plan. The stock of government debt offers a strong incentive for governments to lean on their central banks to allow inflation to run higher. This is particularly the case in countries with less fiscal and institutional capacity than others. But even in major economies, highly indebted households may prefer a higher inflation rate, too, and vote for politicians who say they are leaning that way.

The increase in volatility that is coming may be felt most acutely in the labour market. Spells of unemployment will be more frequent and larger, but they will be punctuated by periods when workers are in short supply. The natural rate of unemployment will be higher. The predicted high rate of job churn, technological disruption, rising inequality, and other risks being borne by workers are likely to motivate a renaissance in labour unions. Working careers will be longer, while jobs evolve continuously.

The tectonic forces point to moderate economic growth and persistently low real interest rates. This combination will favour growing household indebtedness and a continuing upward bias in house prices, absent a major change in housing supply and immigration policies. Rather than looking for ways to control or otherwise distort house prices, it would be better for governments to promote innovation in the mortgage finance sector. Many of today's norms around mortgage debt are a product of the Great Depression. Today, people live longer and work longer, and there is no reason why they cannot build up equity in their home without owning it in its entirety before they retire or die. Financing a house purchase should be as easy as leasing a motor vehicle, except that the house generally appreciates while the motor vehicle depreciates. There is a multitude of risk-sharing or co-ownership models that could be applied to mortgage finance, given the right incentives. There will be more highs and lows in interest rates, too, making the regular renewal of mortgages a riskier process. The form of mortgages offered by financial institutions will probably evolve beyond today's standard as a consequence. House prices may also be more variable, in both directions, which adds to risk for people who may need to make geographic moves for employment.

It seems a natural role for governments to protect society from rising economic risks, because reducing risk and uncertainty is for the greater public good. The tectonic forces point to economic volatility at a societal scale, for which private insurance markets are ill equipped. As a parallel, insurance companies underwrite flood insurance or earthquake insurance and often reinsure that exposure into global insurance pools, but a catastrophic natural event will always fall to governments to backstop, regardless of its source.

Even so, some governments are better at managing economic and financial risk than others. There is no question that governments have become better at it over time, as evidenced by the responses to the Third Industrial Revolution, the Global Financial Crisis, and most recently the COVID-19 pandemic. However, the challenge of dealing with economic volatility will grow, and the state of local politics and global geopolitics will make policymaking difficult. Increasingly polarized democracy, practised at maximum volume through social media, is not conducive to the sort of grand bargains or "new deals" that may be needed in the years ahead. Even if enlightened policies do float to the surface, we cannot assume that governments will have the capacity to insure society at large against increased economic risk. There are indications that some of the fiscal tools deployed during the pandemic will become permanent, which is promising. A stronger, more automatic social safety net is a helpful response to the uncertainty that lies ahead, but it will not insulate the economy from all new risks. Further, fiscal capacity is not unlimited. The rising tide of risk will place unbearable demands on policymakers, leaving the economy more volatile than before.

Fortunately, citizens have found other channels to influence their future. They see problems in the world and ask that their companies contribute to solving those problems. They have savings to invest, but they demand that companies they invest in also contribute to solving those problems. Companies increasingly see it in their best interests to put resources against those problems, especially climate change. There are also signs that companies are willing to address income inequality stresses in the absence of government intervention. I believe that this thinking will broaden in the years ahead to include a wider array of risks faced by employees.

What used to be called corporate social responsibility (CSR) is now environmental, social, and governance (ESG) accountability. Since those who practise ESG well are likely to be rewarded by ESG-aware investors and see their stock prices rise, there is no inconsistency between this practice and the adage "maximize shareholder value." Behind the scenes, the company must find the right trade-off between pure profitability and ESG-enhanced profitability, matching the trend in societal and investor sentiment. The values of the public will become the values of the firm and its leadership, and the bottom line will be maximized naturally.

While some companies may see the emergence of a broadening ESG trend as an obligation, others will see it as an opportunity to create a new competitive advantage over other firms. In a world where workers become scarcer, companies will increasingly see their employees as an asset worth protecting from rising risk. Extra investment in recruitment, retention, lifelong training, and risk management—provided they translate into improved company performance over time—should be viewed favourably by investors and be reflected in market valuations. Companies will help employees manage economic fluctuations and will see the benefit in helping them manage their biggest financial risk—housing. This could take many forms, including mortgage risk-sharing with an individual's employer, mortgages offered by employers, and even employer-provided housing. Those who invoke purist arguments that companies should stick to their knitting and let governments take care of people are drawing a false dichotomy, in my view, and will be left behind.

This book has been about identifying dynamic forces in our environment and thinking about how they will evolve into the future. It is not forecasting really, but an attempt to peek into the broad sweep of our future and become more comfortable in its anticipation. The conclusion that the future is likely to be even more volatile, and therefore even more uncertain, than the past will frustrate many. We should not be surprised to be surprised by the future.

For companies, this will mean dedicating meaningful resources to risk management. A similar conclusion was also drawn by Nassim Nicholas Taleb in *The Black Swan*. His advice was that companies should carefully protect their core business from risk but hold back some capital to invest in both defending against bad luck and in capitalizing on good luck—a reminder that volatility and risk are two-sided, even though we habitually think of risk as only applying to the downside. This means investing most of the firm's capital in the baseline business plan, investing real resources in managing or insuring against bad luck, and keeping capital in reserve to enable a quick pivot in case some good luck happens. Good luck would include such things as the emergence of a new general-purpose technology that costs real money to incorporate. Taleb calls this allocation of capital a "barbell strategy." If no good luck arrives, the capital saved may incite some regret on the part of the company, for it could have been invested in more organic growth along the baseline business plan. However, the essence of the point is that one can never regret preparing for a black swan, whether unlucky or lucky.

A useful parallel is the question of automobile insurance. Perhaps at annual renewal time, a driver regrets having paid for insurance during the past year because they did not have any accidents. In an age where uncertainty will be an order of magnitude greater than in the past, operating a company without insurance against a bad outcome or without the ability to take advantage of a positive outcome will be a very high-risk strategy. To paraphrase Donald Sull, successful companies will need not only a chief risk officer but also a chief opportunity officer.

To manage risk, many of us turn to experts for advice, so it is worth asking what this analysis may mean for economists. I believe that the five tectonic forces are shifting our economic foundations, and this will wreak havoc on the practice of economics. Today's models may have little value in the new era. This has happened to economists before when there was a similar confluence of forces in the early 1970s: the workforce was bulging with baby boomers, income inequality was rising, skyrocketing oil prices were disrupting technology, global inflation was surging, and the postwar global monetary system had broken down. Economists struggled to understand the new reality of the 1970s. John Kenneth Galbraith's 1977 book *The Age of Uncertainty* explained why, and *The Next Age of Uncertainty* explains why they will do so again, fifty years later.

Just as the residents of Bali, Indonesia, have adapted to the ever-present risk of a major earthquake, so, too, will we adapt to a riskier world. Our economy is evolving in real time in response to the growing risks posed by the five tectonic forces. This is Mother Nature at work. Among other things, the evident power of green investing, the emergence of ESG accountability, the Business Roundtable, and other forms of stakeholder capitalism all stand as evidence of the ability of humans to adapt to the next age of uncertainty and prosper. History demonstrates that humanity has a right to be optimistic about the future, for there is no challenge that cannot be overcome with hard work and ingenuity.

ACKNOWLEDGMENTS

Over the years of leading two outstanding organizations, I have been extraordinarily lucky to know and to work with great people. The biggest risk of trying to thank everyone that played a role in getting me to where I am today, is that I will inevitably forget many important contributors. Best that I appeal to the core premise of the book: that we all represent the cumulation of many random events, encounters, and decisions, and changing any one of them would have taken us to a very different place from where we find ourselves today. So, thank you, everybody—hopefully I have paid it forward often enough to balance the books!

The idea for this book first came to fruition in a lecture I delivered at the Spruce Meadows Changing Fortunes Round Table in Calgary in 2019. Two top researchers working at the Bank of Canada, Thomas Carter and Jacob Dolinar, helped me with the background research for that lecture, and a host of other colleagues commented on my work. Carolyn Wilkins and Jill Vardy deserve special thanks for their counsel. Given the high-quality participants that Spruce Meadows attracts, I left convinced that I could turn my little lecture into this book. I thank Nancy Southern and the entire Southern family for inviting me to test my ideas at their world-class forum and for their generous hospitality, year after year.

Writing a book is a lonely and selfish enterprise which often involves long days of effort stolen from family, friends, and other pursuits, overshadowed by a reluctance to discuss it in fear that it could be for naught. This experience was shared with characteristic tolerance by my partner of over 50 years, Valerie, without whose loving support, wise advice, and unending patience, none of it would have happened.

Once the hurdle of admitted purpose has been cleared and a book begins to take shape, getting it into the reader's hands requires some good luck and a lot of professional help. The talented and energetic Amanda Lang at BNN Bloomberg, with whom I have enjoyed collaborating for 20 or so years, kindly read my first version and responded with enthusiasm. She introduced me to her literary agent, Rick Broadhead, who was kind enough to take me on. Rick worked tirelessly to help me understand the publishing world and to get my book into a pair of sure hands. These hands belong to Nick Garrison at Penguin Canada, who embraced my ideas and helped me give them more oxygen so I could explain them more clearly. David Detomasi at the Smith School of Business at Queen's University also read an early version and provided valuable commentary. Thank you to copy editor Crissy Calhoun and the Penguin editorial team who made very important contributions to the final product, especially Alanna McMullen. And everyone in the Penguin creative group, who worked so hard to capture the essence of my thinking in the book jacket, all deserve medals.

Over the years, I have grown accustomed to being surrounded by bright and dedicated people who have challenged me, done most of the hard work, and kept me out of trouble. In contrast, this post-retirement pandemic project required a return to self-sufficiency, so I take full responsibility for all errors.

BIBLIOGRAPHY

Bernanke, B. 2012. *The Federal Reserve and the Financial Crisis.* Princeton, NJ. Princeton University Press.

Carney, M. 2021. *Value(s).* Toronto. Signal.

Chellaney, B. 2013. *Water, Peace and War.* Lanham, MD. Rowman & Littlefield.

Diamond, J. 1997. *Guns, Germs, and Steel.* New York. W.W. Norton and Company.

Edelman. 2020. *Edelman Trust Barometer 2020 Global Report.*

Freeland, C. 2012. *Plutocrats.* Toronto. Doubleday Canada.

Friedman, T.L. 2005. *The World Is Flat.* New York. Farrar, Straus and Giroux.

Galbraith, J.K. 1977. *The Age of Uncertainty.* Boston. Houghton Mifflin Company.

Goodhart, C., and M. Pradhan. 2020. *The Great Demographic Reversal.* Cham, Switzerland. Springer Nature Switzerland AG.

Greenspan, A. 2007. *The Age of Turbulence.* New York. Penguin Books.

Harberger, A.C. 1998. "A Vision of the Growth Process." *American Economic Review* 88 (1): 1–32.

Harper, S.J. 2018. *Right Here, Right Now.* Toronto. McClelland & Stewart.

Haskel, J., and S. Westlake. 2018. *Capitalism without Capital.* Princeton, NJ. Princeton University Press.

Keynes, J.M. 1936. *The General Theory of Employment, Interest and Money.* London. Macmillan Press.

Koonin, S. *Unsettled.* 2021. Dallas. BenBella Books.

Mian, A., and A. Sufi. 2014. *House of Debt.* Chicago. University of Chicago Press.

Piketty, T. 2014. *Capital in the Twenty-First Century.* Cambridge, MA. Belknap Press.

Roberts, W., 1985. *The Leadership Secrets of Attila the Hun.* New York. Warner Books.

Roberts, W., and B. Ross. 1995. *Make It So.* New York. Pocket Books.

Roser, M. 2017. "Tourism." OurWorldInData.org.

Ruben, J. 2020. *The Expendables.* Toronto. Random House Canada.

Schumpeter, J. 1942. *Capitalism, Socialism and Democracy.* New York. Harper and Brothers.

Schwab, K. 2016. *The Fourth Industrial Revolution.* New York. Crown Business.

Schwab, K., and Malleret, T. 2020. *COVID-19: The Great Reset.* Geneva. Forum Publishing.

Sull, Donald. 2009. *The Upside of Turbulence.* Toronto. HarperCollins.

Taleb, Nassim Nicholas. 2007. *The Black Swan.* London. Penguin Group.

Volcker, P., and C. Harper. 2018. *Keeping at It.* New York. Hachette Book Group.

World Economic Forum. 2020. *The Future of Jobs Report 2020.*

INDEX

Note: SP = Stephen Poloz